Nobody Ever Told Me Anything

Rachael "Steak" Finley

This book is a memoir. It reflects the author's
present recollections of experiences over time, which
are fallible. Memories are not to be treated as fact;
rather, they are an interpretation. Some names and
characteristics have been changed, some events
have been compressed, and some dialogue has been
recreated. There are no bad people in this book and no
victims. There are only people, and their impression on
the author is subject, like everything else, to bias.

Written and Recollected by Rachael "Steak" Finley
Edited by Tia Harestad
Cover Photo by Zak Quiram
Interior Layout and Typesetting by Lizette Chavez

For my flat tire friends, for Mars, who is my whole world, for Liz.

For Joe, Josephine, Skip, and Hannah. I had to take you out because of page count but you're always here.

For the people who have loved me along the way.

For the Internet community who brought me Tia, who helped make this possible.

For the help of people like Shannon Byrnes, M.A. LMFT, thank you.

For Zak. For loving me through all of it and encouraging my evolution.

For my Mom, and for every version of myself that came before today.

Introduction

I don't have the authority to tell you that there are more ways to die in Florida than anywhere else in the United States, but what I can say is that it *feels* like there are.

Venomous spiders, alligators; pet pythons let loose in the swamp, the people who hunt them with revolvers for government change. In Florida, the only thing that looms larger than death is the sky. Mercurial. Blue, to thunder-struck gray. And even it can, you know, kill you. It was underneath those clouds that I met Rachael for the first time.

"I don't want you to tell me what you think until the end."

I didn't know whether she was talking about her hometown or quoting our first phone conversation after she sent me her book, but there was a cheeky, inimitable grin splitting her face. We were standing the distance of her truck's front bumper apart, each of us unsure of the other's COVID-19 comfort level, but slowly inching forward in the way that people with a shared secret do. The way that everyone does around Rachael.

She's disarmingly honest, easy to talk to, sincere. All of the things you'd want in an advice columnist, and then some. For one, she doesn't call herself a columnist. She won't even call herself a writer.

"I just want this story to live somewhere else. A place where I don't have to feed it every day, but where it can feed other people. You know?"

I told her that I did know. And, that it was a pretty writerly thing to say.

The thing with Rachael, with *Nobody Ever Told Me Anything*, and with all of us is, is that no matter how self-possessed, satisfied, or successful we may seem, there is a version of ourselves that we'd like to forget. A skin we've shed. There are those who spend their entire lives trying to destroy this link to the reptilian world, and those who embrace it. People who, like the gecko, swallow their shed whole—not as a means of hiding their former self, but in order to nourish their present.

In a way, *Nobody Ever Told Me Anything* is this digestive process. There are few people who have lived as many lives as its author (foster child, cancer survivor, designer, television host…the list goes on) and even less willing to examine those lives up close. By sharing her story, Rachael doesn't just teach you how to reconcile with your past or the people in it, or open her decisions up to speculation—she grants her readers the same unique privilege she always has, from Tumblr to podcast to Hot Lava, even when it was so often missing from her own life. Safety. To share and to learn, and share so that others might not have to learn the hard way.

Rachael did that for me in Florida. She showed me where to step, how to spot sandspurs, promised to look out for sharks when I jumped in the water, and pointed which way to run on the golf course in the dark (yes, *that* golf course). For someone who claimed to have never been told anything, she seemed to have an answer for every danger. Was it an act, this unknowing? Or, was it the only way to respond to knowledge of her kind?

I've followed Rachael in her backyard, and I'd follow her in places she's never been. She is that kind of presence, that kind of writer, that kind of friend. I don't believe she will ever be in her final form; I think she is the kind of reptile that was born to disrupt.

Tia Harestad

June, 1996

"Rachael, get up."

"Rachael, *up. Now.*"

I hear the urgency in my Mom's voice and my eyes snap open. I prop up on my elbow.

"What is it?"

Mom doesn't respond, but I feel her opening drawers, shifting things. I hear a few coins clatter together in her palm and turn to the window to see if it's still dark out. The shades are black, but the shades are always black because we're not allowed to open them, so that doesn't help.

"What time is it?" I ask.

I'm trying to get my bearings, blinking through the shadowy shapes, scanning the room for anything out of order. Once my eyes adjust, I see that Mom is already dressed. In fact, she's showered, her hair set in tight curlers. She has a squiggly brown line drawn and caked around her eyes. She looks 'okay.' She's breathing, she's present. There's a tinge of happiness and a lot of hurry on her face, and it makes me feel uneasy. I try to look unsurprised, wondering how she managed to get ready without me noticing that she left the bed or turned on the shower. I feel guilty for sleeping, like I missed something important.

Then, she leaves the room and I leap up, chasing after her as she flits about the house checking vessels for loose change.

"Where are we going?"

Mom doesn't say anything, so I listen to her body, her movements. She holds out her fist and hands me her credit cards, motioning for me to follow her to the kitchen. I see her duffel bag and a pair of shoes against the front door as we walk past. The kitchen is slightly brighter than the bedroom, an early, grayish light pushing against the shades. Mom points a shaking, sloppily painted finger to a bright blue piece of paper, taped crookedly on the wall.

"Emergency numbers," she mumbles, reading through them.

I nod, acknowledging the same old suspects: my grandma, my aunt, the number for the hospital, poison control, and Mom's friend, Ms. Kilroy, one of the other teachers at school. Her name is at the top of the list, circled in red ink.

Ah, an ally, I think to myself.

"You call her first," Mom says. "Then don't call anyone else unless you're dying."

It dawns on me that these are the first instructions of their kind, ever.

1

When Mom leaves, she doesn't usually make an announcement, or even acknowledge that she's left; the click of the door, or the distant sound of her high-heeled footsteps, are the only things that tell me I'm alone. But here, in the kitchen, she's giving me a list of contacts, pushing her cards at me, telling me where I can find the wads of cash she keeps hidden around the house.

"Where are you going?" I ask, finally.

Mom leans down to speak with me. Her uneven eyeliner gives her tired eyes a look of surprise.

"Rach, Mom is very sick."

I nod. Of course she's sick. This is old news to me. We've been discussing her sicknesses my entire life. It's why she lays on the couch with her headaches, why she sometimes throws up and needs to be alone in her room. I am comfortable with sick. In fact, I think it's great, because it requires no preparation from either of us.

"I'm going to go somewhere to get better," she continues. "I'll be back as soon as I can."

"Oh, okay," I nod.

I follow her to the door, watching her put on her shoes. She tells me not to go outside under any circumstances, and not to open the door for anyone. *Easy*, I think to myself. *A plan.* I like plans, and find it easy to follow them, because plans mean boundaries and boundaries give me the security that I don't realize I'm desperate for. Mom continues talking, her eyes looking up to check the list inside of her head, to make sure she doesn't miss anything. She opens her duffel bag and looks inside, still talking, telling me that this is for the both of us, that it's the right thing to do. Stay inside, stay inside, stay inside. She zips the bag closed again and hoists it over her shoulder, her keys clanging loudly at the lock on the door as she opens it.

"I love you," I remind her. She steps out onto the front porch. "And don't worry. I *promise* I'll stay inside."

It's still dark outside, the crown of the sunrise visible beyond the golf course. There's dew on the grass. Her junky Gremlin, typically hidden from the neighbors, is pulled in the driveway. I wave to her as she walks to the car and she motions for me to close the door. I do as I'm told. I hear Mom's keys hit the ground, hear her footsteps as she run-walks the rest of the way to her station wagon. I watch her headlights turn on through the wavy, decorative glass in the panel lights on the door. Her perfume is strong still. I can smell her in the house. Signs of life.

Sighing, I walk to the kitchen, looking at the list of names she's written for me before rummaging up some stale Cheetos, flopping down onto the couch. I turn on a marathon T.V. show, feeling the energy leave the house, not knowing those ten minutes together that morning were going to change everything.

The Villa

Before one day alone turned into ten, and ten days turned into ten weeks, and those weeks then became nearly a year, Mom and I are sitting side by side in the Gremlin, driving into Foxfire for the first time.

"That one looks exactly like the Brady Bunch house," she says, pointing a chipped, red-polished finger out the window.

"Yeah, it does," I nod in agreement, though I've never seen the show before.

We pass countless new cars, baby blue Mercuries and Lincoln Continentals, all parked in their driveways. Mom snorts.

"Tourists always park in the garage," she mutters, wiping her forehead on the back of her hand. "Unless they *want* you to see their fancy new town cars."

Within Foxfire are a number of subdivisions, each with their own wooden sign designating a fox-inspired name—Foxhunt, Foxtrot, Foxmoor, Foxwood. One after the other. The entire idea of a fox loses its meaning as I read the signs, *fox fox fox fox fox fox fox*, and my eyes are swimming in beige. Beige ranch houses and beige condos, beige duplexes and green grass. My head is spinning by the time we pull up to the country club at the center of the development: the building is tall, Mediterranean-style, with a sign boasting a golf pro shop, restaurant, pool, and fitness center. There had been a pool at our old apartment, too, but we couldn't afford the few extra dollars every month in fees to use it—I think it's why we sit in silence until the country club disappears from the rearview mirror.

"That's the place!" Mom finally exclaims. "Grandma's Villa."

It's beige, like all the others. Mom pulls out a garage door opener I don't recognize and parks her dented station wagon inside. This is a one-time thing, she says in a fast voice, because we can't have the neighbors seeing the garage open every time we leave the Villa, but we also can't park on the street because a car like ours would stick out like a sandspur.

"I'll find us a spot tomorrow morning," she tells me, plopping our dinner—a greasy bag of burgers—into my lap. I catch one last glimpse of the fading evening light as the door comes to a close behind us.

"How will we get food?"

"We'll take the car out at night to go shopping."

We get everything inside in one trip. The Villa has the musty smell of an unopened vacation home, which we quickly replace with the deep-fried perfume of fast food.

"Where am I when you answer the phone?" Mom asks, pointing to me like a drill sergeant with a soft french fry in her hand, the way they used to be before Burger King changed their recipe. We're sitting together at a table for the first time in months, which feels like a cause for celebration, even if it is happening in the dark.

"At work," I reply, chewing on a Whopper Junior.

"Good," she nods. "Who answers the door?"

"No one."

She refills my Coke with half of hers and walks to the refrigerator, topping hers off with what's left of that morning's pink drink—her 'moms only' concoction. I wonder if she ever gets sick of that flavor.

"What if the neighbors see us?" I ask her. "What do I say?"

She brings the drink to her lips, swallowing several times before speaking. When she emerges above the rim, her voice is breathless, hushed.

"They won't."

At that age, there was nobody more important to me than my mom, and no one more beautiful. She was tall and athletic, toned and tanned, with shimmering red hair that caught the sunlight and threw it back into your eyes like gold. She was the only teacher at school that dressed in brightly colored clothes, coordinating her form-fitting skirts with her shoes and handbags, never leaving the house without her signature red lipstick and nail polish. She took up space and she liked that about herself; when she was younger, she was criticized for being loud, catching looks. But once she became a mother, she would appraise herself in her bedroom mirror before going out with friends, turning slowly and smiling. I would watch her run her hands down her flat stomach and cup her large breasts, laughing, "Look at that *floozy*." In a good mood, Mom's eyes were the color of mountain water, clear and blue. When she was depressed, they were foggy, obscured by mist.

No one could charm like she could, nobody could keep up with her banter—it's what made Donna, *Donna*, and brought in the tips at her second job at the restaurant. She seemed impossible, like a trick of the light, and when she held out her hand for me to hold, I felt her energy seep into my body. At school, I was shy and uncomfortable, always struggling to make friends, wearing the same clothes day after day, but Mom made me feel unconquerable. She knew how to fix things, could change her own tires and haggle for the best deal and persuade people to do things they normally wouldn't, like extending a return policy or holding a spot in line, all with a simple smile. Men held doors for her, pushed her chair in, gave her their parking spots. And I would watch in wonder, marveling at the way she thanked them with a wink and a toss of her hair, her biggest fan of all.

And then the world hurt her. So, she hurt herself.

The drinking started in the Big House, which wasn't even that big at all—it got its name because every place we lived in afterwards was smaller and smaller. My dad cheated on her, so she threw him out and a cup took

4

his place; she poured herself drinks when she woke up in the morning and finished them when she came home from school. Always pink, and always in her 7-11 Big Gulp mug. I didn't know what it was exactly, but I knew that it wasn't just juice—I accidentally drank it once when we were living at the Big House, and the taste made me scream, like nail polish remover. She carried it with her everywhere.

My dad was a criminal in flip-flops—half fisherman, half ex-con, with weathered skin and a round belly that bounced when he laughed. He was an anomaly, someone who hid illegal weapons in the ceiling tiles but also taught me the names of all of the native plants and animals in Naples. On our street, he was famous for putting on shows for the neighborhood kids by hooking chicken to a fishing line and coaxing alligators out of the swamp behind our house. But after Mom threw his things into the driveway, he drained their shared bank account and fled town, so she couldn't afford the house anymore. In the days before the bank foreclosed it, she locked herself in her bedroom. I ate canned pears until the pantry was empty, waiting for her to come out. When she did, her eyes were dull, and she had lipstick smeared across her cheek. I followed her to the kitchen, where she handed me a black garbage bag, a constant figure in all of my life's upsets. She started wrapping her crystal glassware in newspaper.

"*Your dad*," she hissed, "has fucked us, Rachael."

She punctuated her words with her movements, thrusting open kitchen drawers, pouring utensils out with a *clang*.

"Every cent I saved taking orders from those goddamned pissants in the restaurant? *Gone*."

My eyes were wide as she cast aside photographs, kicking over the calypso footstool from their first apartment together.

"He could care less if you had a shirt on your back," she spat, and I believed her. Mom spoke to me as if I were one of her teacher friends, bitching about the superintendent over a drink at Applebee's. It made me feel like…

"It's you and me," she said.

And that was exactly it. It made me feel big, the two best friends, like I was part of a team. No time to be sad, to drag my feet, whining. I knew what losing her savings meant for both of us. Whenever she took a sick day, Mom would tell me exactly what the time at home had cost her, and what she'd have to do to make back the money lost. Money was the reason she fixed the holes in my jeans, bought all of our shoes at Payless and chose the steaks in the separate freezer at the grocery store, where all of the meat was stamped with yellow stickers. Money was the reason her parents had never wanted her to marry Dad in the first place, and it had even sent her out on the boat with him, helping him pull gill nets onto the boat. I knew that what my dad had taken would not be replaced quickly. And, judging by the way Mom was muttering to herself, I wondered if it would ever be replaced at all.

You're right, Mom. Let's get out of here.

5

Signs of Life

At first, living in the apartment was exciting, but once the commotion of the move died down, so did the adrenaline. And once the adrenaline was gone, so was the dopamine high. The apartment complex was dirty and tired, and so was the one-bedroom Mom and I shared. There wasn't space for me anywhere except the couch, but either Mom didn't like seeing me in the apartment, or she didn't want me seeing her, so most days, she'd kick me outside, telling me not to come back until I was ready to eat.

Every day was hot, but it felt like it was always the hottest days that she sent me out of the house to hang around. I walked the cracked and broken walkways looking for signs of life, for families taking bike rides, siblings sitting on porches spitting watermelon seeds, the things I'd seen along the dirt road to the Big House. Even when I did see people walking around, lugging their trash to the big dumpsters in between the buildings, the place still felt abandoned, desolate. I missed seeing ibis plunging their long, hooked beaks into our dewy yard, looking for bugs. I missed the pepper hedges and my treehouse, the canal, the eight acres that tucked us in at night. I didn't know which was worse: knowing that the Big House was only a few miles down the road or knowing that I'd never get to see it again.

Summer is a time when my paradise turns back to its old self, back to the swamp it really is, no longer desirable to those who want an escape from the freezing temperatures and slush-filled gutters of their homes on the East Coast. Once their pools are no longer able to shield them from the tropical heat, the snowbirds flee for home; summer storms in Naples turn the sky a flu-like grayish yellow and the humidity hits record-breaking numbers again and again, so much so that you stop paying attention to the weather. It gets to a point where talking about the temperature just makes you hotter than you already are, but at the same time, your brain is so dulled by the sizzling rays that it's all you can think to say. The heat and depression would get trapped between the apartment buildings in the complex, and gnats drunk on mating season would swarm at head-height, sticking to the sweaty corners of my eyes every time I stood up. Even the clunky, rusted cars in the complex were struggling, their engines coughing, the plumes of exhaust choking anyone who dared pass by. I would walk past the parking lot with my shirt pulled up over my nose, but could still feel the fumes.

For hours a day, I slung my body at the end of our stairwell. Sometimes drawing circles in the sandy dirt with a stick, but mostly, imagining myself somewhere else. The apartment buildings in the complex formed a kind of half-circle around a grassy knoll where stringy, underwatered silver buttonwoods and a few live oaks had been planted, all too far from the canal banks to thrive, but put there to give the illusion of waterfront property. Sometimes, if I got out early enough to beat the heat, I could find geckos skipping along the leaves in the hedges by the dumpsters, or watch a centipede climb over the curb, looking for damp soil to curl up in. Watching them, I started to think that if they could survive here, maybe I could, too, but by the afternoon, when the other kids in the complex started to make their way to the pool at the edge of our building, that thought evaporated like the sheen of sweat on my upper lip. We didn't have the $25 for membership, so I would sit on the end of my stoop, listening to their laughter echo across the pavement, jealousy and shame wrenching my gut like hunger pangs. Whenever I saw them coming back with their wet hair, I would duck down and hide so that they wouldn't ask me to play with them, even though it was what I wanted more than anything else. I didn't want them to know why I couldn't swim with them.

By 6:00, when the block began to smell like greasy fast food and good Cuban home cooking, the mosquitos would get thick enough to urge me indoors. It took my eyes a long time to adjust to the darkness; Mom closed all of the blinds and kept the air conditioning blasting at all times, so it felt like the inside of an industrial refrigerator. Cold and damp. Shuffling through the dark, following my path to the kitchen, I pulled the food Mom forgot to eat from the inside of the microwave before nuking some Bagel Bites. I would eat as slowly as possible, watching whatever had been left on the T.V. because I couldn't find the remote. After a few shows, I'd brush my teeth, and pick something to sleep in off the ground. I never had an actual pair of pajamas, and slept on couch cushions that I smashed together on the floor, using my stuffed pig, Piggy, as a pillow. Then, I'd wake up, go outside, and do it all again.

Bills began stacking up, and in our messy apartment, we didn't need any more piles collecting dust. I learned to answer the collectors' calls and pay the bills with Mom's credit card because the checkbook had run out of checks, my grown-up Donna voice getting better every time I used it. It was 1995; I memorized Mom's social security number, her PIN numbers, her account information. I did all of these things not because I felt a sense of responsibility, but because I knew that if another collections notice came in the mail, my mom would move from the couch to her bedroom, and that when she did that, it sometimes took her a week to come out—that, and I also knew that if the power got turned off it would greatly affect my ability to make Bagel Bites. Everything felt better when Mom was at least on the couch, in the comfort of her giant sleep shirt, her pale, bare legs glowing blue in the light of another crime show marathon. I was happy to help her, and happier knowing that there would be fewer moments of panic when the phone was disconnected or water got shut off.

This was not the life we painted for Grandma when she called. My grandmother had a suburban home with wall-papered rooms and color coordinated bedspreads, a sprawling garden and a lawn with no weeds. She no longer had a gardener, but the weeds never grew back—they simply *knew* better. Of her three daughters, two were divorcées, but my mother was, in her eyes, the wild card. Grandma was never sold on my dad, with his being a convict the first offense, and his uncertainty about his Jewishness a second, so Grandma was happy that my parents were separated, glad that we were moving on with our lives, living someplace new. But when Grandma's agreeance started to feel more like a lecture, Mom began avoiding her phone calls. She didn't need to have her nose rubbed into her mistakes: she was living in them, every decision piled up like the shit all over the floor. Any time she sounded hopeful, Grandma made Mom doubt herself, her judgment seeping through the receiver like noxious fumes; she might have been glad that we'd moved away from my dad, but she wouldn't have liked the apartment, either. So, when she called, it was my job now to assure Grandma that Mom was at work, happily so, easy. That things in the apartment were great, that I'd just come inside from playing with my friends at the pool. And if she were to ask what I was up to, or how I was doing in school, I was to keep things positive. I sold not just our location, but both of our lives to Grandma.

"We have our own garden now," I told her. "We're growing tomatoes on the balcony"

I looked at the balcony full of boxes, wet and rotting from the last rain, deciding it was better not to worry about their contents.

And while we prepared for phone calls like most families did earthquakes, a knock on the door meant something far worse. Mom would press a finger to her lips, motioning for me to turn the T.V. off. There was no way for anyone to see in, but we went into the bedroom anyway, huddling together for a tense minute or two until footsteps echoed down the stairs.

"*They know where we are*," Mom would whisper, her eyes wide.

"*Who?*" I mouthed back, clutching her sleep shirt.

When she decided the coast was clear, Mom would tiptoe to the front door and peer out the foggy eyehole, shoulders shaking. She would stand like that for several minutes, a black shadow in the black apartment, pressed against the door. What she was waiting for, she never told me, but she would devise plan after plan for some future date when it would be time for us to leave the apartment, when it would be too dangerous to stick around.

"We'll have to leave in the dead of night," she'd tell me, popping a waffle into the toaster for dinner. "Only the clothes on our backs. Nothing else."

And the door wasn't all we needed to be wary of: there were also the people who followed her on her rare outings to the liquor store for sustenance. If I didn't go with her, she would come back with her hair humid and wild, face frantic, like she'd narrowly escaped some kind of hostage situation.

"They were tailing me! The whole way here!" She'd pant, angry and in disbelief, tossing ice cubes into her big red cup. The way she talked about it was both urgent and flippant. Like, it had been a thing—a big thing—but there was nothing to worry about once the door was closed.

"Had to circle the parking lot three times just to be sure. But there they were, sure enough."

Every time she talked about it, I kept quiet, understanding that whatever Mom saw, or thought she saw, was best left to her. We had made it this far, hadn't we? I trusted that she knew how to deal with almost any threat. Mom's strength only waivered once, when the mice showed up in the middle of the night.

"GET 'EeemmmmmmM OFFFFFFFF!!!"

Her voice rang out from the other side of the wall and I leapt up from my cushions, heart beating in my throat. Body tight, fists clenched, bumbling blindly into the coffee table, slamming my knee.

"MOM! *MOM?*"

"GET 'EM OFF, GET 'EM OFF! *GET THEM OFF OF ME, RACHAEL!*"

From the light of the T.V., I could see that she was jumping up and down like she'd stepped on a fire ant colony, her arms waving wildly, brushing at her skin, completely naked. I ran to the light switch and flipped it on, turning back to her.

"IF YOU DON'T GET THESE FUCKING MICE—"

There was nothing on her bare skin except for the red marks of her own scratching, little lines carved into her beauty spots by her long-nailed fingers, scrabbling from her thighs to her breasts, up and down her neck and face.

"*Mice?*" I strained my eyes to see better.

"MICE!" She bellowed. "CRAWLING! They're everywhere, I—"

I grabbed her hands and lowered them to her side, gasping for breath, feeling like I was about to pee my pants, but forcing my voice to be level, calm.

"Let me look, let me see."

She was breathing heavily, her eyes clamped shut. I brushed my hand along the scratch marks, looking for bites, a rash—anything that might have caused her to shoot out of bed like that. But there was nothing.

"They're—they're off you." I told her, locking her fingers in mine. She opened her eyes slowly, peering down at me, and her skin, from beneath her lids. "Let's check your bed."

I went into her bedroom and heard her following behind me. Her breathing was uneven but slowing, and as I stripped her bed, I saw nothing more than a few chip crumbs. No bugs, no ants, and definitely no mice. I have never even seen a mouse in Florida—something bigger would have eaten it.

"They were all over," she said, voice cracking. "Crawling on my face, my bed. *Hundreds* of them."

"Well, they're gone now," I reassured her, unsure of what else to say. We didn't have a script for invisible mice. I turned to give her a hug, and nearly jumped back.

It was the first time I'd seen Mom in harsh light in weeks. Her skin had a purply undertone, like a bruise as it heals, and her lips were chalky, chapped and cracking. Her eyes were deeply lined and bagged, absent of their blue sparkle, her pupils inky black and oversized. I could see her ribs and the nodules of her spine very clearly, noticed the hollowness in her cheeks, the brittleness of her hair. It was the sickest I'd ever seen her, but what it was, I couldn't say. I walked back to the living room with her behind me, pulled my cushions up off the floor, and placed them back on the couch. The T.V. was still on, so I turned up the volume.

"Let's sit."

We stayed up until the sun rose, until the panic in the room hung like a thin mist instead of a dark cloud. Mom fell asleep with her head on my shoulder, with the sheet I'd been using as a blanket draped across us, over her nakedness. I liked helping her. I stayed there, feeling her breath on my skin, until morning.

That was our cycle. Little ups, big downs.

I wanted to be as big for her as I could, but I couldn't see the ways in which she was hurting, and neither of us could see the ways that she was hurting me. When we had arguments, they were explosive, brutal, physical. One day, our electricity got shut off, and Mom dragged me up the stairs from down on the stoop, her grip piercing my arm painfully.

"*LOOK!* Look what you did!" She screamed, clicking the remote in front of a black T.V., pointing to the unlit clock on the microwave. I started to cry, already feeling blood pool below the indents of her fingernails, a bruise forming.

"HOW could you do this? *Huh?*" She shoved a pile of mail off of the counter, slamming her fist down on the cheap laminate countertop. I couldn't tell if she was yelling at me or at herself, but I watched her move around the room, kicking things, yelling, flipping the light switches on and off, shaking. Finally, I couldn't take it anymore. The calculated commitment to being grown up met reality head on.

"I'M JUST A KID!" I shrieked. "*JUST. A. KID.*"

"Don't you scream at me. Don't you ever fucking scream at me! Do you hear me? DO YOU HEAR ME?"

Her voice chased me as I shielded my face, running into the bathroom and locking the door. I curled up in a corner of the bathtub, feeling Mom's stamping feet, and the slam of her bedroom door, shake the bottles of shampoo around me. I cried big, hot, angry tears, sloppy and loud, smearing my runny nose on the back of my hand. By the sliver of light under the door, I watched a palmetto bug run across the edge of the tub, my sobs scaring it out of its hiding place. I buried my face in my knees,

10

and when I looked up, the cockroach hadn't moved.

"What are you staring at?"

"You okay, kid?" It flicked back with its pokers.

"Shut the fuck up."

Sniffle. Swat hand.

"AHHHHH! MY LEG!"

I had only meant to scare it, but I smashed it into the faucet by accident; a broken leg landed a couple inches from its body, while the remaining limbs kicked stupidly from its overturned belly.

"I'm sorry! I'm sorry! I only meant to scare you, you're gross, you know?" I cried, scrambling to hand the leg back, feeling like even more of a monster than I had when Mom screamed at me. And when it didn't magically reach out and reattach its missing limb, I crumbled.

"I'm REALLY sorry!"

"SORRY ISN'T GONNA TURN THE POWER BACK ON!" Mom hollered from her bed.

She was right. And I was talking to a bug. I scooped him up, flung him into the toilet and flushed. *It's quieter without him,* I told myself. *More peaceful.* I stayed in the bathroom another hour until I heard Mom snoring. It had only been a day without power, but the apartment was blindingly hot, even with the shades drawn. I cracked one open, trying to get some light into the room, and crouched down on my hands and knees, sifting through the stack of mail that Mom had thrown, searching for the misplaced bill. When I found it, I took a handful of coins from the change cup on the counter and went outside to find a payphone, the snot on the back of my hand drying tightly in the hot sun.

As the summer progressed, so did the intensity of Mom's emotions. More people following her, more fights, and with every spike in emotion, a deep, depressive pit. When she was low, Mom mumbled under her breath, little words trailing behind her as she brought herself from her bed to the bathroom or to the fridge. Sometimes, I caught my name. Other times, Grandma's, her first husband, Mike, or even her first boyfriend, Harry. I stopped asking "what" when she chattered—the conversations weren't for me, and my interruptions just seemed to irritate her.

But I couldn't look away.

"Mike...Dr. Mike...Dr of what, he can't fix shit ..."

The tone of her voice gave me goosebumps, and I'd turn on the couch, barely raising my eyes above the back cushion. Too creeped out to interrupt, but unable to ignore the robotic way she jerked her arms and legs, the way her eyes didn't blink. There was no way for me to know what was going on, so I listened for clues.

"Harry, oh Harry...I should have married you."

A sad voice meant more ice in her glass.

"Rachael...can't listen...fucking brat..."

Anger told me to keep my head low.

And then, the baby voice. It was the worst of all, going beyond pity.

11

"Why, Mommy? Why me?"

Hearing her like this made me sick with wanting, pulled like a rubber band between running out of the dark apartment into the piercing sun, and wishing I could pick her up in my arms. Usually, I'd bring her a blanket and sit next to her as she sunk to the floor, my small hand on her back as she rocked herself back and forth, whispering for her mom, until she was ready for me to lead her back to bed and off to sleep. She was a wrecking ball, but even if it meant getting knocked down, I always, always, *always* preferred to see her in motion.

I left early one morning to go grocery shopping for us, and as I lugged several sweating bags of frozen food with me down the side of Highway 41, I hatched a plan to feed Mom back into normalcy, to get her body back to the comfortable, strong, protective shape I remembered. Honking cars and the *whoosh* of semis lifted my lank hair, tickling my bare shoulders; someone yelled something I couldn't understand out their window and I ducked my head, focusing on the plastic bag handles digging into my palms. I had a couple of boxes of Stouffer's mac and cheese and a frozen Welsh rarebit, her favorite. *She's going to love this,* I reminded myself. *She's going to love me for this.*

When I came into the apartment, I was expecting to find her still in bed, and to win extra points when she woke up to the smell of cheese thawing in the oven, but she wasn't there. Except for a suitcase on her bed, her room was empty. Even stranger, she'd turned both of our T.V.s off. I quickly put away the groceries and walked to the parking lot, but I couldn't find the Gremlin. I went back upstairs and waited for her, hungry but unable to eat, tapping the toe of my shoe anxiously against the laminate floor.

A few hours later, she was back. Her skin was streaky, like she'd put on makeup but sweated right through it, but other than that, her face was normal—she even had a little lipstick on. She kept her keys in her hand as she walked to the fridge, pouring herself a drink; I could almost catch a glimpse of the person that met me in the kitchen of the Big House after school, but there was a vibration to her, like the outline of her body was tickling, static. When she saw me looking up at her from the couch, and the open garbage bag of clothes strewn around the room from the day we moved in, she cocked her head.

"You haven't packed yet?"

That was the day we drove to Foxfire.

Shhhhh...

The rules for the Villa are simple: never turn on the lights, except the one in the bathroom, which doesn't have a window. And even though the newly-tarred streets are perfect for roller skating, never go outside unless it's dark. We got our calls forwarded so we 'wouldn't miss a beat,' but Mom never rose to answer, even when it rang.

At first, it's strange to wake up in the Villa. There are very obvious rental touches throughout, like matching towels and baskets of potpourri, but it also feels baldly unwelcoming, like a double suite at the Holiday Inn, trying to disguise the fact that it used to be a smoking room. The floors are tiled, and the kitchen looks out into a sparse, rectangular yard, lined with thick ficus hedges.

I sleep in what appears to be the kids' bedroom. It has two twin-sized beds, each with a white wicker headboard. The nightstand between the beds is also white, decorated with a seashell-encrusted lamp with a mauve shade. There is a dresser and a closet, but I don't unpack my clothes because Mom doesn't tell me to. I like to think that if my mom had unpacked hers, I might have, too, but it's one of those things kids definitely don't do on their own. I'm just glad I don't have to sleep on the floor.

Mom never asks me how I like the Villa. She never asked me about the apartment, or how I felt about leaving the Big House, either. But she is moving with energy, excited, it seems, by the change of scenery, and the distraction of developing our 'plan of attack.' I absorb her energy, happy just to hear her talking again, happy to be part of a plan, happy that she sits next to me on the couch during the day instead of burying her face under her covers.

"Tonight, Winn Dixie, KFC," she tells me for the tenth time in a row, her drill sergeant voice drowning out Olivia Benson's as *Law and Order* flashes across the T.V. screen. Her legs are crossed in front of her, thin and mottled like fish scales, and she's kicking one of her feet, shaking the glass coffee table.

"Uh-huh," I nod. If I don't respond, this will go on even longer, but I really want to find out who threw that mutilated body off the Brooklyn Bridge.

"The sun sets at, what, 7? So, we wait an extra fifteen, make sure those old biddies really can't see through their glasses, and then we move. Back

13

door, back alley."

Mom found the back alley while snooping around the backyard one night. Pushing through the ficuses, the grass changes from sod grass to Florida's native crab grass, leading to an alleyway that lines the entire block, perfectly hidden and completely undetectable from the street. Looking back, it was probably so that maintenance could spray all of the houses with pesticides to keep the precious golf course bug-free, but it's perfect for sneaking to the Gremlin, running like a seam down the entirety of the development before stopping at a large green transformer three blocks down from our Villa. Instead of feeling ashamed about hiding our dingy car, I'm having fun—I've always liked the nighttime in Florida. The humidity evaporates, giving way to crisp, open air. I like it even more now that it's the only time we go out. Every movement feels like our little secret.

Out the backdoor—quiet, *quiet*.

Don't let the screen door slam, duck down behind the hedges.

Careful, quick footsteps. Avoid the corner where the neighbor's motion light will trigger!

To the car, to the car! *Hurry! Hush.*

I know how this looks, but keep in mind: I was 10 when we moved into the Villa. I didn't know we were squatters. I didn't know what that meant or looked like.

Now, I know why Mom didn't want to ask her parents for help. They were generally disapproving people, the sort who never lent a hand without mentioning the distance of the stretch. So, not telling Grandma that we were secretly living in her vacation home didn't arouse any suspicion in me. Instead, it felt like another part of the game, and Mom went to great lengths to get me in on the script, to make sure I wouldn't slip up. But it wasn't long before she was breaking her own rules—slipping out during the daytime, snapping twigs, bumbling home through the alley when the neighbors were still awake. Sometimes, she'd be gone the entire night, and I'd wake up and find random grocery bags filled with beads, glue, and craft supplies on the floor, her red hair peeking out from behind the couch. I couldn't explain any of it, and the more I asked about it, the more annoyed she got.

"*Errands*," she would always tell me, like the answer was obvious, flicking through the channels on the T.V.

For my mom, everything was errands, everything was work. Maybe that's how she justified leaving me, or maybe she didn't even think about that.

"For what?"

"Rachael, please. I'm tired."

And that was that. I tuned myself to Mom's moods like a radio, allowing her to baby herself if she wanted to, or following her orders, watching as she bossed everything into place, out of control in her need to control every second. I'm glad when school is just around the corner, looking forward to a routine for both of us.

"WE'RE GOING TO BE LATE!"

"Wha—?"

"GET UP! GET UP!"

A plastic clock lands on my chest with a hollow *thud*. I kick back the covers, too scared to look at the time.

"SCHOOL. NOW."

"I'M COMING!"

Now that I'm in middle school, I no longer take the bus. Instead, I go with Mom to work, but since she's expected to be there earlier than her students, I'm expected to be ready so that I can eat the free breakfast they give out in the cafeteria before school starts. But Mom is still coming home late at night, so she rarely sets an alarm; if she *does* remember to set an alarm for herself, she often forgets to wake me up and take me to school with her. Those mornings, I run through the house looking for her, pulling my clothes on only to realize that she's long gone, and the bus is, too. Then, I sit in an unfocused daze in front of the T.V., fretting over what to say to my teachers. Late or absent, only the return of Mom can ease my stress; the rustling of trees in the backyard, and the *clunk* of ice dropping in a plastic cup, is medicine for my anxious heart. She'll gossip to me about the other teachers and students with frenzied cheer in her voice, and I'll forget that our morning began in flames.

Our mornings are always worse when she leaves in the middle of the night. So, in order to keep track of her, I move from my bedroom to hers. I wake up in the middle of the night in a cold sweat, gasping for breath as I slap out an arm, feeling for her body beside mine. Nothing. I run down the hallway and look for her on the couch, hoping to find her tangled in blankets, but she's not there, either. My footsteps are as loud as the heartbeat in my ears, thoughts whirring, twisted, fighting back worst-case scenarios as I crawl back onto her damp mattress, sheets sickly soft from weeks without washing. I picture her crashing the car, getting followed by strangers, losing her way home, and stay up until the sun begins to rise. When I finally do pass out, it's only until she shakes me by my shoulders, screaming that it's time to get to school. We spend nearly every morning flapping through the house like this, one of us crying out for the other to get dressed, Mom throwing things at me, reaching for whatever pile or shoe is within reach.

It makes me angry that I'm tardy for school, that I miss breakfast and get detentions during lunch, but I can't say that to Mom. The frenzy of failing *her*, making *her* late, and jeopardizing *her* job, grips tightly around my throat. She rages at me and I sob back, tears shooting out of my eyes like bullets. The Villa is complete chaos by this point, with bags of clothes and junk piling in every corner, just like the apartment. No matter how hopeful it felt at first, coming back to this place all alone, eating my microwave dinner in the dark, implies that as long as Mom stays in this state—angry, lost, so far from what she used to be—I will, too.

Had my mom not been such a beloved teacher, there probably would have been some backlash to her—or, by default, *my*—behavior. Her mania translated beautifully in the classroom, and students clamored to be in her English class, loving the unconventional, high-energy style of her lectures. She would move around the room wildly, calling on people at random, asking them to make different voices for the characters in a story. Kids actually completed their reading assignments because they wanted to hear my mom discuss their subjects, annihilating some characters and lauding others, or throwing books at the wall if someone fell asleep at their desk during independent study. She reapplied her red lipstick between classes, keeping her 7-11 cup close at hand, though I'm unsure what she filled it with during the school day. Her ability to morph into anything functional at all made our life outside of school feel like a dream.

Even if Ms. Finley was the most popular of the eighth grade teachers, our shared last name did nothing to corroborate any popularity of my own. Those with a 'Cool Parent' know that unless you've hit an early puberty, your parent's hype only makes people talk about how little you share in common with them. I sat alone at lunch, my outfits usually wrinkled from the clothes pile in my bedroom. If Mom was in a screaming mood in the morning, I'd reach for the closest shirt and pants, oftentimes wearing whatever I had on the day before. Bird-faced Blonde Brittany, the pinnacle of the popular table, pointed this out during lunch one day.

There she was, positioned directly under the fluorescent cafeteria lights, making the shine in her off-the-mannequin rayon top, and the roll-on body glitter applied like glue to her bony clavicles, unmissable. Everything about her was intentional, from the way she coordinated her layered camisoles with her Sugar Floatie flip-flops, to the way she raised her voice whenever she talked about her weekend plans, making sure uninvited guests were within earshot. The fact that she wasn't a natural 'alpha girl' like her older sister made her crazy.

"Can you *believe* that's Ms. Finley's *daughter*?" She shouted, applying her Bonne Bell lip gloss. I'd only ever seen Bonne Bell while flipping through *Seventeen* in the grocery store checkout line. "My sister's in her class and she says she's like, the coolest teacher ever."

I always sat at the abandoned end of the 'It' table, pretending to read while I listened to their inane conversations, hoping to pick up on their secrets, or to learn about something that we could become friends over. But this, I did not want to hear. I debated getting up, but whenever people laughed at what she said, Blonde Brittany's voice grew in volume instead of confidence, though she was hopeful that it came across the same way. I had seen this happen to other kids before and ducked my head, praying that it would be over before my eyes welled up.

"But, like, *look* at her. She wore that outfit yesterday, didn't she?"

When I didn't say anything, she continued, leaning over the table. The color rose in my cheeks, eyes stinging; I leveled them with the Diet Coke she was sipping for lunch, staring behind it to the center of her chest, right at the padding of her 'real' bra, to the harsh underwire outline protruding under the stretchy magenta fabric, as if to say, *You may not need me now,*

16

Blonde Brittany, but I'll be here when you do.

My eyes widened as I imagined her boobs growing right before my eyes, like two fleshy balloons inflating. I wonder, do *I* need a bra? They seem itchy, and I think about the 20 minutes I spent that morning looking for underwear—it's not like I need another thing to lose in the house.

"*Hello?* Earth to you?"

I look up, and a tear perches itself dangerously at the edge of my eyelashes.

"I said, *didn't you wear that yesterday?* I know you can hear me. You're always listening to us at lunch."

When I get up from the table, burying my face behind my hair, I can still hear her talking.

"Oh my *god*, you guys! Look at her baby shoes! I swear I saw those in the window at Payless."

It wouldn't have mattered what I wore, if my lips were glossed or my hair was crimped. I was fundamentally different from the girls at that table, and no mask would have helped me disguise myself as one of them. They were the kinds of girls who knew more than they should, whose older sisters and brothers taught them everything you couldn't learn at school, the things nobody ever told me. You could see it in the way they walked, the way they stood around their lockers with a hand on one hip, back arched, like nothing was new to them, like they'd seen and done and heard it all before. And maybe that's because the world they lived in was so small, they really *had*—I mean, if all you have to worry about is acting like you've been there, you don't have to concern yourself with what other people are thinking or feeling. You don't have to tune into the changes in their voices, the shine in their eyes, where they go in the middle of the night. You just wake up with a white-toothed smile plastered on your face, knowing that it will be there tomorrow. And the next day, and the day after that, no matter how nice or mean of a person you are.

When I told Mom what happened at lunch, she tried, in her way, to sooth my insecurities.

"I was the tallest girl in school, from the time I was 11 until I graduated high school," she barked, handing me a bag of Cheetos. "No boys liked me, and every girl that wasn't one of my sisters made my life hellish."

"At least you had sisters at school," I mumbled. "I don't have anyone."

"We fought all the time then just like we do now," she said, waving away my words with her hand. "I had the biggest boobs you can imagine, and Grandma made me wear the ugliest things to cover them up. Think I felt good about myself?"

I shrugged, thinking about Blonde Brittany's padded bra and balloon boobs again. I was a pinhead with a worm's body and a flat chest. Mom and I couldn't have looked more opposite if we tried.

She got lost in her storytelling, ending her rant sometime around when she was a student at Cornell, and all the men wanted to date her. Comfort felt like a lost cause, so I started making plans to go lay in my

17

bedroom and breathe deep into Piggy's fuzz.

"I'm gonna go do my homework," I lied.

"That's my girl," Mom smiled, eyelids already beginning to droop.

I stayed in my bed for the rest of the night, half of my mind wondering what it was that made people like Blonde Brittany popular, and the other half hoping that Mom wouldn't try to drive after all those trips to the refrigerator. Before I fell asleep, I heard her push open my door.

"Rachael, honey?"

"Yeah?" I whispered.

"Brittany is a little cunt. Her *and* her sister."

Thanks for getting it, Mom.

Where Are You Going?

Waking up to an empty house is like waking up to a car accident.
One minute, I'm sleeping, head leaning against the cool window. The
air conditioning is on, and the palm trees brush against the window in a
whisper. Everything is fine. I trust that Mom is driving us, that she knows
where we're going. Then, I take a breath, roll in my sleep, and glass is
flying everywhere, and I'm jolted awake by a sharp pain in my chest. The
panic of finding an empty room presses in on me like an air bag squeezing
my heart. I'm screeching out for help, but except for the shadowy musk of
Oscar de la Renta and vodka, there's no one in the driver's seat.

Night after night, I lose her. That is, until she goes from eight-hour
disappearances to days at a time.

She's put in a leave of absence at school, so I take the bus there and
back, letting myself into the empty house, leaving the back door unlocked
in case Mom comes back. My teachers ask me how she's feeling and tell
me to pass along wishes for a speedy recovery, the care in their voices
betrayed by the hungry looks on their faces, hopeful for gossip. I give them
our spiel, bent into a shape that fits this scenario. Vague answers with just
the right amount of detail. I tell them that we're waiting for hospital test
results, that she's hoping to be back on her feet soon. In truth, I don't
think Mom has any intention of coming back to the school, and I start to
worry that if she doesn't, the cards I use to pay the bills will stop working.

One day, I come home and find her laying naked on the tile floor in
front of the T.V. I drop my backpack and run over to her.

"Mom? *Mom?* Are you okay?"

It's the first time I've seen her in four days, and the sight comes as
a shock. Her skin is grayish, pooled with sweat, the curves of her body
illuminated by a Thigh Master infomercial. I feel a lump rise in my throat
like I'm going to puke and stick my head down in front of her mouth,
silencing my own breath to listen for hers; it's quiet but it's there, barely
audible above the perky music of the commercial. The woman on the
screen is sitting by a pool with the Thigh Master between her legs, but
that's not really what she's selling. She's selling you her smile, selling
white teeth and tanned skin and a life with a pool, selling, selling, selling
until you don't know what you're buying, but whatever it is, it sounds
like a deal. Mom and I have laughed at this commercial together a dozen
times—when the scene changes from the pool to the more attainable

cubicle, she never misses an opportunity to point out the strange eye contact that the woman makes with her coworkers, squeezing her legs together at her desk.

"Can you imagine me doing that in my classroom?" She usually laughs. "Don't mind me, kids, just slimming these thighs!"

But right now, the woman and her thighs and her bright blue pool and the pitch of her voice feels violent, and Mom is lying prostrate on the floor, her strawberry blonde curls concealing her face, unlaughing. The bright-eyed woman on the screen, squeezing away. I try to remember the last time Mom looked like that. Eyes wide open.

The longer I look at my mom, the more her skin looks like wet newspaper, as if the smallest movement could tear her apart. I gently push back her hair and can see the veins on her face, extending from her cheek to her neck, splaying like violet lightning bolts on her inner wrist. I snoop around and find her clothes piled in the bathroom, her purse and keys next to her bed. I pick them up and put them in my pocket, planning to hide them so that I can get some rest that night. When I come back to the living room, she has shifted in her sleep, and I see that much of her body is bruised, white mottled with purple, like a wine-stained carpet. I grab a blanket and cover her with it, then nestle myself against her, watching the television through her wild hair.

"*For just three easy payments of $13.99...*"

When she wakes up, Mom does not acknowledge the strangeness of my finding her naked in the living room. She rises from the floor, blanket wrapped around her body, and staggers into the kitchen, yawning. A heavy June rain bounces off the skylight overhead.

"Gloomy morning, huh Rach?"

It's the next day, two in the afternoon.

I am thankful school is ending. I'm tired of my teachers asking me where Mom is, sick of feeling their eyes on me when I shuffle through the hallways. When I'm at my desk, I stare at my classmates, wondering what their heads are filled with. How do they have time to look the way they do, to choose new clothes every morning, to smile and make friends? I keep my head down. I look forward to summer, thinking, *less to manage.*

When my classmates discuss their vacations, I give myself a reason to chime in.

"I'm going to my grandma's lake house," I say. "In New York."

This is a lie, but everything is, so what does it matter? When I was little, Mom used to send me to my grandparents' lake house with the rest of the aunts and cousins so that she could stay home and teach summer school for extra cash, but we don't do that anymore. But as soon as I say it, several kids scoot their chairs in closer to me. I like having their attention, and the words fall from my lips with ease.

I'm in a good mood when I get off the bus. A patch of night-blooming jasmine has grown on someone's fence, and the air smells sweet, the perfume of the sugary flowers mingling with the freshness of mowed grass.

20

I picture myself bringing friends to Foxfire, wowing them with my big neighborhood, the surrounding wealth distracting them from the fact that we have to duck down and run behind the bushes to get inside.

When I come in through the back door, Mom is splayed out on the couch. The heavy slider is the only thing that shows the age of the house, and as I push it, my eyes fight to adjust to the dark interior. I can make out her shape in the kitchen, the red glare of her favorite cup.

"It's nice outside," I say.

"Hmm?"

"It's nice outside," I repeat. "The neighbor's flowers smell pretty."

"Jasmine," she says, waving a hand. "Sickeningly sweet. Makes my stomach turn."

I say nothing, opening the cupboards. I find a stale bag of Doritos and bring them to the couch, sitting down next to her. She waves her hand like she's downwind from red tide, her face pinched and queasy.

"Eat those in the kitchen, would you? No wonder this couch is so stained."

I get up stiffly and return the bag to the cupboard. Then, I go to my room. Maybe if I had known she was going to leave me in a few days, I would have stayed and sat with her. But there was no way for me to know what was going on in her mind, and no chance I could have predicted that when we did say goodbye, when I said 'I love you' to no reply, that she would be leaving me for as long as she did.

21

We're All Stardust

She needed to get better—that was obvious. From *what*, exactly, was a little more complicated. Did I think Mom's moods were a problem? Yes. Did her drinking worry me? Only when she had her keys in her hand. I didn't know anything about mental health, but she was so far from the person she'd been in the Big House, and the woman that she was before her divorce, that I was terrified to see just how different she could become. If I had to be home alone for a couple of weeks, maybe a month, so be it. We'd been working our way towards that, anyway.

That first weekend alone, I don't have a plan. I eat a sleeve of Saltine crackers for breakfast and pace the house, wandering from room to room, looking for something to do. I haven't been inside of the garage since the first night Mom parked the Gremlin, assuming that she filled it with boxes just like she did to the rest of the house. When I turn on the light, I'm surprised to see only a stack of boxes in the corner, a bucket and a few hand tools. The room smells like my grandparents and pesticides, and the concrete floor is cold under my bare feet. As I have already studied every other inch and corner inside of the house for something to eat the sunlight away, I decide to spend my day in the garage, going through the boxes. I pick a wet wedge of gummed-up crackers from between my back teeth and reach up for the highest box on the stack.

Nothing but cords. This must be the contents of Mom's old office or maybe some stuff from a school computer lab. I push it aside, dragging the next box towards me. This bin contains a CRT monitor, some AOL CD-ROMs, and a pack of old gum. I pop the gum into my mouth as I move for the third bin. The gum is a clear mistake, crumbling like flour against my tongue, but the final bin is a gold mine: taped up in bubble wrap is the tower of a desktop computer, something that the county sent all of the teachers to help them prepare for the transition to digital classrooms. It was untouched. I spit the gum out onto the garage floor and glance around, half expecting someone to yell at me. When they don't, I unwrap the desktop, remembering the many late nights spent in Mom's classroom while she graded papers, going between Minesweeper, Solitaire, Pinball, and an old *Jurassic Park* game someone left in the processor. I untangle the plugs from the first box and try them, one after the other, in the back of the desktop.

Four hours later, I have the monitor and the desktop connected, plugged into the wall of the garage. There's no *Jurassic Park* but, having followed the AOL setup steps, I know entertainment is fast approaching. The afternoon heat barely warms the cavernous garage, only half-lit from the single bulb hanging from the ceiling. I go inside to disconnect the cord from the only phone in the house and bring it back to my new home office. I plug it in and click *Test* on the setup screen. *Connection Ready.*

For a moment, I feel keenly aware that I will no longer need the T.V. to be on all day and night for company. I am about to enter a space where everything and everyone will be at my fingertips.

Then, the screen changed. *Enter username and password.* I pause, fingers suspended above the keyboard.

Today, we have multiple screen names. Sometimes, a new one for every app. But access to the internet was limited in 1998, and up until this moment, I have only ever used a computer at school. Some kids would brag about the computers they had at home, the chat rooms they entered, who they talked to. Selecting a screen name was something taken very seriously, like naming a dog. Who is this dog today, and who will he be tomorrow? What are his attitudes? His taste in music? His hobbies? With fewer hobbies than a dog, the chance to reinvent my space is a newfound freedom. Who and what would I be in the digital world? What would I choose?

I thought about the book I had read at my grandparents' lake house one summer, a fantasy about pixies and dragons. The thrill of logging onto the internet for the first time filled me with the same sense of wonderment that the book had; Pixy53 came to mind, as five and three were my first and second favorite numbers. But that was taken, as was Pixie53, then Pixiedust530, and every other combination of numbers and letters I could come up with that kept with my theme. 53Pixie. Pixie053. 5PixieDust3. Next to the boxes was a pile of *Reader's Digest* magazines that Grandma kept for guests who she willingly rented the house out to, in case they wanted to spend their vacations inside. I swung out a skinny leg and kicked them over in frustration, convinced that I was never going to find something special to get me online. As the magazines slid across the slick concrete floor, one of the covers caught my eye. A purple galaxy, shimmering in the black universe. I jumped up, rushing back to the computer. *STARDUST.* Then, with shaking fingers, I typed in the first three numbers that popped into my head. *871.*

It's true, kids. If your parents didn't tell you not to, or were in a rehab facility 90 miles across the state, there's a chance you did the thing that every episode of *Dateline* tells you not to. You put your address numbers into your screen name.

I chew on the inside of my cheek, waiting for the approval of my screen name for what felt like hours, but was probably only ten minutes. And there it was—the sound every one-time AOL user has heard before. Imprinted in our brains, our adolescent DNA, like the baby back ribs jingle from Chili's.

"You've got mail!"

I typed in every address that I knew, every name that I could think of. I went from the MTV homepage to Ask Jeeves to eBay, ecstatic as I scoured the endless pages of CDs, my mind and heart racing. I taught myself everything there was to learn on the computer, spending almost 20 hours sitting in the garage that day, my eyes dry and salty from staring at the screen. Finally, I settled on my first internet purchase: a $35 Blink-182 clock. When the mail came later in the week, I also experienced my first lesson in internet scams. My prized possession was just a printed *photo* of a Blink-182 clock. As a child who had once slept in the summer heat without air conditioning because the power was shut off, I appreciated money enough to understand the consequences of taking from an empty pot. I never bought anything off eBay again, though I did pin the clock to my wall to soften the blow.

The internet was good to me for a while. I logged into chat rooms with strangers, describing my face in detail and asking them which celebrity I looked like—a common practice in the nineties. Mostly, I just told them about my life, including the lies that kept us safe, making up some of my own. Watching the way people reacted. I told Mom about the things I'd looked up when she called, like how she'd come up on a Cornell graduate list when I'd searched her name on Ask. At first, she was good about checking in every few days—initially from a facility just outside of Naples, and a few weeks later, from a hospital someplace else. Once, she called me from a payphone where I could hear traffic screeching in the background, and I couldn't make out what she said, except for the "Soon, honey," that followed every time I asked when she'd come home. But eventually, the calls stopped coming, and I was lonely for human contact—*real* human conversation—and the internet wasn't cutting it.

I couldn't walk past the front door without thinking about her. What she'd been wearing when she said goodbye, the way her shaking hands had dropped the car keys on her way out. I was starting to worry.

I was also worried about how much money I had to live off of, so whenever I snuck out to the grocery store, I shopped for one box of Bagel Bites a day and made use of the grass alley. When I got home, my stomach would growl, but I'd shove my meal into the freezer, pushing myself to last as long as possible without food. I propped the door to the garage open with one of the boxes so that I wouldn't miss the phone ringing if Mom called. Which felt like wishful thinking, until one day, while looking at puppies that I had no intention of adopting, a call finally cut through the stale air.

"Hello?"

"Hi, sweetie."

"Mom!" I didn't care how desperate I sounded. Mom's voice was bright and she sounded like she was safely inside somewhere. "I miss you."

"I miss you, too. How are things?"

"Good," I heard myself say. Which, in that moment, was true.

"How are you feeling?"

"Better. Not perfect, but better."

My heart faltered. More time.

"When, um, do you think you'll be home?"

"Soon, sweetheart."

I wanted the word to swell and fill the empty kitchen where I stood, but it didn't. Instead, it made everything tunnel around me, like I was staring down at myself from a telescope miles away until I was nothing but a pinprick. A pinprick in a messy house with an overflowing garbage bin and blankets lumped up on the couch so that she could be closer to the door if her mom came home. There was no point in reminding her that school was about to start—if she wasn't good enough to come home, she wasn't good enough to work.

"Okay."

"Has Grandma called?"

"Yeah. She thinks you're avoiding her," I add this last part in hopes of maybe guilting her home sooner, but it doesn't work.

"You told her I'm teaching summer school?"

"Yep."

"And she still asks about me?" Her voice sounds prickly now, and I regret saying anything.

"Not for a while, no."

"Okay. Well, you know the drill if she calls again. I gotta go, sweetie, my call time's up."

"Love you," I squeak, fighting back tears.

"Love you, too."

On my eleventh birthday, Mom calls. She sings to me in her sweet soprano, with the voices of other patients echoing her in the background. She tells me that this is going to be my best year yet—*our* best year—and I hold the phone with both hands, pressing it into the side of my head, trying to bring her closer. Her voice is a little sluggish, like she just woke up or something.

"Be a good girl and we'll celebrate when I get home."

Brand New

She said to stay inside 'no matter what.'
But that didn't mean school, right?
She didn't know she'd be gone this long.
You didn't know she'd be gone this long, did you?

Back and forth, I argued with myself in the bathroom, first in the
shower, then in the mirror as I brushed my clean hair, parting it down the
middle. I found a stack of books in my bedroom that I thought I lost and
quickly put them down. Then, picked them up. I fought with my shaking
fingers as I tied my shoes, which were suddenly too small for my growing
feet. The front door felt like one of Mom's icy blue eyes, glaring down
at me, but once I hurried out the alleyway and onto the street, I felt the
panic leaving me. The morning was still, the air was humid, the process of
finding a wrinkled outfit from the floor had been unhurried, and I found
myself breathing deeply as I boarded the bus. *I look brand new*, I thought.
And I get to have breakfast. It was only my second time on that bus, since
I'd only ever managed to catch it once when Mom left me behind the year
before, and the morning crowd felt less intimidating than I remembered it.
This year, I'm going to be just like everyone else. No bugs, no jokes, no weirdness.

I went to school because I knew that if I didn't, the school would call
to try and find out why, and that could open an investigation. This was
something that I'd learned in the room with other kids of divorced families
years earlier, when the school counselor brought us all aside for a 'check-
in.' While she tried to assure us that everything was normal, and that
divorce happened and that we'd all be fine, the fact that we had all been
pulled out of class to talk to her in some side room near the principal's
office made me feel the *opposite* of normal. All this to say, I didn't want the
attention of my counselors or teachers more than I didn't want to break
Mom's orders to stay inside. And while many kids would have jumped
at the chance to skip school and watch T.V., I followed my instincts,
convincing myself that, in her sickness, my mom had simply *forgotten* what
September meant. Besides, I was excited to be around people again. I
told myself that things would be fine, that I would smile at my teachers
and they'd tell me what a pleasure I was to have in class, and the same lies
from the year before about Mom would hold up just as well.

It was strange how normal a day it was. How easily the hours passed,
how fine things could actually be with Mom away. I had time to eat the

free cafeteria breakfast, find my locker, and get to class before the tardy bell rang. I ripped out the used pages of my sixth grade notebook to make way for seventh grade assignments, feeling confident, like I could reinvent myself in the remaining pages. When the day ended and it was time to board the bus again, I noticed some eighth graders swapping CDs from their Walkmans in the backseat. Despite being called a Walkman, I had never taken mine out of the house; I make a mental note to bring mine on the bus the next day, thinking, *Tomorrow will be better. The same exact day, just a little better.*

December 25, 1996

I watch holiday movies on *Lifetime* and make Rice-A-Roni. Mom doesn't call.

Last Call

Then, the phone rang. You told me you were fine, your paper skin okay, safe, somewhere. I told you that I hadn't left and assured you that we were doing well—the both of us, me *and* you—with the tone of my voice, the grip of my small hands on the receiver. I promised to keep on that way, and you promised to get better. I love it when you promise newness, even if it never comes, and I feel calmer knowing that we are intact, that things are going okay, that you think you can come home soon. You seemed very 'up,' and I know when you're feeling up you like to talk quickly, jumping from place to place, and I was happy just to listen, to hear your voice.

The truth was that I still didn't know where you were, exactly—a hospital somewhere? You never clarified when I asked—but it has been a week or two since we last talked, and now the power has gone out. And even if I had power, I wouldn't have been able to call because you never gave me the number. So, I can't tell you that it's dark now, that without the air conditioning, the humidity has started to sneak in around the house like your mice. It's stifling, hot, and sticky inside, and I need you to tell me what to do about the electricity, how to get it fixed without a phone. I *need* to talk to you about the Blink-182 clock, how it was paper, how stupid that was. How sorry I am for wasting your money. I need to know what time it is. I need to talk to you about the bunny, too. Honestly, I'd really like to leave out the part about the bunny, and just forget his little soft bunny head. I feel terrible about it, but you need to know if I could change it, I would never have caught him at all. I didn't know he'd die so easily, but I thought he'd last more than a day without water and the guilt of finding his rock-hard, rigor mortis body is something I am still trying to process, something I probably wouldn't have shared if you *had* called, unless you asked me about it. I buried the bunny out back with Grandpa's tiny garden shovel thingy that I found in the clean part of the garage, but I still see his glossy, lifeless marble eyes on the back of mine when I try to fall asleep at night. Unlike packed-clay soils, the Florida earth is sandy, and pretty easy to cut through, and I could dig plenty of graves, if ever we should need them.

After I dug the grave, I was really thirsty, so I slipped through the hedge to get some lemons from the neighbors' trees. It's easy to get lemons in the pitch black because they glow, and I think you'd be proud of how I knew how to do that without asking. How I didn't trip their motion light

29

while I plucked them from the tree. I mix the lemon juice with sugar—so much sugar—but use less now that the power is out, and the ice machine won't work. The lemonade has to be made with less sugar or the sweet, warm lemon water tastes like chemicals. This is my personal recipe, my personal taste. I drink it while sitting on the patio furniture that, I should tell you, I have moved into the garage. It feels like we've added onto the house, and I pretend that you are with me. That we are sitting on a balcony in our rich-person house somewhere far away from the Villa, maybe as far away as you are from me now.

Honestly, if you *were* to have called, I might have also left out the part about the water. That, since the electricity has been turned off, so has the water, but that I found a stock of gallon jugs from the last hurricane season in the back of the pantry. I can get more—it's no problem, don't worry—but I know that if I use them to fill the back of the toilet tank it will deplete the supply too quickly, just like they teach you in the hurricane prep infomercials. I can't carry more than one at a time from the store, so this system doesn't really work; instead, I've decided to ration the water jugs the smart way. I drink a lot at school and only use the jugs for necessities, like my warm lemon water. As far as flushing the toilets goes, well, like I said, the sandy soil moves easily under Grandpa's shovel, so I've just been digging a few more holes outside, but you don't have to worry about that, either, because the privacy hedges are taller than me. I'm only 11, you know? I try to only go out at night still, but sometimes nature calls. The crabgrass sod picks up easily like a rug, and after I fill the dirt back over, you'd never really know I was there. The problem with this is that you have to remember where all of the holes are, because you don't want to step in one. I started on one side of the yard but I'm moving towards the middle now, and without a light in the backyard it's kind of hard to tell where I've been. So, I went on another nighttime mission through the neighborhood to pull the red and yellow stake flags from all the new construction going on, and I put them near the holes. It kind of looks like our own mini golf course, actually.

Thanks for listening, Mom. I love you and I hope to see you soon.

Adaptation

Men have started knocking on the door.

I see them when I leave for school in the morning, parked under the pink-flowering oleander tree across the street. It scatters flowers across the hood of their car, and I wonder how long they've been sitting there. I don't have a lot of experience with men in suits, but I assume these guys are collectors because whenever the bills weren't paid and someone knocked on the door, Mom and I would hide in the closet.

Assholes. They probably followed us from the apartment.

I take the grass alleyway so they don't see me leaving, but sometimes they catch up to me as I'm walking to the bus stop.

"Where's your mom?" One of them asks.

It's a hot day, and I squint up at their faces, shadowed and serious.

"She's at work," I say, hurriedly. Then, again because their suits purported some kind of authority, I add, "We will be ready to pay the bills soon."

They stand back as I walk past them, gripping my backpack straps tightly, still feeling their eyes on the back of my neck as the bus pulls up. I keep my face blank.

They're tricky bastards, always waiting when I creep home from school, switching up their parking spots, knocking when they think I'm inside. Mom wouldn't answer, so I don't, either; I press my back into the wall so they can't see my shadow, and watch them through the wavy glass framing the door until they disappear.

The electricity, the internet, and the water have been out a month, now. I think this is fine because I was never *You've Got Mail*-ed by anyone except the program itself. And after the eBay fiasco, I've decided that life outside of the walls of the Villa, and into boundless cyberspace, is not for me. I do miss having a clock that tells time; not knowing what time it is has been confusing for my sleep cycles, and I think I've been going to bed awfully early. Partially out of boredom, and the exhausting, painful heat, but also because it's difficult to tell the time in a place like Florida where the nights are just as warm as the days.

The Villa has become unbearably quiet, and my panicked arousal has become a near-nightly occurrence, just like it was when Mom and I first moved in and she would disappear from her bed. Only now, I'm the

31

one disappearing; after many unsuccessful hours of trying to fall asleep, watching the condensation drip from the windows of my terrarium, I decide it's time to pull on a pair of shorts and walk outside, as if leaving the house alone in the dark was as casual as a midnight fridge raid.

Fog hangs over me like a blanket as I slip through our yard, cutting silently across the street. I skip past the oleander tree, glad to see that there's no car beneath it, then run several houses down and out to the golf course. The course is perfectly trimmed, and dew is scattered over the grass like a limitless net of pearls. Seeing it like this, free of golfers and noise, gives me a rush—it's like I'm bursting with secrets, or part of a fantasy, a fairy pixie tiptoe-dancing through the night.

Every time I wake up this early, I try to make it further and deeper into the refuge. Of the 385 acres of manicured golf course, much of it is cut with medians, sand traps, and oases. By law, it is also a nature preserve, safe from developers *and* safe for nests, holes, and dens of all shapes and sizes. I like being out here with them, the day's rejects. The way they come alive, out of hiding once no one is looking, just like me. Sometimes, I catch the beaming white crown of an egret glowing in the light of one of the illuminated fountains and I spread my arms like wings, sprinting from hole to hole. I put a safe distance between myself and the water hazards, knowing that alligators enjoy the safety of these man-made lairs.

I am terribly afraid of the dark, but somehow, the blank, black golf course isn't as scary as the Villa, which has taken on an achingly familiar, sinister air, the way that the apartment felt when Mom would lock herself in her bedroom. It's a raw deal, but I'll take the uncertainty of the outdoors, the endless sounds and hidden inhabitants, over the certain emptiness waiting for me on the other side of the ficuses. Every journey outside makes me bolder, braver; I sprint through the manicured grass, feeling the cold dew tickle my feet until my skin adjusts. I feel like I'm part of the air, cutting through the course, hair whipping behind me. It's an electric feeling, hearing the buzzes and chirps of the other night creatures, the occasional twig snapping behind me. And I go, go, *go* until I'm completely winded, body aching with exhaustion, just in time to tumble into a cold sand trap and lay there, head spinning, until the moment where my body softens against the sand, feeling held. Then, I stumble back home and sleep until sunrise.

Hungry for contact, sticky and hot, I leave the bedroom with purpose one morning, the foggy darkness stretched out like a cloudy carpet. I cushion my bare footsteps, breathing silently from my nose. In my hand, I hold a leash made of my only set of shoelaces.

At first, it was the dragonflies, something I could trap, train, watch, and wile the time away. And once I discovered the sewing kits Grandma left in the Villa for her guests, I knew exactly what to do. Half of my childhood had been spent chasing bugs, and I was an expert at cupping dragonflies in my hands, never crushing their wings—what was tricky was

32

creating the perfect loop, small enough to fit around the middle, but not so tight that its head would break off. It took hours to make them, but once you got it right, you had every bug girl's dream: a fly on a leash.

Okay, so I said I wasn't going to be a bug girl in seventh grade. I promised myself twice. But it was too hard to deny myself the *ooohs* and *aahs* of what I had accomplished. Unfortunately, when I flew the shimmering blue dragonfly on a thread through the halls of my middle school, it was met with everything I had tried to avoid—being seen as a creepy crawly myself. I let my dragonfly go at lunch, string dangling as it disappeared into the sky.

I thought about this as I crossed the golf course, shoelaces in hand, wondering if my classmates had ever seen the electric blue of midnight golf course grass, or if they'd ever chased a flock of spoonbills towards the pond, watching them rise like a pale pink mist. If they felt the way I did whenever I went outside. Then, I shook my head. *I am on a mission.*

I am looking for the Muscovy ducks.

Having chased every lizard and solved every snake from the Villa to the far reaches of the golf course, I have moved onto the ducks. I'm so completely lost in my imagination that catching the ducks is all I think about; I spend my inside time hatching a plan, crafting lassos and mapping out the places that I've seen them, imagining myself with my new best friends, learning from them, loving on them. Compared to the raccoons, opossums, and reptiles that are hidden on the 27 holes, the ducks are both less toothy and less shy when it comes to human interaction. They know that if they stand close enough, there's a chance someone might share part of their dried-out sandwich from the country club pro shop—ducks don't care how terrible a sandwich is, or if it's one of their cousins between the bread. But I haven't been able to locate the ducks after dark, and am determined to find wherever the hell it is that they tuck themselves into when the day comes to an end. Why? Because if I approach them with a snack, they might not notice when I slip a homemade leash around their necks. And if you leave an animal-girl alone long enough, she's going to try her hand at domesticating whatever it is that might not kill her in her quest for company.

Chasing the ducks makes me think of the Big House. Of wandering around with my Critter Cage ™, looking for someone to take home with me. I have always thought of animals as individuals, probably because I spent so much time alone with them instead of kids my own age. When I catch my first one, it pulls against the leash, squawking in fear; my heart drops in an '*oh no, what have I done to this thing I was just trying to love??*' kind of way. I fumble with the rope, trying to loosen the knot and let it go. I get a good nip from the duck in the process and make a mental note to bring scissors the next time I'm back on the golf course.

Several nights later, three ducks waddle feverishly around our screened-in back porch. They've made a terrible mess, smearing their shit across the tile, their webbed feet dragging and smearing the muck. The porch is disgusting. The smell, equally horrifying. But with no running water, I have no way to wash it away, nor do I have anything to offer my friends in terms of food. After a couple of days of throwing stale chips and leaves at their toes, listening to them jabber angrily in the night, pressing their bills into the screen walls and trying to get out, I let them go. I have abandoned all dreams of taming new pets and accepted the reality that hits most pet owners, no matter where you get them from—these guys *stink*. They chatter nervously before taking flight, and I watch their black-and-white tail feathers until they're pinpricks in the sky. I like to think that no ducks were truly harmed in the making of this childhood experience, although many protested being held against their will.

How to Be a Woman

The unpaid credit cards are as worthless as the plastic they're made of. I fling them like frisbees around the house, pinging them off the windows, trying to entertain myself. My only joys are Monday mornings; I have never been so excited to go back to school, to get to eat two meals a day instead of one. The joy of being a seventh grader—which had always felt so significant—is second to a carton of 2% milk.

Lately, I've been getting off at the stop near the grocery store so I can use their bathroom to freshen up, wash my hair, and do anything else that feels sanitarily necessary with the water from the sink, using the hand soap in place of shampoo, body wash—everything. Toothpaste, even. When my hair dries it feels like plastic, but it's better than nothing. I remember to shoot an awkward smile at the cake decorator in the bakery because I know she sees me entering the bathroom fully dry and exiting, 20 minutes later, with damp clothes and a freshly wet, slicked-back hairdo. She's small and brown, with long, clean, shiny black hair that she keeps tight under her hairnet, smile edging off her square face. Even if I don't feel like smiling, her big grin coaxes me into giving her a small one. Sometimes, I think she knows me, that she knows my secrets, but she never mentions anything or even flags me down to ask. The one time she waved me over, she silently gestured to a stray mini cupcake on the counter. I took it wildly into my hands and swallowed it in one bite. It *was* a mini cupcake, after all.

I go to school one day with a wad of cash stuffed into my pocket, something I found while digging around in Mom's closet, trying on her shoes—the kind of hiding spot only a drunk person could come up with, but never remember. When I get off the bus, I march through the automatic doors of Publix, on the hunt for things to make a woman smell nice.

Some of the popular kids were talking next to me at lunch the other day, and I sat extra still so that I could poach their popular tips. Like, how women should smell nice, among a list of other womanly things. I've been wearing the same outfit since the washer and dryer went out, and Blonde Brittany loudly pointed out, once again, that women need to wear new clothes every day. I sat silently, wolfing down my cafeteria lunch. They talk about other girls as if their body splash bottles never hit empty, as if their water always runs freely from the tap. In the bathroom during break,

I asked Nice Jennifer if I could borrow some of her vanilla jasmine body spray, but she said no, so I quickly moved behind her as she sprayed it. Some of the small droplets hit my skin, but a period later, the tiny amount of jasmine vanilla mist had fizzled away, and I was back to smelling like old clothes and the blubbery pink hand soap from the grocery store. I needed more.

Unfortunately, body splash comes from the mall and the mall is straight across town. Skipping school in an attempt to walk there would violate both rules one and two of the Mom-and-Me secrecy pact, so I am going to have to get resourceful in this grocery store. Once my hair is relatively clean, I wander the aisles. I lift my shirt to my face and breathe deeply, smelling the sour staleness of the cotton. A tourist in a "Naples" poncho, basket laden with diet snacks and shrink-wrapped sandwiches, glares at me. I roll my eyes big and far back into my skull until they touch a headache—she sees. Satisfied, I walk down the laundry aisle to find something for my clothes, but fabric refreshers are too far out of my price point, so I grab dryer sheets and a ninety-nine-cent squirt bottle, and make my way towards the baby aisle for the final ingredient to pleasant-smelling womanhood: baby powder. Ah, you sweet, versatile dust. All of my lunches spent close to the 'It' table has granted me the knowledge that baby powder is key to all scent unity; I heard Nice Jennifer say that she read in *Teen People* magazine that a light dusting of baby powder across your body after a shower would keep you smelling fresh, and a small shake into your two-day-old hair would revive it back to life. Everyone at the It table had really great hair. Mine was leaking the last of the grocery store sink water onto my shoulders as I checked out.

At home, it took 10 minutes to mix five dryer sheets and water into the spray bottle and spray down my entire clothes pile, another five to drench my body and hair. It then took two days before anyone noticed, but finally stupid, annoying Bowl Cut Sean from science class said that I smelled like fresh laundry, which I wouldn't say was bad. But the rash I got from the bouillon of chemicals sprayed directly onto my skin took about a week to go away, and stupid Sean mentioned that, too.

May, 1997

Guess what, Mom?

I stacked the dining room chairs against the front wall and finally got my hands on that tree frog you liked to say 'good morning' to! But then I saw the bus coming and had to rush to make it on, so I brought him with me to school. Everything was going fine until the first bell rang and he jumped off my shoulder, right onto Softball Dierdre's hair, and then Blonde Brittney was screaming from one desk away and he jumped at her eye, right onto her shimmery white eye shadow. I really fucking hate Blonde Brittany, Mom. I know you say she's an idiot but it's hard not to feel like I do when I can still hear her laughing down the hall, telling everyone how weird I am for bringing the frog to school, saying that I really must live in the swamp. I carried him from the hallway to the bushes outside and set him on the windowsill outside your old classroom, just how he liked to sit at the Villa. We can visit him there when you come home.

Also, I'm sorry about the scratches on Grandma's nice dining room chairs. I don't think she'll notice where the stucco notched into the wood under my weight when I was trying to get the frog—I filled the scratches in nicely with Sharpie, but we only had black and orange so I mixed them together.

It's weird how, in elementary school, everyone likes you if you successfully smuggle an animal into class, but in middle school, people think you're gross and weird. Why do you think that is, Mom?

Fuckslugs

The men in suits think they're sneaky, think they're *so* sly sitting in their car watching me come and go, but they don't have a garage to hide in so I can see them clearly every morning, every day, late spring sunlight glowing from the hood of their car. Unlike the rest of the seashell-colored town cars in the neighborhood, theirs is dark and tinted. They got out of the car three times this week, asking for my mom. The last afternoon, they tried to catch me at the end of the block before I went down the alleyway. I told them that I had a few dollars in cash that I could give them if they would *just* stop coming around, but it didn't really phase them. All they said was that they would come back again later to check in on me. Greedy fuckslugs—you can't scare me. GIVE IT UP!

I didn't lie to the men when I told them I only had a few dollars. I'm hungry all of the time, and it's hard to focus at school with my rumbling stomach and itchy, sour skin. My teeth feel furry from all of the lemon water I've been drinking, and I have big, persistent sores across my gum line. It hurts when I talk, and I think people are starting to notice them. Thankfully, something exciting has happened! I was sitting on the bus this morning, thinking about which mini box of cereal I was going to choose for my free breakfast, when I spotted an orange tree on the other side of the neighborhood. I couldn't figure out which lawn it was, but I knew it was somewhere adjacent to the 14th hole because I recognized the house with the big, bright camellia tree, which I know means it's time to make a left and get home off the course; after school, I waited until it was dark before running out the slider. The pouty, round bodies of the oranges glowed against the blue-black leaves, not as bright as the lemons, but enough to catch the eye. I cradled them in the pouch of my big t-shirt and smiled down at their cheerful faces, holding them close as I sidestepped a freshly dug hole in the yard. I unpeeled two of the oranges for dinner, and set the rest aside for later. When I finished, I stood up a little too quickly and saw stars, but once I caught my balance, I dragged Mom's pillow into the bathtub with me and closed my eyes, feeling the coolness of the tub swaddle me as I picked orange pulp from my teeth.

Unfortunately, by the next afternoon, trapped in the house with all of the windows and doors shut, steaming behind the glass, the oranges have gone bad. They leaked through my fingers when I tried to peel them and were too soft to eat. I went out again to gather more, and the

38

same problem occurred. Suddenly, I was ripped out of the trance of preoccupation. Worthlessness screamed inside of me and all around me, my situation suddenly magnified, every emotion, peaking. Something inside me burst: I shrieked and whipped the oranges at the wall, watching as the fruity guts and pulp streamed slowly down to the floor. The shock of my voice and the sound of the violent splatters wrapped around me, and I felt satisfied. I reached for the rest and disposed of them in the same manner, my screams echoing through the house in an angry, empty way. The room smelled sugary sweet, citrus covering decay, and my body shook as if I'd run the golf course ten times over. I fell asleep that night with sticky hands, and when I woke up to go to school the next day, I told myself that I'd clean up the mess before going back out for more oranges. They smelled nice at first, but now that the carcasses have been left exposed and rotting, flies have started appearing out of nowhere to suck on their spoiled, fermented blood, and the house smells like a garbage can, room to room.

The Villa creaks its ribs under the dampness of the night air. By sleeping in the bathtub, I feel cool enough to still want to wrap myself in a blanket, because sleeping without a blanket feels like a crime against oneself. Having no blanket feels sad. I'm not sad, I'm just heavy, as heavy as the humid air. I miss my mom, and in the bathtub, I can smell her perfume as it drifts from the surface of her vanity. I think about her paper skin, like I always do at night. The way small ridges honeycombed around the dark spots on her arms, about the blueish tones underneath, thinking about all of the times her thin skin had bruised. I dig my fingernails into the pillow, gripping it tightly, smelling the remnants of her perfume, and hoping that her skin is flesh-toned again. That wherever it is, it's keeping her warm.

CRACK! CRACK! CRACK!

I am up and moving my feet across the carpet before my brain is on, or my eyes have even opened. My arms and fingers are outstretched, feeling for something, for the small fire she's started, for the noise of her bursting in through the back door. For a moment, in those soft seconds between sleep and wakefulness, I'm reaching for my mom. Then, my brain comes-to and I know, once again, that I'm alone. But now what? It's quiet again, and a light is shining through the beveled glass sidelights at the front door. I'm trying to make sense of the moment, unsure when I fell asleep. Someone outside is saying my name, my mom's name, calling for us. *Fuck,* I think. *They're calling for you.* I crane my neck to glance out the side kitchen window, trying to figure out what time it is. The sky is black-black—it's late-late. I hear my name again, this time in a large, booming voice. *Shit.* Another light shines through the window, just behind the other one. I slump down, scratching my tangled hair. *What do I do, what do I do, what do I do?*

I know I'm not supposed to open this door, but they ask me to. Their voices aren't angry. They say they want to help me and I pause, but answer

39

sooner than I expected myself to.

"Alright!" I yell hoarsely. "I'm coming."

I know this is wrong, know it goes against direct orders, but I'm tired. Tired, not just because it's late, but because I'm hungry and I'm hot and I'm tired of everything. I'll take anything, any little change to shock the system, even if it hurts, no matter what it costs. I toss aside the rules and peel back the bar lock on the door, and the door gently pops open. The paint is sticky from the heat. My skin is damp, hairs on my legs and arms, prickling. Through the crack I can see the bill men and they can see me. Their suits are ill-fitting, pants covering too much of their shoes, stressed buttons stretching across their big bellies. Slugs.

"Hello?" I rasp.

"Rachael? Is your mother here? We need to speak with her."

I step back because I don't have the answer for this and they know it. The heat from inside the house hits them like a concrete wall.

As one of them looks over my shoulder, I can feel his eyes landing on the pile of split, rotting oranges on the carpet. He continues to scan for signs of life, but there are none. I wince as he steps forward, but he only lifts his hand to the light switch. When no bulb flickers on, the other man points his flashlight into the house, and I see the gold badge on his hip, and I know it's all over. *Mom, I'm sorry.*

Alone

Alone is not one feeling, one emotion. It is hundreds of feelings, a spitball of complexes, a soul and a mind rolled up and chewed through and spat on until everything gets compressed, pushed, forced through a straw. Sadness, anger, guilt, fear, shame, anxiety, resentment, terror, regret, confusion, SO MUCH confusion, the kind of confusion that claws at your stomach and crawls out your mouth, barking, red-hot and searing, "*Why am I alone?*" Because loneliness isn't dark and ominous, loneliness rarely keeps you up at night—it's how you *became* alone that haunts your heart. What could you have done differently? What steps did you take along the way? Could you have avoided any of them? The loneliness is simply the final form. A quiet that is more than quiet, a steady, reliable silence whose calm is filled by the emotional spew that brought you to the final place: here, alone. The dust of all of those other feelings has finally settled, and until you take a clean finger and swipe it along the caked-in dirt and lift it to your face, you won't see the specks, the shaking moments siphoned off like dead skin, like dander, smudging not just your finger, but the very air you breathe. And then you'll watch as the white track below the dust, the imprint of your fingertip, fills just as quickly as you cleaned it, until alone is the only thing you see, room after room, no matter where you go.

That's what will keep you up at night.

827.10
Female, Age 11

Ms. Kilroy picks me up at the station. She's crumpled under her mumu, a housecoat wrapped tightly over her round body, a thick pair of glasses hanging onto her nose. I've only ever seen her in contacts and it takes me a moment to recognize her, eyes shriveled and small behind the lenses. She doesn't hug me when she sees me, doesn't reach out a hand. She talks to the officers in their ill-fitting suits, my name sounding strange in their mouths. I sit in a plasticky leather chair down the hall, shuffling my feet over the fibrous carpet like I'm running in place. Blue, red, gray, green. None of the colors go together, but they form a muddled gray pixilation, background noise for this room and whatever happens in it. It's what I stared at while the therapist talked to me, so much so that the low, buzzing hum of the blurry colors drowned out her voice while she talked. When she was done, the officers walked me out to the hallway, handing me a cup of apple juice and a few graham crackers. Baby food for the baby. The juice stung my dry throat, and I resumed my watch of the carpet while the officers joined the therapist in the room. By the time they're done, Ms. Kilroy is there. We walk out to her car, dawn light reminding me of the morning Mom left.

"Well, your mom really did it this time," she says in her East Coast accent. Now, she hugs me. I can tell she wants to comfort me, but I feel blank, static filling my insides, bubbling like carbonation.

"*What* was she thinking? I mean, *honestly*. You know she's been calling me about once a month. Huh! She said you two were in New York."

Ms. Kilroy prattles on, occasionally glancing into the rearview mirror to look at me in the backseat. Her minivan smells like Windex and onion soup. I shiver in my big t-shirt, toes numb in my flipflops.

"You cold, honey? Oh, what am I *saying*? Of *course* you're cold, look at you. What on *Earth*, well…"

Ms. Kilroy is a Jewish mom stereotype, overbearing in opinion and hyper-focused in her care, her love-language translated by way of constant picking, prodding, micromanaging. She's so unlike my own mom that I don't even know what to think, and can't imagine them actually being friends outside of the school; I remember going to Applebee's once with Mom and Ms. Kilroy, but it was a long time ago, well before the apartment or the Villa. She was expecting the call from the officers as much as I was expecting them to come pounding on our door.

42

Ms. Kilroy stops her New Jersey minivan in the driveway of the Villa. It's the first time I've ever actually seen the place from this angle, and although I've been living here alone for nearly a year, it looks strange and unfamiliar. I quiet the instinct to tell Ms. Kilroy to pull the car down the street so that the neighbors don't see us and unbuckle my seatbelt.

We go inside together, and I hear the sharp intake of breath as Ms. Kilroy looks around the house, the early morning light illuminating the chaos of the kitchen, the rotten oranges, the stains on the floor. Flies buzz around our ears, and Ms. Kilroy waves a fretful hand, shooing them away.

"Do—d'you have something for your clothes, *Rachael*?"

Ms. Kilroy says my name with a *huchh* in the back of her throat, the Yiddish way. I know it comes from a place of care, so I don't correct her; when she was talking to the cops, she sounded like she *knew* me, and although I could tell she was upset with Mom, she was protective of our situation, giving them only mandatory information and not a syllable more.

Now that I've left the Villa, I am finally smelling it for the first time: the hot, humid air, the contents of the toilets that I couldn't flush, the unwashed clothes, spoiled food, the swampy smell of the pipes creeping out through the drains. Ms. Kilroy follows me into my bedroom, where my pile of old clothes sits stinking and sweat-logged in the corner. As she bends down next to me and starts grabbing shirts, shorts, I become aware of her hurry, aware that she doesn't want to spend another minute in my smell, and I start to feel wrapped in it, embarrassed. I cast wads of clothing aside, trying to find things like underwear and socks.

"Whatever you don't have, we'll get for you. I'm sure you can fit a few of Arielle's old things…"

She's suggesting this so we can leave and I know it. She doesn't want to breath this place anymore.

Quickly, I try to hide Piggy underneath a couple of shirts and shove the clump into the old grocery bag on the floor. Once we've scrounged up enough clothes to fill it, Ms. Kilroy walks me back to the front door. I turn and look behind me, at the kitchen, the hallway, my feet in the place where Mom last stood. I shift, locking my footsteps perfectly into hers.

"Let's get going, then. Breakfast and a shower."

The soupy smell of Ms. Kilroy's car matches the smell of her house. Parsley. It's dark inside, shades drawn, but I know that she will open them once the sun comes all the way up, and that the white tiles in the kitchen will shimmer with their light. Ms. Kilroy has the same job as my mom, but she lives in a house that she actually pays for, well-kept and tidy, in a development similar to Foxfire. She has more side tables and coffee tables in her place than anything else, each one cluttered with pictures of her kids, Arielle and Shawn. Seeing their faces, and the orderly, intentional way the house is made up, makes me feel out of place, like I'm messing it up just by being there. It's not overly tidy—it just feels like there are rules inside. Rules that I am bound to break.

43

Arielle is six years older than me, her brother, a few years younger than her. Unlike kids my age, Arielle is *scary* cool: she wears a ball-chain choker around her neck, skinny jeans, and tight tank tops that flaunt a Hebrew symbol tattooed in the center of her back. I knew about the tattoo because, during the Applebee's dinner a few years earlier, I remembered Ms. Kilroy freaking out about it at the restaurant—her daughter was only 16 at the time, after all. While Arielle smoked cigarettes and went to punk shows, Shawn wore button-down *Dragon Ball Z* shirts and collected throwing stars, but they both shared the habit of spending as little time in the house as possible, rolling their eyes every time their mom asked where they were going or why they were dressed the way they were. Their dad wasn't in the picture, either, so I was the one Ms. Kilroy dragged around, the new object of her motherly attention. Divorced women have a lot of love to give, and they dollop it in excess, sometimes at a cost to themselves. It's a lesson I'll learn in 20 years, but in this moment, I am ready to hold her love.

The first few days at Ms. Kilroy's really rocked me. I quietly slumped from room to room, out of the way of her kids. I was as poorly socialized as a shelter dog, even more terrified of talking to older kids than I was those my own age. I wanted to hang around Arielle, but at the same time, I didn't want her to talk to me or see me sitting on the couch. And I definitely didn't want to get close enough to where she would expect things out of me. I was still dealing with the humiliation of everything that had happened; I let my mom down and now I'm here, interrupting Ms. Kilroy's life, adding another spot on her morning drop-off, sitting behind Shawn. I still haven't spoken to Mom on the phone, but Ms. Kilroy has given me enough bits and pieces to understand that she's not coming back anytime soon. Whenever Mom does come up, I like that Ms. Kilroy's tone is pointed and direct, I haven't been spoken to in such a clear way before. I like that she sees my history, and understands that I can handle the truth.

Mom *was* in a rehab facility but then left and started drinking again. Now she's somewhere around Miami, staying in another facility; what she doesn't tell me is that Mom got a DUI and has to stay there per the terms of her arrest. *That* part was on a paper I found later on, sitting on her kitchen island. And as I went through the papers, I found something else: CPS had contacted my grandparents before getting in touch with Ms. Kilroy. But when they were asked if they wanted to take over as my legal guardians, they said no. It said so right on the paper. *Declined*. Rejected by my own family.

Summer vacation started, and I still felt like I was walking on eggshells around the Kilroy's house. I no longer felt the need to hover around Ms. Kilroy like a shadow, watching her make dinner and listening to her gossip about women from the synagogue, but I didn't feel comfortable enough to take up much space. Mostly, I laid in my room reading Arielle's old schoolbooks, or listening to the angry music blaring from Shawn's bedroom, nodding my head along and mouthing the words. He listened to the same few tracks over and over again, so although I didn't know many of the band names, or anything about them, I was starting to have favorites. It wasn't the same kind of stillness as the Villa, but my body begged for movement, and I found myself missing those nights at the golf course, how the smooth palm of the sand traps curled around my burning muscles. Ms. Kilroy's yard was small and manicured to match the neighbors', but there wasn't much life—a bulk pesticide took care of that—so I would just mill around her front yard, picking at the grass. She must have gotten tired of seeing me lay around, or maybe she wanted Arielle to spend some time with me, because eventually, she suggested that Arielle take me with her to the mall.

Mallrat Opossum

Arielle popped a cigarette between her lips as soon as we were out of sight, and steered with her knee while she lit up. As she prodded me with questions, I quickly discovered that I was a dud. A dud without interests, or friends, or identity—the things that shaped Arielle's world. Was I supposed to have these things already?

"I really like Blink-182, the *Cheshire Cat* album," I threw out.

"*Blink-182*? That's kid shit," she said, shaking her head, not looking at me. "Pick something here."

She reached into the backseat of her car to grab a binder packed with music. Overwhelmed, I grabbed the first CD I saw—it was black, and looked like it was covered in magazine clippings—and Arielle slammed her hand across the dial to turn it up full blast, filling the void left by my lacking personality.

"Huggy Bear," she screamed. "Good choice."

If I had anything to say to her now, she wouldn't have been able to hear it over the sound of the music and the rattle of her car speakers, struggling to keep up with the bass. There was no space for conversation, let alone a single thought. I think she was doing me a favor.

Naples looked different from the passenger seat in Arielle's car. Maybe it was the angry music shaking my shoulders, or the teenager behind the wheel, but I felt like I was actually entering my city for the first time. We passed the high school, then turned into the mall parking lot. When Arielle killed the engine and the music stopped, she turned to me.

"Just try to keep up, okay?"

An order.

The mall with Arielle was unlike anything I'd experienced before. No shopping, no parents, no time limit. The few times I'd accompanied Mom on an errand, she'd dragged me by my wrist through the crowds, the veins in her temples pulsing as she barked at me to move faster. We never walked around like this, never went anywhere without a mission; as Arielle and I approached the pet store, I remembered the time Mom guilt-splurged on one of the puppies in the window. We'd spent the whole drive home thinking of names, and I slept with its tiny head on my foot that night. Two days later, Mom accidentally ran it over with her car. I hurried past the store with a pit in my stomach, realizing what state she was probably in when she drove that day, and tried to push the memory back where it came from, feeling childish.

When Arielle had enough of wandering, she led us to Journey's, where her friend John—an older dude in a couple local bands who wore the same ball-chain choker as she did—had a daytime gig as the store manager. All of her friends looked like men and women, and I sat on the store bench while people tried on shoes, watching them come into the store, listening as Arielle gave them the same careless "Hey." It was funny to me that this whole place was built around the idea of being alternative and different from everyone else, yet all of the shoppers and employees were alike; at home, Arielle was the only one dressed in black, piercings shoved through every inch of cartilage. But at Journey's, where a continuous reel of pop punk music videos and skateboarders played on the T.V., the place and its people looked just as curated and corporate as every other corner of the mall. Just as I was wondering whether wearing black would help me find some people of my own, Arielle tapped me on the shoulder.

"I'm gonna meet up with some friends," she said, pulling another cigarette from inside of her purse and tucking it behind her ear. She looked behind her to make sure John saw her. "I'll pick you up outside the food court at four, okay?"

I nodded, used to having time to myself, but not in a place like this. I watched her disappear into the crowd of people walking and talking, and decided it wouldn't be so bad to disappear myself.

At first, I had no idea which way to go. I moved aimlessly, weaving between tourists carrying big bags with beach hats from Bloomingdale's, jumping around old women speed-walking in matching track suits, finding that the more I moved, the more energized I became. I poked into every store and kiosk that seemed to attract kids my age, or teenagers that looked like Arielle, sliding in behind them and pretending to shop while they chatted with each other, joking and goofing around. I milled around Pacific Sunwear, listening to the older kids talk about music, noticing which kinds of clothes they pulled off the racks. I'd been practicing being invisible for so long that the mall turned out to be everything that the end of the It Table hadn't been—completely anonymous, and completely informative. Cool girls with layered tank tops and low-rise jeans toted bags from Bath and Body Works, and I hopped around the mall until I found that powerfully-perfumed mecca, beelining for the body sprays that had been so out of reach back when I was at the Villa. No dryer sheets mixed with water, here; I couldn't decide which scent to choose, so I doused myself in all of the bubbly, artificial-fruit-scented mists, layering everything from Nice Jennifer's signature jasmine vanilla to cucumber melon before going over to the lotions. I slathered my skin in various shades and scents of body glitter and glitter lotion, appraising the sparkle of my skinny arms in the bright fluorescent lights.

I had been so busy moving around the mall that I didn't notice my growling stomach—not until I encountered the food court, anyway. I walked back and forth, unsure where to start, or how I'd pay for a snack. As I did, I was passed not one, not two, but *three* mini pretzel bites

47

smothered in cinnamon swirl frosting by the girl holding the sample tray outside the Auntie Anne's. I tried the same tactic in front of the Orange Julius and left with several paper cups of milky smoothie. It became obvious to me that the minimum-wage employees carrying the free sample trays in the food court could not give less of a shit if you asked for one, five, or the entire tray of their lukewarm products, because minimum wage means minimum attention to the face of the kid who has passed you three times in a row. I mean, the whole *'manning-the-sample-tray'* gig might've beat punching numbers at the register, but all of it was just another way to wile down the hours until they got to take a smoke break in the parking lot, or switch to another equally mundane task behind the kiosk. If the employees didn't have the painfully disinterested look of Arielle, they were middle-aged moms, dads, aunts, and uncles who knew hunger when they saw it. They happily passed sample cups my way, and I wolfed them down, mirroring their smiles, grateful that the sample people—like the cake decorator—told me how they wanted me to feel.

When Arielle met me in the parking lot at 4:00, I was full, stimulated, and smelled like six conflicting types of plants, desserts, and citrus. As we pulled out onto the interstate, I stared out of my window, watching the glassy rooftop of the Coastland Shopping Center gleam in the evening sun, Riot Grrrl screaming in my ears. For the first time in a long time, my world felt large, almost infinite. I felt optimistic.

Arielle's mall drop-offs became a routine, the kind of structure I didn't know I needed. Sure, I had aimless hours to myself in a shopping center, but the dependability of getting to and from the mall, of seeing the same stores, the same food court, even the same security guards, was a comfort to me. And I had been so isolated when I was living at the Villa that all of the crowds, the employees, and the families eking out of every corner stamped out the loneliness I was used to. I would sit at a table in the food court with my handful of free samples spread out on a napkin, stacking free sugar packets in front of me, watching families do family things, friends be friends. Even though their lives were happening around me, I felt like I was part of the moment.

China Hut, an intentionally obvious riff on Pizza Hut that was saved from copyright infringement only because of the small size of our town, was another place that taught me that politeness, and just the right amount of ass-kissery, could get you anything. Aiko, the middle-aged man that worked there, gave me a free scoop of orange chicken as long as I remembered to say, "Thank you, mister Aiko." I was never sure whether this was his first or last name, but I learned that as long as I sold him a smile and assured him I was having a "fine" day, I could count on China Hut for snacks. Whenever he asked where my mom was, I told Aiko that she was coming to pick me up. It was the same lie I told to the mall security guards when I was still seated at my table, food court employees hanging up their aprons, the metal doors swinging shut on the shops, waiting for Arielle to come get me.

48

I never felt like anyone really wanted to *know* how I was doing, anyway. And, truthfully, I didn't want to talk about it. There was anger towards my mom, stress over her whereabouts, a feeling of not being enough, of being the kind of kid you can leave behind. How do you put that into words without crying? Toeing the line between the perfect amount of kiss-ass and anonymity, saying enough to not tip anyone off, was better for me. I didn't want to cause concern for my lack of supervision, so I mimicked adults' expressions back to them to put their minds at ease. And in return, the people at the mall got the warm, fuzzy feeling that happens when a smiling near-stranger remembers your name, or follows up on a story that was told to them last week. I asked about Aiko's wife, the security guard's son, the smoothie girl's shitty boyfriend. I was selling, selling, selling, and in return, I got people. People who had things, a lot of things, even if it was just an extra caramel sauce meant for the side of a giant pretzel, or the opportunity to walk down the dark hallways that run behind the storerooms and food court restaurants, helping the security guard check all of the locks. I got a playing field to test out every kind of personality trait I wanted or maybe didn't, an audience to practice who I was and who could handle knowing what about me.

After a few test-runs of telling people why I was at the mall or where I lived or where my mom was, I was met with questions, long faces, '*Oh, honey*'s,' and sad eyes, all of them reflecting the very obvious hope that I was going to jump in and say, "Just kidding!" at the end of the conversation. And I learned that it was honestly a chore to answer these questions, because the answer is never the right one. I saw their wincing, concerned looks, could stare into their disbelieving open mouths and practically see the wheels turning, the '*What Lifetime movie is this again?*' cogs pushing through the brain sludge. I *definitely* knew I didn't have the answers or emotions that they were hoping for, and was fully aware that it was a drag to *be* a drag. So, I dropped the helpless-preteen-angst-shtick at the Coastland Center doors, adopting a more positive spin. "My single mom works long hours and the mall is safe," "she picks me up before close but today she'll be here early." That's what they wanted. Not just to hear that it wasn't *really* that bad, but also that today was better than the day before because I was going home early, that we were going to go to the movies after she picked me up, or whatever other lie I felt was appropriate for my audience. This was the beginning of my education on giving people what they wanted, on pitching, positioning, propping up and selling myself for the minor gains that lead to larger gains. And if now you're thinking that the cusp of eleven, twelve, or thirteen years old is too young to be aware of what the world wants from you, then you are wrong, because the right time to learn this is exactly the time when you are handed the opportunity.

... The Skatepark

The mall was my teacher, and one of the first lessons that I learned was that there was a right and wrong way to look at boys, and the right and wrong kind of boys to look at. Boys with suntanned skin and blond highlights were laughers, the kind of kids who pointed and hollered when they noticed your gaze—in other words, scary boys. Any time I saw a shared team sweatshirt, I kept my eyes down, knowing the jock-y types were never afraid to shout at you to get a laugh. The older boys with car keys jingling in their pockets rarely returned my glances, but they also smelled like weed and drugstore cologne, and pretty much only hung around the piercing kiosk, flirting with curvy girls whose noses and eyebrows were decorated with cubic zirconia. Finding the space between too long and too short of a look was difficult, but I learned that the right glance would allow a boy to see me seeing *him,* but wouldn't leave enough room for him to come up and talk to me. It would be another year before I actually started harboring affection for boys, but learning that I could bat an eye or steal a glance from a 15-year-old pushing a floor sweeper around the carpet at Pacific Sunwear before they closed for the day gave me hope for my future. When he quickly averted his gaze, I felt warm, almost empowered, like I was someone worth looking at, maybe someone who, someday, could have a boyfriend like John from Journey's to stand near in a stock room or Paul from PacSun to loiter at the trashcans with. So, the mall was good for that, too. In fact, it was the epicenter of many teenaged milestones, not just for myself, but for the entire pubescent population of Naples.

Because of its location, the mall in our town *was* our town. Limestone carved with leaves, fake fronds in massive pots next to the garbage cans, and a palm tree-lined parking lot all reminded you that you were still beach adjacent—0.8 blocks away from the beach, to be exact—but it felt different from the rest of Naples. During the summertime, tourists were reminded to put a t-shirt on over their bikini tops before going into Nordstrom's.

My parents used to say "when they built this, it was in the middle of nowhere. Then the town filled in around it"

Coastland Center was built across the street from Naples' eponymous high school, with Jungle Larry's bordering the east end of the mall entrance. Jungle Larry's was a local zoo, the kind of animal-rights nightmare that could only exist in 90's South Florida, but somehow still managed to hang on by a thread up until a tropical storm one season blew it to shreds. The newly homeless troop of orange monkeys that had been running amok at Jungle Larry's moved into the trees surrounding Naples High School's football field, and could sometimes be seen scurrying across the campus holding lunch trash.

In a couple years, I'd attend this high school—one of three high schools I'd enroll in non-consecutively across my four high school years, actually. There, I'd fight for my space amongst kids whose parents spent weekends on their yachts, whose parents' parents grandfathered them into one lucrative industry or another, trouncing around town like they owned the place. Which, in truth, some did.

But this fact would not only remain completely unbeknownst to me, as the school and mall were on the entirely opposite side of town from where I ever lived, but also, I would never have attended Naples High School at all if it weren't for a random, extra boring day spent at the mall. One that saw me slumped over a chair in the food court, flicking a chicken nugget around the chrome perimeter of my table with a straw. Fate, and a gentle giant named Josh, would connect a pink sugar packet to the back of my head, and I would ignore both of them, as most of us do when fate drops hints, but neither fate nor Josh took very kindly to being pushed aside and ignored that day, and eventually one of them flung enough pink sugar packets to force me to not only accept the fact that yes, indeed, I was being pegged in the back of the head, and no, I could not just ignore the person launching them. The interference into my every day programming caused me to whip around, annoyed, my daily descent into anonymity interrupted. My scowl was met with a smile by a 16-year-old boy towering at six-foot-four, whose awkward, big body and baggy jeans spilled over the Cookie Company kiosk. His feet were propped up on the counter against the plexiglass window, just under the soda machine, and back against the opposite wall of the plastic booth was a pile of pink sugar packets waiting to be hurled in my direction, had I not turned around.

"What?" I snapped, doing my best to look cool and unbothered by the sugary assault, but also cool and *also* bothered by the world around me.

"Why are you always in this mall?" He asked, his voice about two octaves higher than I had expected for a person of his size, as soft as an unbaked cookie.

Instantly, he became non-threatening, and despite what I had learned from hanging out with the adults in this mall, this was a kid. Or, some kind of hybrid. When I looked at him, I saw a person that, like me, didn't quite fit the mold. Unlike most of the teenagers in the mall, spending their parents' money and driving away in brand new cars, Josh was earning minimum wage at the Cookie Company behind a counter that was five sizes too small for his body, with a voice equally mismatched to his shape. It might have been that I was simply tired of making up excuses for why I was at the mall, or maybe that I was tired of carrying the real story inside of me, I spilled my guts.

Josh and I sat at his kiosk and talked until the end of his shift, when a quiet girl named Amanda came to relieve him. Amanda had very dark hair and shockingly pale skin, and the contrast of her size to Josh reminded me of a little mouse; as they muttered to each other in their equally tiny voices, I tried to figure out if she was 16 like Josh, or 30. I never did establish her age, but over the next few weeks, I started my mall days at the cookie counter, where I would learn that Josh and Amanda would occasionally have sex in the fridge behind the kiosk where all of the cookie dough was kept, and I made a mental note to avoid eating any of the cookies kept back there. I also learned that sometimes Josh would hook up with other girls back there, too. Girls that came to see him at the cookie counter for that reason alone. The simplicity and casualty of it all seemed odd to me at first, and made Josh seem much, *much* older than me, but I assumed that, like most things, I just didn't "get it" yet. In fact, I had never really thought about *it* at all. I would eventually learn to look and see if there were two backpacks behind the counter when I got there, and if there were, I would use this cue to determine whether or not to wait around and grab some free chicken from China Hut or to take a few laps around the mall until Josh would be free to sit around and hang out like normal.

On that first day, when Amanda got there for her shift, Josh began to gather his things. I could sort of picture his size when he was crumpled up in the Cookie Company kiosk, but once he was standing, I really got a good look at how awkwardly giant he was for his age, and tried not to laugh at his voice in comparison.

"Hey, Rachael, have you ever been across the street? To the skatepark?"

I shook my head, busily chewing my third free chocolate chip sex room cookie. When Josh spoke to me, he made sure to avoid slang or phrases that I wouldn't understand so that I could keep up with his stories, which I appreciated.

"Do you want to walk over there with me? Now?"

Josh rattled off questions without any expectations as far as an answer because, really, both of us were well aware that I had no place to be. Watching Josh as he rose from the kiosk, no longer a kid, but now a towering man with a baby face, I had that feeling that happens when you see someone you know outside of the only place that you know them, like seeing a teacher in a restaurant. As he peeled the Cookie Company polo shirt off of his sloped shoulders, now standing in front of me in an oversized t-shirt (do they even make oversized shirts for oversized people??) and jeans and torn-up sneakers, I felt like I had been talking to a separate person. I had spent about five hours with the first version, Cookie Josh, but this Josh? Did I technically want to go anywhere with this brand-new person?

Eager for a plot twist in my Lifetime movie, my gut said yes. I wiped the cookie crumbs off of my mouth and stood up from my table, coming up to Josh's elbow.

"Yeah, sure. I'll go."

Of course, I knew the skatepark existed. How could I sit in a mall every day and *not* notice packs of sweaty, loud boys coming through the food court to get drinks multiple times a day? But did I really know what was over there? No, not at all. And I preferred it that way. Large groups of any kind were a 'no' for me.

"I can't believe you've never been over here," said Josh, shaking his shaggy head. "With all that time spent in the mall, you could be a cool skater chick if you wanted to by now."

As he said it, I knew that's what I wanted to be. He included me, grouped me in, and I was willing to do whatever it took to belong. But also, cutting through the mall parking lot, the thought made me sweat. It difficult to keep up with Josh and his long-legged strides. I walked a little faster, By the time we reached the hedges on the outside of the mall property, Josh left me with a final piece of advice.

"There's a lot of boys over there, Rachael. Don't kiss any of them. Okay? You don't, I mean, you don't even think about that stuff yet, though, right?"

Josh treated me like a baby, but in a way, that made me feel even safer around him.

"No, no, of course not," I said hurriedly. "Gross."

I stayed close to Josh as we walked through the front gate, hiding behind his big body, probably standing a bit too close because his skateboard had already hit me twice in the thigh. Which hurt like hell, but I wasn't about to chance it with the kids surrounding me; I'd take pain over social humiliation any day.

It was loud in the skatepark, and the stadium lights made me feel brand new after the long hours spent under the fluorescent bulbs in the mall. The sun was already setting, and a nice tropical breeze set in. The time of day when all of the tourists say, "Isn't it amazing here?"

In a way, the skatepark *was*. There were boys everywhere. Moving really fast, talking really loud, taking up space. They all looked exactly like Josh with their big t-shirts, baggy jeans, and *really* messed up sneakers, and I noticed that, like all of my shoes, none of them were brand name. But nobody seemed embarrassed—they huddled around in support to watch as someone lined a split seam with glue and sat it in the sun to dry, sweaty-socked feet propped up on the railing for some air. I sat down on the edge of the bowl as Josh nosed his board forward, chin resting on my knees, folded in front of my chest, eyes on the boys' sneakers. Already, I was picking up on a new life hack—by looking at someone's shoes, you can tell if they're your people. Every brand-new classroom, every crowded bar, every new work environment: if you look at the shoes, you can find your crowd. Because, more than stylistically, shoes indicate a lifestyle.

The skaters weren't my people yet. I knew that from the cramped knockoff Keds on my feet, to the confused looks the boys shot me over their shoulders. Josh introduced me to his group, going down the line of names—Brett, Quin, Dan, Jesse, Billy, and Joe—and they nodded in my direction. No one talked to me, and I liked it that way. It gave me time to study them all, sitting quietly under the bright lights, watching Josh skate around and laugh with his friends. When they needed a break, they came up and sat around me, making crass jokes. No one seemed to care that they had never seen me before, or that I wasn't contributing to the conversation. Sitting next to Josh bought me the kind of social currency that I'd never had in elementary or middle school. Whatever I was— whoever—I was vouched for. And I liked being vouched for more than I had even liked walking around the mall alone.

Once the sun went down and the stadium lights turned on, the younger kids went home. I watched Josh disappear inside of the doors of the community center set at the back of the park, listening as moms ushered their kids into their minivans. When he came back out, the boring, family-friendly 80s rock that had been playing from the skatepark speakers was gone. Rap started blasting, and everyone in the skatepark cheered. I watched as a stringy kid high-fived him, narrowing my eyes.

Eric "Butchie" Perry and I first met in the second grade. He was small and quiet with thick glasses that broke once after we got into a fight. He blamed the whole thing on one of his brother, Derek's, friends. Although he had absolutely nothing to do with it, that kid was still not allowed over to their house, but in second grade, anything beats admitting to your family that you lost a fight to a girl.

We'd met again in fourth grade when Butchie didn't let a single person in the school miss the fact that I had "accidentally" dyed my hair bright red with a $1.99 henna hair kit that my mom had stocked up on during a manic episode. To be honest, I picked the red from the other colors in the bag because I wanted to look more like her; the box had promised golden strawberry, but had turned me into a fire engine redhead with a borderline mullet, more faux pas than bombshell. It had been years since then, and although the departure of his glasses gave way to a barely recognizable entanglement of disheveled hair and lanky limbs, I still felt the burning desire to tell him to go away. This, and the worry of what a familiar face might mean for me at the skatepark, where I was trying to reinvent myself.

I felt my whole body tense up as he walked over to me, dragging his skateboard behind him. The half-smile on his face did nothing for me; I had so many questions and concerns, beginning with whether or not *he* would ask *me* a lot of questions. The most important of them being, why does he look like *that*? Why does he look like Josh when I feel like such a little kid, yet we're practically the same age? I stared down at my shoes. Kid's shoes. Butchie was only a year older than me, but somehow, in the stadium lights, it looked like he needed a shave.

"Hey. Rachael, right?" He asked, sitting down next to me. "Do you remember me? We had second grade together."

"YES," I blurted, loudly and abruptly, before he could mention my mullet or anything else. I knew the mullet would do me in—and would much rather think back on them as "deep bangs," anyway.

54

Satisfied, he asked me where I'd been and how I got to the park. Then, he asked me about Josh.

At this, his tone becomes slightly stern. Whatever I knew about Josh's escapades, from the backpacks at the cookie counter to the jokes made around the skatepark, Butchie certainly knew more. Boy-and-girl interactions were mostly new to preteens, and almost always fleshy. I stared at the bleachers while hoping to make it clear that, no, Josh was not *that* kind of friend.

A week after I played it cool, Butchie invited everyone over to his house for the weekend. So, after the stadium lights turned off, we piled ten of us into two cars and headed to the other side of town. Sandwiched in, small and nestled together, I laughed when everyone else did, trying to keep up the appearance of being someone who was invited places all of the time.

Any person with actual life experience, or who has travelled at least a little bit around the United States, would understand that the neighborhoods that we were driving through were blue-collar, their families, working class. But the local newspaper painted it as an unsavory, unsafe side of Naples, not because of gun violence, or illicit activities, but perhaps because of a DUI or a fight outside of a shitty cantina, and undeniably because the neighbors were brown instead of white. The kind of stuff that rocks a sleepy beachside town with a staggering wealth gap to its core, but that wouldn't have any big city printing articles in its papers. We drove past old tract neighborhoods and a few cozy mobile home parks, peppered amongst the public housing developments that many native Floridians call home. We were 12 miles from the beach at most, with many of these homes accounting for waterfront properties, if you consider the wide sooty canals waterfront. And although going for a swim would be ill-advised, given the water moccasins and alligators that sunbathe on the banks, the lights of these houses reflected peacefully in the shimmering surfaces of the canals, mirroring the dark sky. As we passed, I realized we must've been close to the Big House. In fact, I could *feel* it.

When we got out of the car, there were people outside, enjoying the night. All of them seemed happy, whistling to themselves as they walked home from work, still in uniform. It was after dark, but the neighborhood was alive with the smells of spices and grease, and the sound of T.V.s blasting from open garage dens. Like I said, locals park their cars on the street. Garages are for gathering friends and clinking cheap beer bottles together.

Butchie's house was dark as we got up to the door, and he opened it up with a set of keys jingling in his pockets. But unlike my parentless Villa, Butchie's parentless house was vivid and animated, with a dozen teenagers sprawled around the living room, boxes of pizza being passed around, cigarettes being puffed. Some of the older guys had beers with them, but they all kept their drinks far away from me, insisting that I was way too young while still allowing Butchie to drink a Bud of his own. They sat around the T.V. playing video games while I curled up against the corner of the couch, watching silently, orbiting the conversation, the jokes, and the heckling that swirled around the room, but it was all friendly. The right Master P song would end any argument, and get the entire crew jumping and screaming together in a broken-down living room at 11:30 pm on a school night, soda and beer bubbles spilling out from cups onto the floor.

That summer, we fed off each other, even *fed* each other, and the pride, the safety in numbers, and the security of our circle, glowed inside my chest. I was just happy to be included, to be passed a slice of pizza—never part of the action, but part of the group. And that was more than I'd ever had for the last 13 years of my life, and a drastic reality shift.

Every night that I slept in Butchie's room on the top bunk, I listened to everyone breathing around me, piled up on the floor. *I am not alone,* I would think to myself, hopeful that, wherever my mom was, she was feeling this, too.

Enter Master P.

It wasn't long before I left Ms. Kilroy's entirely, and moved into the Perry house with Butchie, his brother, Derek, and his dad, Richie, but it wasn't a formal arrangement. I'd been staying with Ms. Kilroy for a little over three months, and had gone from hovering around the house to spending almost as little time there as Arielle. As far as Ms. Kilroy was concerned, I'd never smelled like weed, so she trusted my judgment; she was emotionally exhausted, finally processing her divorce, and as long as my custodial papers were signed and my skin was tattoo-free, she didn't care where I slept. Everyone called Butchie's top bunk my bed, and even though that was mostly because I was the only one that wasn't afraid of hitting their head on the ceiling fan, I felt claimed. It might have been just scraps, but I would have slept on the porch if it meant being allowed to hang around.

Usually, I was the only girl in the friend group, and the only one around the guys at the skatepark. And, truthfully, I liked it that way. When they would talk about girls, they bragged loudly about their conquests, who did what with who, what they heard about so-and-so, who had the best boobs, whose arms were too hairy and who was fun to make out with but annoying when she talked. I avoided the same treatment; my prepubescent body functioned like a shield, as did my silence in their spaces. I used my time in the audience to formulate an invisible checklist of what *not* to do. Sure, focusing on which type of girl I didn't want to be wasn't the best foundation for future female friendships, but I would remedy that line of thought later in life. It wasn't like I felt any sort of loyalty to girls at the time, so I didn't really see any problem with the way that my friends talked about them.

I never stopped to consider what kind of guys I wanted to attract, or what they even saw when they looked at a girl's straightened hair and body glitter. Turns out, they don't notice anything at all, not even your signature scent, unless of course you have *none* of the desired traits and are therefore "sloppy," but if you *do* hook up with them and you leave a little sparkle on their bedsheets. *That* was what was considered hot. It was complicated territory, and I preferred the non-pressure of being ignored entirely. The lowest spot on the totem pole, but still above ground.

Slowly, I ditched the pink florals Ms. Kilroy had bought me and pulled Butchie's hand-me-downs over my head instead—threadbare skate

57

tees with stretched necks, holey shirts with band names I didn't know, three sizes too large. I would have told you it was out of necessity, being out of clothes and money, but I'm willing to show my cards and say this was more of a choice, another means of fitting in with my brothers. I mean, I *buried* myself in men's clothing, and started high school wearing clothes that I never would have imagined myself in: big tees and baggy sweatpants with nothing more than a pair of boxer shorts underneath. As for the boxers, I learned that if you were going to do it, you had to do it right, and that meant sewing the boxer holes shut so that you didn't flash the entire second period gym class your pubes when you reached up for a frisbee. Thanks to my experience with Grandma's sewing kits, I was one step ahead, but you had to be prepared to sew the hole shut again every few rinse cycles. Which, to me, was a very small price to pay for an identity; I would've sewed all my own clothes to look like my friends if I had to.

Footprints, Everywhere

My unofficial stay at the Perry house came to an end when Mom got out of rehab at the end of September. I was a few months past 13 and already a student at Naples High, and had been spending almost every night with my friends after school, checking in with Ms. Kilroy only when the social workers required me to. When I told Butchie that my mom would be coming out of rehab, he rushed to help me rustle up a pile of clothes, stuffing them into a Winn-Dixie bag.

"If you don't like it, or, like, something doesn't work out," he began, dragging his voice along the words as Derek drove us towards Ms. Kilroy's fancy neighborhood, "You can come back."

I nodded, twisting the handle of the shopping bag nervously in my lap. I wasn't sure what to make of my situation, or which version of Mom would be waiting for me in the dented station wagon. When we got to Ms. Kilroy's, the two of them were standing outside together, talking. I swallowed hard before grabbing my things.

"I'll IM you," I said. Butchie nudged me with his elbow, less than a hug but closer than a high-five, and I waved goodbye to Derek, stepping out onto the street. They drove off quickly, sparing me the pain of lingering eyes. I kept mine on the pavement.

Nervous, excited, I finally looked up at her. Her red hair had grown out a little and her grays were showing, and the old clothes on her body looked a few sizes too large, like she'd shrunk while she was away. But her eyes weren't glassy, and she didn't have the rapid, fretful twitching that she usually had whenever she made a stop somewhere, like she was itching to get back home. My teens melted off of me, and I stood there, trembling. Her baby. When she pulled me in for a hug, I realized how much I'd grown since we had last held each other, my face almost reaching hers. She smelled exactly as I remembered, and I inhaled deeply, fears melting to nothing with every exhale.

"I was just telling your mom, and I'll tell you," Ms. Kilroy said, her arms folded as we broke apart. "If *either* of you need anything, you call me. Anything at all."

"Thank you, Ms. Kilroy," I said, pushing the toe of my old flip-flops into the gravel of her driveway.

"Barb! Just Barb!" She said in my ear as she gave me a quick hug, patting me hard on the back."

"Take care," she shouted into the car. Then, commandingly, "Of each other."

I had imagined that no one had been inside of the Villa since I'd left it almost six months earlier, but I was wrong. My neck prickled as we came in through the front door, and I had the panicked feeling that we were being watched; I checked over my shoulder to where the men in suits used to be, parked under the tree across the street. No one was there. The heat was trapped in the front walkway, bouncing off the tiles as Mom fumbled with the keys. When we walked into the house, I looked up to check the corner where the tree frog should've been. No one was there, either.

Mom must have been back for at least a day, because all of the piles of laundry were washed and folded, and the rotten fruit was gone, with only a yellow stain left behind on the walls where the oranges had made impact. There were no more puddles on the floor, no more tar-like Pepsi smears blackening the countertops. No more flies. The lights were back on, and the house was cooled down. I sniffed the air nervously, worried that it might still have that gluey, terrarium-air smell. It didn't. It smelled like bleach.

"What do you want for dinner?" Mom asked, dropping her purse onto the kitchen table.

"I don't care." I said, stuffing my hands into the pockets of my mesh shorts.

"Barb said you made some new friends," Mom replied, eyes wandering up and down my outfit. "That's nice."

"Yeah, it's been good."

"The look does nothing for your shape."

I ignored her, chewing on the inside of my cheek, watching the unfamiliar way that she moved, hearing the slowness in her voice. This Mom—sober Mom—was new to me, and in some ways, the chaos of the old Mom felt safer. For a moment, I wished she were here instead. I didn't want to have the responsibility of keeping her calm, of not saying or doing anything to tip the scales, to send her away again. I questioned whether to even address all the time we'd spent apart, to ask her where she went. She looked exhausted, like she'd been chewed up and spat out and chewed up again, forced back into her old life, forced back to me. She swayed a little, and grabbed the counter for balance, trying to look casual. I took a deep breath.

"Wanna watch T.V.?" I asked.

At first, things felt okay. Not normal, and very slow, but okay. Mom stayed glued to the couch, her T.V. marathons flickering across her face once again, awake but unaware. She was unresponsive to things that normally would have set her off, like the lights being left on or a knock at the door. A woman from Child Protective Services came to do a home check and Mom just stood there blankly as she walked through the Villa, opening the fridge and poking her nose into the bathrooms, probably to

60

make sure our toilets had water. She turned the tap in the kitchen sink on and off before pulling me aside to ask how I was doing. She made notes on her clipboard while I talked.

████████████████████████, she wrote. ███████████. ████████
███████. ████████████████.

"I'm fine," I told her. "Everything's fine."

The woman's pen scribbled on for much longer than I spoke.

"Alright, I'm going to have a word with your mom, now. Go on outside."

I sat on the back stoop, our tiny, rectangular yard pockmarked from where I had dug all of the holes. Most of the electrical flags I had taken from the construction sites to mark my sod toilets had been removed, but a few were still piled up on the edge of the grass, and I tried not to wonder whose job *that* had been.

As the days dragged on, it became clear that Mom had only been treated for her drinking while she'd been away. While I never fully understood what it was that led her to behave in the ways that she did, didn't know what to call those stretches of feverish intensity, or the sullen drag of depression that followed, I knew that it was something that she wanted to heal from. Close to when she left the Villa, she had mentioned it to me, saying she wished she had more control over her thoughts. I had chalked it up to something that came with the drinking, but now that she was home and sober, I recognized that it was her constant, with or without vodka. She'd barely be awake when she dropped me off at school in the morning, but when I got home, she'd be hunched over the kitchen floor, brushing at the tiles with a toothbrush.

"Oh, *good!* You're here!" She would say breathlessly, her eyes shimmering, pupils opening and closing in the light like hungry mouths. Then, she'd lower her voice. "You don't see them anymore, do you?"

"See what?" I asked, crouching down.

She would get down as low as possible, pointing a finger down the seams of the tiles.

"Footprints! There and there!"

I'd press my lips together and shake my head.

"No, I don't see anything."

When she turned to look at me, her expression changed, frenzy replaced with anger.

"You think I'm crazy, don't you?"

"No, Mom. I don't."

"You think I don't know? Don't know how *stupid* you think I am?"

"I don't think—"

"Shut your *fucking* mouth," she hissed, her voice barely above a whisper. "And get the fuck out of my house."

Those afternoons, I would walk around the block feeling defeated, waiting for her to cool off. I would sigh deeply, frustrated now that I knew that there was life outside my mom's house. A life that was robust, open,

61

waiting. I wondered if I should just risk it and go back inside to use the phone and call Butchie, or wait until she went back to her room. But then, to think about leaving was to think about what Mom might do if I left her behind. *What if she hurts herself?* I thought. *What if she needs me?* Feelings moved around inside of me like waves, anger crashing into desperation, desperation pushing and pulling against guilt. It had never been this complicated before, and it was painful to hear myself asking the questions that crept into my mind as I circled the block. Was our relationship only mother-daughter in the biological sense? Check the box, split the D.N.A., boom. Done. And if that's all we were, could I leave to save myself?

Or, was she Mommy? My other half, my whole heart, the center of a world built just for two, us against it all?

It went on like this for weeks, the fights and the anger and the guilt, until I started seeing the bottles pop up, rolling out from the kind of poorly planned hiding places you'd only pick if your mind wasn't right. Knowing that she was back to drinking meant that it was only a matter of time before she was back to her nighttime wandering, and I knew that my presence was the only shot at keeping her inside. A panic settled into my chest every time I was away from her, and the only way to soothe it was to go home, see her sleeping, crawl into bed next to her, and hope that the alarm I set wouldn't pitch her into a rage the next morning.

But keeping both schedules—mine with her, and mine with my friends—started stressing me out more than it did provide relief.

"Where have you been?" Mom would scream, throwing things.

"School, Mom."

"*Liar.*"

"I'm serious!" I would shout, ducking her blows.

"You're talking to them, aren't you? Telling them all about me. Your '*horrible*' mother. Ungrateful bitch."

Everyone seemed to sense that things weren't quite right with my home situation because I never wanted anyone to leave the radius of the mall. When people started getting tired of skating, or the stadium lights got turned off, I would suggest things that would keep us out.

"It's a school night, Rach."

I began to itch, thinking about their structure, their rules around school nights, quiet, long hours. Then, I began to itch thinking about Mom, sitting at home alone.

"And you're sure you don't want to stay?" Butchie would ask when Derek got home, jingling his keys impatiently.

"Now or never." Derek would say, sighing like he had somewhere else to be.

"Yeah. I'm sure." I'd say to Butchie. Then, to Derek, "Shut up, prick."

My days got long again, and my CDs started to feel stale. There was no more escape in the lyrical angst; there was something inside me building pressure, coming up from my diaphragm and settling behind my eyes. It craved change, movement, a burst, an explosion. And any thought

62

or promise I fed it, things to keep it from detonation, things that worked the day before, washed right over me. *She's going to get better. Just one more day. Look! No alcohol. Things could be worse.* I bounced my leg to take the edge off. I bounced my leg until my shins ached. I felt like a volcano, hungry for something—anything—to take me away from myself.

Cellie

"Come on, let's go over to Bloomie's."

"What, why?"

Josh stood up from our table in the food court, cracking his knuckles. We'd just finished our smorgasbord of samples and I was expecting us to follow the usual routine. Digest, wait for the other guys. Then, skatepark. We never went to the department stores.

"I got a friend coming. He wants to go shopping."

Shopping? We didn't have any money. I raised an eyebrow and followed Josh as he swung his backpack over his shoulder, giving a little wave to one of the Orange Julius girls who sometimes met him in the refrigerator. I ran to keep up with Josh's NBA-sized strides.

"Who is it?" I asked.

"Mike. Mike Wheeler."

I'd heard about Michael before. Many times, actually. It was evident from the way that people talked about him that Michael was the kind of guy whose cool preceded him, but I hadn't seen him at the skatepark, not since I'd started hanging around. I'd heard about his taste in music, how he knew of every rapper, every punk label, even unsigned bands— the kind you had to scour the internet for hours to find. I'd also heard that his house was the first one to have DSL cable internet installed, not that I knew what that was, since my friends and I were all dial up. There were plenty of rich kids that palled around us at the skatepark, and our group had been to a few of their houses; their families were just like ours, only everyone seemed to smile more, and to care a lot less about material things, like having 'it all' didn't make them happier. We'd leave with clothes that still had the tags on, free skateboards, and video games, careful not to smile too big in a way that gave them power over us. We smiled once we got to the car, once it was in reverse, precious about the few items we stuffed in our backpacks. They always told us to come back soon. But Michael never had anyone over. He was elusive, a mystery.

Josh swung his big arm out in front of me, stopping us before we rounded the corner and got to the north entrance. I tried to adopt the suddenly aimless way he was walking, all slow and cool, like he had nowhere to be.

"What's up, Miiikey?" Josh said suddenly.

I saw Michael's watch before I saw him—it caught the ceiling lights

64

and flashed in my eyes. When I looked up, I felt my breath catch in my chest. I forgot about the shiny watch. I forgot about everything.

Michael was the same height as Josh, 6'4, but impossibly thin. His dark hair curled a little around his ears and the bottom of his neck, long like the rest of him. He wore an XL red t-shirt over his medium-sized frame (by height alone) and unlike ours, Michael's jeans were brand-new, un-distressed by either design or wear, visibly heavy in the way that only expensive jeans are, cinched around his waist with a shoe lace, but barely clinging to his bony hips. His plaid boxer shorts were puffy, exploding out of the top of his low jeans, as if the only reason he wore them this way was so that he could fill out his pants.

I scanned his shoes and saw that, yep, he was one of us, only his skate sneakers were brand new. Later, I would find out that these were Mike's *mall* shoes, only used for such outings as this. He kept a more familiar-looking, torn-up pair in his backpack. The laces of his mall shoes were footballed and taut around the fat, stupid tongue found on all skate shoes from that time period but, in keeping with his look, were still untied. It's not like Mike had any need for laces; he looked like he never tripped. He looked down and gave me a nod.

"'Sup?" He asked, clear but lispy.

"Hi," I squeaked. I tried not to think about his eyes after he looked away.

I followed the two of them, trying to poke Mike's mystique apart in my head in order to make him feel less intimidating, but I came up short. The more that I looked at him, the more that I wanted to look at him. And even though he was 15-and-a-half, and I was 13, I felt like he was many years beyond me. I lagged behind Josh and Mike as they walked into stores, the two of them several long-legged strides ahead of me. Whenever I caught up, I would laugh along with the park drama Josh was filling him in on, trying my best to straddle the line between attention-grabbing and nonexistent. It wasn't long before they dimmed the lights in the mall and announced that we all had to get out, and the three of us walked to the curb together.

Unlike Josh, almost every word that Michael said was shortened, slanged, and abbreviated.

"Do you have one of these?" He asked me.

"What?" I heard him very clearly, but wanted him to talk to me again.

"A cellie. You have one?"

A cellie. Of *course* he calls it a cellie.

"No, um, I don't," I stammered. Michael was the first kid I saw with one of his own.

"Here," he said, holding out his hand. "Try it."

When I reached out to take the phone, Michael's fingers grazed my palm slowly. His pale skin turned one shade pinker and I tried to stifle a grin, but accidentally ended up looking like a frog. A large white SUV pulled up, quiet and quick, as shiny and new as everything else surrounding him.

65

"See ya later," he said, swinging his backpack over his skinny shoulder, jeans bagging.

"We probably won't see him again for a while," Josh said out of the corner of his mouth, waving goodbye.

"Why?" I asked, unable to look away from Mike. Our eyes met as he flung himself into the passenger seat, and I felt my stomach drop.

"Mike's agoraphobic. He doesn't leave his house."

"What do you mean? We're at the mall right now!" I raised my voice now that Mike's car was gone.

"Yeah, he only comes here like once or twice a year, that's why we had to meet up. He doesn't even go to the skatepark anymore," Josh sighed. "The only time you'll catch him is if he randomly has a craving for Chik-Fil-A, those nuggets are stronger than any phobia I know of."

Josh laughed at his own joke, but I pretty much ignored him, enamored with what I'd just seen. Mike Wheeler, the big mystery, *blushing* at me. *Looking* into my eyes!

I thought about Mike the whole way home. I thought about him when I stepped over my mother sleeping peacefully on the tile floor, on my way to heat up my Bagel Bites. I thought about the feeling of his hand on mine as I punched the numbers on the microwave, thought about the way we'd stared at each other. He had been a stranger to me in the mall, but by the time I laid down to sleep that night, I knew him in a thousand different ways.

Naples Daily News, Police Beat

Mom got another DUI. And this time, I was in the car.

It was kind of a miracle that it hadn't happened sooner, really. Driving drunk was as routine in our house as driving sober. By the time I was old enough to know the difference, to see it in her eyes, feel it in the sway of the station wagon and the bumps along the curb, I was still getting in the car with her, afraid of what she'd do to me if I didn't. On this particular night, I'd seen it from a mile away, but I had the fresh sting of a slap on my face and knew better than to argue about it. As I sat in the passenger seat, watching the palm trees weave in and out of the headlights, I could feel it coming. And when she crossed the center line, I didn't even say a word. I just didn't care anymore.

Thanks to the local newspaper, the incident generated a lot of buzz, most of which felt 'too little, too late' as far as my safety was concerned. I mean, I'd survived a lot of shit thanks to Mom's choices, and having my head slammed into the dashboard and a seatbelt burn was the least of it. Don't get me wrong, "Local Teacher Drunk, Wrecks Car. Child Inside" was a snappy headline, but the district's decision to sever ties with Mom over the incident wasn't going to do anything to prevent shit like that from happening again. In fact, the way Mom responded to the firing, you'd think it was an open invitation to burn all of the progress she'd made since coming back from rehab.

Losing her job was just the nail in the coffin, and a badly timed one at that. Grandma wanted us out of the Villa, and the stress of finding a place to live without a job made Mom desperate. She had very little money saved up and a mountain of credit card debt. So, she did what she felt was best.

Tropical Acres Mobile Village was a 65-and-up community located not just on the opposite side of town from the Villa, but what felt like the opposite of *everything*. From Butchie's, the Big House, even my high school. Which made sense, considering I'd used Butchie's address to get into the fancier high school in the district to begin with, but still. We were in the sticks.

And Mom wasn't 65.

"Rachael? For chrissake, are you even *listening*?" Mom yelled, jamming her finger into the dash and killing the radio.

Her gray hair was splayed around her face, as electric as her glare, station wagon grumbling along the road to the trailer park, bumping and lagging. Neglected like the rest of us. She drove extra slowly, mostly because she didn't want any pieces falling off, but also because she didn't want to catch the attention of any cops, now that her license had been taken away. All of which gave me plenty of time to stare out the window.

"Yes, Mom."

"We blow this, and we're on the streets. Completely fucked. All we have now is my severance package."

"I know."

"Oh you do, do you? Well, then I'm sure you can repeat after me," she snapped. "How old am I?"

"Sixty-five." I said, dully.

"And who are you?"

"Your granddaughter."

"And where are we from?"

"Miami."

"And where are we going?"

"Tropical Acres Mobile Village."

"Good," she muttered, drumming her fingers anxiously on the steering wheel. "Good job."

She lightened up and put the music back on, her voice humming ahead of the tune.

I watched as we rolled past all of the familiar parts of town, far and away from all of the miles of golf course and in-ground swimming pools that marked the 'nice part' of Naples. Here, all of the houses and apartment buildings were practically built on top of each other, or were lonely little shacks pasted together, miles away from the nearest neighbor, their chicken wire fences strung with KEEP OUT and BEWARE OF DOG signs. We crawled down a busy road, cars honking behind us, until we came to the sign. Tropical Acres.

I had expected the place to be awful. I really had. I expected rusty old bikes and junk in people's driveways, hoarders with boxes stacked so high that no light came in through their dusted-up trailer windows. In other words, trash and shit, the way kids at school talked about trailer parks and the people in them. I'd been dreading the shame the entire drive over, sure that I would feel the same way. But actually, Tropical Acres was nice. Like, *really* nice.

"This—this is where we're staying?" I stammered. We passed a small lake at the entrance of the park, and I could see another in the distance, behind several rows of bright, pastel-colored trailers. When I turned to look at her, Mom was smiling.

"Pretty good, isn't it? These seniors only places, they sure know how to maintain a garden bed."

I waited in the car while Mom went into the leasing center to grab the key; suddenly, my eyes felt wet. Not with sadness, but with gratitude.

"The old lady at the desk asked me my skincare secrets!" Mom laughed, swinging the car door open. I watched her sit down and smile at herself in the rearview mirror, mussing her hair. "I do feel a little bad about lying, of course, but it's kind of fun, isn't it? Letting them think I'm some sexy granny."

Buzz Buzzzzz

Inside the trailer, Mom's cellphone—another perk from her severance package—started to buzz. I watched her from over a stack of boxes as she dug through her purse, putting a finger on her lips like she always did when she answered calls.

"Hello?" Mom asked. Then, her tone dropped. "Oh, hi."

I figured it must have been Grandma, given the way her face fell. But then she was gesturing for me to come over and take the call. "I'll put her on. One second."

Mom covered the receiver with her hand and stared at me seriously. I was practically eye-level with her now.

"It's your father," she said, her tone flat, annoyed.

"Okay?"

"You tell him we live in a nice place. But don't use the word trailer!" She added, hurriedly. "Tell him it's a manufactured home. *IF* he even asks…"

"Got it."

I took the phone and held it to my ear while Dad blathered on, telling me about fishing, some new girlfriend, a rowdy night with Uncle Jack. I nodded, accepting his bi-annual phone calls for what they were: obligatory.

"So, where you living?"

"Over by the lakes," I said casually.

"The lakes? The lakes by the airport?" Already, I could hear the disgust in his voice, unwarranted for a man that spent most of his time in pay-by-the-hour motels.

"Yeah, the place is nice."

"Is it, now?" He asked, skeptically. "One of those ol' trailer parks back there?"

"It's a development," I said, shooting Mom a look. "We live in a manufactured home."

"You two shoulda never left that old house," he cut in.

"Alright, Dad. Nice talking to you, *love* you," I said, slamming the phone shut.

"What'd he say?" Mom asked, trying not to look too curious as she continued her granny pout, now in the vanity mirror.

"Nothing. Like always."

I wasn't ashamed of the trailer, because when you don't have a trailer, you have nothing at all. Not even my dad's ignorance could take that away. Sure, we hadn't come into something this nice in an honest way—well, as close to honest as Mom could manage—since the Big House. But none of my friends even batted an eyelash when I told them they'd be dropping me off at our new place, no one made a single comment when they rolled past the other mobile homes. They pointed to the ones that were two stories instead of one, nodded in approval when we passed the lake, asking me if I'd checked it for alligators. These were people who understood poverty and didn't live in denial like my dad, people who knew what it felt like to scrape the bottom of the barrel, knew some of what I'd gone through to get here. Everybody else had to tread lightly, especially the people that put us here in the first place. For Mom, my dad was that person, but since she didn't speak to him, the burden fell on me to punish him for this.

Salvation

Mom hadn't meant to do it. I *know* she hadn't. She was sick—*is* sick—and was just mad, scared, worried out of her fucking mind. I had been walking up to our doorstep when one of our neighbors waved me down.

"Um, hello? Over here, dear."

It was a woman with permed gray hair in a blue tracksuit. Her wrinkled brow was knit with concern, and she had a gray-faced pug on a leash, wheezing and drooling over her white sneakers. They looked a lot alike.

"Um, hi," I said, awkwardly.

"I don't mean to pry," she began, her tone indicating the very opposite. "But I was hoping you could tell your grandmother to stop putting her—" she lowered her voice, but not by much—"*bottles* in my recycling bin."

I swallowed. *Great.*

"Sure thing," I said, sweetening my tone in preparation for a lie. I'd heard my friends do it a hundred times, cans of spray paint behind their backs. "We had some guests over this weekend for a dinner party. I'm sure we just ran out of room in ours—it won't happen again."

She pursed her lips, nodding stiffly.

"*Right.* Well, *do* let her know that I'll be filing a complaint with the park association, should I find that it does."

"I sure will. Thank you for your time, ma'am."

I turned back towards our door, eyes rolling into the back of my head. *A dinner party? Really, Rachael? When was the last time Mom even ate dinner?* I had barely turned the knob when the door swung open, Mom's locked fist yanking me inside. She kicked the cheap wood shut behind me and held onto my wrist as she spoke.

"What the fuck did you say to her?"

"*Nothing,* Mom."

She tightened her grip, spitting through gritted teeth. I looked down at my hand, blue veins popping against the raspberry-color of my skin.

"OW!" I shouted, but she held on tighter.

"What. Did. You. *Say.*"

"Mom, *please,* you're hurting me—"

"You told her my age, didn't you? Hate it here so much that you want me on the street?"

71

"Mom, let GO!"

The pain was overwhelming, but she was just picking up speed, pressure increasing with every word. I felt my breath catch in my chest, eyes welling with tears.

"Oh, you'll be fine living with your little friends, but me?"

"STOP IT—"

"You don't care about me. Not one *bit*."

She finished the sentence with a surge of strength; then, a crack echoed between us. She dropped my wrist, her face white. I held it in my other hand, sobbing, the pain sending spasms up my arm and into my back. My skin felt like it was on fire, and I crumpled onto the floor, cradling the growing purple lump as my body shook. The room was silent for a moment; then, I heard the sound of keys.

"Get up," she said.

I stayed on the ground. I didn't want to look at her.

"Rachael. Get up." Her voice wasn't scary anymore—it was pleading. I peeled my eyes away from my wrist. She looked terrified.

"We—I'll get you a splint. Let's go."

She didn't say another word. Not when she stepped outside, head swiveling to look for neighbors. Not when she opened my car door for me. Not in CVS, where she grabbed the cheapest splint she could find, me following behind her, tears streaming down my cheeks. Not even when we got home, when she opened the box so I wouldn't have to. When she moved to touch my wrist, to help me put on the splint, I turned away from her. Still wordless as she walked to her bedroom and closed the door.

When I was sure she was gone, I picked up the phone and called Butchie.

Richie had insisted on taking me to the walk-in clinic the second Derek and Butchie brought me inside, and it was a good thing he had—my wrist was broken, and if I hadn't got it set in a cast, I probably would have had a fucked-up arm for the rest of my life. I wanted to forget about the whole thing, but the weight of the cast made it difficult. For the most part, everyone seemed to understand that I didn't want to talk about it, but when I got tired of the sympathetic stares pointing towards me, baking in the bleachers, I went inside the mall.

It was the first time I'd gone into Coastland Center since meeting Mike. Josh had been right—Mike was *never* around, and no amount of thinking about him could make him materialize in front of me, his pants bagging. I thought about walking around like I used to, but the last time that had been exciting was, well, when I met him. Unsure what to do, I sat down at a table and felt my brain drift off.

"Hello? You alive? Skinny kid. Hey. YOU."

I jolted my head up in surprise. A girl in a red visor was glaring at me.

"Do you want an application or something?"

"Huh?"

"Do you want a *job*? You've been sittin' there all day, staring off into space."

"I'm fourteen," I said, shrugging.

"Yeah, *so?* The girl that just quit was fourteen, too. She had both her hands, but she was lazy as shit," she smirked, staring at my wrist cast.

"What's it pay?" I asked.

"Jack shit."

I stifled a sigh. "When can I start?"

Within a week, I was murmuring prayers of thanks to the nugget gods. Michael had come by not once, but *twice,* each order complete with an awkward smile and the kind of eye contact where you look and then you get immediately sweaty and then hate yourself for looking, but then you look again anyway and *oh, great, now he's looking, too.* But the humiliation was worth it because, by the third visit, it led to the much larger success of having Michael asking me for more than just extra Polynesian sauce.

"Do you ever get a break?" He asked one afternoon, our hands touching as I passed him his drink.

I had daydreamed about this moment so often that you'd think I would have been prepared, but I could barely speak over my heartbeat.

"Uh, we're supposed to," I spluttered, "but I just eat when I'm done."

"What time is that?"

"Eight."

"Cool," he said. "I can meet you after today, if you want."

"Sure," I replied, mouth going dry.

"Um, okay. I'll see you then." He swallowed his Dr. Pepper, Adam's apple bobbing, and turned away. I watched his thin, broad shoulders hunch as he walked over to the cookie counter to see Josh, staring at him until my manager barked me back to reality.

At 7:58, I cut to the back to peel off my sticky Chick-Fil-A polo. I had on one of my only tank tops (a slightly-too-big-gift from rich girl Karen Lawson) but it smelled better than my uniform. And while I normally wolfed down every piece of free chicken that I got in a bag after my shift—often the only real meal I had each day—I shoved my nuggets down into my backpack, too nervous to eat. I milled around the register until I saw Michael's tall frame out of the corner of my eye. Then, I went over to my old table.

Michael hurried over to meet me, rushing ahead of the rest of our friends behind him. He had a big smile on his narrow face (small by normal standards, but big on him), and sat down and pulled a cigarette from his back pocket, tucking it behind his ear.

"Do you...want to go outside?" He asked.

Giggles. Our friends had caught up. They were heckling us from one table over, but I could hardly hear them. I gave Michael a nod, and as we stood up, he took my hand.

"*Ooooh!*"

"Wheeler's got a girlfriend!"

He tensed up a little but I relaxed—chanting like that was something

73

all my brothers did, and he didn't deny it. We floated out of the food court and into the back lot. The sun had set, and the lights from the skatepark glowed above the palm trees. We got to a bench that most mall workers used for smoke breaks and sat down.

"Hang on," Michael said tenderly, letting go of my hand to cup his palm around the lighter, blocking the wind.

"Can I have one?" I blurted, hoping that my confidence suggested that no, this was *not* my first smoke, even though it was. I could feel him looking at me as I took the cigarette, and I looked down at my tank, hoping that I looked pretty, or cool, or a cross between the two, even though I felt like I had a sandspur trapped inside my throat.

Even though we had only said about 20 words to each other, I could feel the same restless quivering in Michael's movements, and that calmed me down. He was watching me, in the way that I had been looking at him since the day we met. When I peeked up from behind my hair, I knew that he loved me, too. He looked over his shoulder and saw our friends snickering in the corner, pretending to trail off to the skatepark, and he lowered his voice.

"So."

"*So*." I replied, smiling.

He puffed on his cigarette, blowing it behind my head. Our knees were touching, and he slid an arm to the top of the bench, dropping it little by little until I could feel its weight on the back of my neck. It was light and warm, his touch, impossibly gentle. I couldn't remember the last time someone touched me.

"Chick-Fil-A, huh?"

I smiled. The cigarette felt hot and awkward between my lips, so I pulled it out, hoping that I was holding it between the right fingers.

"It's not the worst job in the world."

"It isn't?" He asked, taking another drag.

I shook my head.

"I'm glad to hear you say that," he said, slowly. "Because, you know—I came down there to see you. I like seeing you."

My heart leapt in my chest, turning my small puff into a full inhale. Instantly, I flew into a fit of choking, sputtering coughs. When I was sure that I'd caught my breath, I looked into his face and he let me, staring back. I could feel myself shrinking in his eyes.

"I like seeing you, too, Mike."

"You can call me Michael."

Totally Bald.

There was a rumor circulating, because there was always a rumor circulating at the skatepark, about some older kids hooking up in the baseball dugouts at the far end of the lot. We, Butchie, Josh, and myself, decided to sneak over there and see if it was true.

We huddled into the announcer's stand and waited, giggly and loud and not sneaky at all, until a girl with short, bright blonde hair came darting out from across the unlit field, some shaggy-haired dude whose pants were halfway around his thighs hopping behind her. They ran and we screamed and Josh lunged to try to flip the awning spotlights on, but nothing happened. Butchie and I fell over in a fit of laughter and finally, when the coast was clear, we sauntered back to the skatepark to tell everyone what we saw, or what our imaginations *told* us that we saw.

Catching people in the dugouts got added to the roster of activities that staying late at the skatepark offered. One evening, Hugh—a kid in our group who already had stubble on his chin at 14—came by the park with his girlfriend, Jade. While she was in the bathroom, he told us that she was completely shaved *down there*.

"Totally bald."

I tried to imagine what that looked like, which wasn't difficult since all of us had been naturally bald just a few short years ago. Where is pubic hair even meant to stop, anyway? Mine would zig-zag down to my knees if I let it, or maybe all those dark, thick hairs on my legs *were* pubic hairs, down to my big ankles and across the toes of my big feet. Jade was tan, and I wondered if her crotch was tan, too. Her bouncy brownish-blonde hair was long and silky, and met the top of her long legs at her Hollister micro-shorts. Everything about Jade is small—her face, her stature, her hands. I'm long and tall, with arms swinging down at my sides like a gangly ape's. My wrist bones are big and bell-shaped; hers are tapered and tiny. Where her perfect tops grazed her waistband, mine were bra-length, awkwardly short, and I had to hunch to make them school-appropriate. Jade sat with her narrow shoulder blades all pinned back, arching upwards so that her breasts could soak in the sun, so that the sun could gaze upon her—there was no telling who was more golden.

Maybe this was why I hadn't seen or heard from Michael in two months. Or, maybe it was because he knew I'd slept with Derek.

I shook my head. *Forget that.*

We all watched Jade, glowing and glittery, as she came out of the community center. The guys jumped to help her down from the top of the mini ramp as she met us at the bleachers, coconut spilling from her pores. She pulled a compact out of her bulging purse and dabbed the pad across her nose, turning her head to look at her hot reflection in the tiny mirror. She never talked to us, and she knew that she didn't have to—her hotness was loud enough.

I squirmed in my seat. The entire time Hugh was talking, it felt like Butchie was staring at me. I knew Derek didn't talk about me to the guys since none of them really talked to him. He only came around to the skatepark when somebody wanted their tricks filmed, since he was the one with a video camera. *Low stakes*, I'd thought at the time.

Later, on the drive home, I fought to get Butchie to look at me, but he acted like I wasn't there. That's when I knew I'd been wrong.

Sex with Derek had been stupid, simple. *You're a virgin, I'm a virgin,* poke, poke, poke.

Sometimes, I try to dissect why he felt like the best choice, but there really wasn't much to it. He was goofy, an oddball, one grade up; he carried a briefcase instead of a backpack and claimed to be working on his 'novel,' whatever that meant. Because we were so different, and only related to each other through Butchie, he felt like a safe bet. Someone I could get it over with and feel no obligation to. A person that could get me ready for sex with someone I actually liked.

When it was over, I crept back into Butchie's room, crawling into my top bunk as if nothing had happened.

What I wasn't prepared for was Derek calling me his girlfriend. Or, the fallout with Butchie that followed. Unlike my brothers, who were slapped on the back and poured an extra beer and seated at the center of the circle on the living room floor, hyped into revealing the details, I was a girl who had sex. And according to Butchie, that was shameful.

"What, did you just *slink* down the hall to Derek's room one night?"

He wouldn't even look me in the eyes. And that hurt. Deep.

The thing was, I didn't value sex. Nobody told me to. My mom wasn't even around when I got my first period, so we both dodged 'the talk' bullet. Considering all of my influences were hyper-hormonal teenaged boys, the fact that I wanted to get it over with is unsurprising. I wanted to free myself of the virgin card and maybe even experiment, and knew that sex with Derek couldn't hurt me because I was not emotionally invested. I didn't go into it thinking I'd get the spotlight—trust me, I was more than happy to keep it a secret—but I also hadn't expected my friends to distance themselves from me, either. Why could they have sex and access all of the cool that came with it, and when I did it, I was 'slinking'?

In a few more years, I would see that giving someone all of you made you easier to keep, or harder to throw away. Not sex as a chip or a card to be played, but sex as the most honest, full version of yourself. Your thoughts, your dreams, your hard work, your loyalty, and your most physical being, you know? I think people find you harder to toss aside when they know these things. It's a slippery slope, though, because the further you're in, the harder it is to get out, and as often as I like to be kept and protected, I find myself looking for a clean exit for the moment I feel the need to run.

I wish there had been someone in my life to tell me not to play along, that I *didn't* have to be Derek's girlfriend. But I didn't have a home to return to besides Butchie's, and I didn't have friends in my corner to back me up. So, I accepted the drugstore flowers pushed robotically into my arms by my locker. I sat with the popular kids Derek was trying to impress with his newfound social collateral—sex, girlfriend—and stared out the window, tuning out their conversations, his desperate attempts for approval. It would never work; they were plutocrats in popped-collar polos and khakis who lived on the beach block. We were...

"Rachael? *Rachael!*" Derek was snapping his fingers in my face.

"What? Did the bell ring?"

He rolled his eyes, skin red. "*No*, we're talking about going to the beach this weekend."

"All the couples are," chimed in one of the girls, scraping invisible dust from the shoulder of her hundred-dollar hoodie.

"Oh. Nice."

When we left the cafeteria, Derek shoved his hand into mine. I heard the *ooh's* of the Abercrombie models behind us, and my stomach curdled. When they passed us, heading to class, he dropped my hand and lowered his voice. It was all for show, just so he could show the rich girls how great a boyfriend he would be to one of *them*.

"We're going to the beach this weekend."

"Are you kidding?" I asked, incredulous.

"And wear a bikini. Seriously. Do you even own a bikini?"

"I can't pay for that!"

"Jesus Christ," he mumbled. "Well, would it kill you to stop wearing my brother's clothes? You look completely *derelict*."

"I don't even know what that means!" I yelled back.

Derek stepped closer, lowering his voice. "Look. I know I'm not Mike, okay? But he's never coming out of his house again, so...this is all you've got."

Lizette Chavez

I felt like I was being punished for every bad decision I'd ever made before I even got to *decide* if they were bad decisions. Why was *I* even at school? My friends weren't hanging out with me, my parents didn't care what I did. What was the point?

Derek and I "broke up." Sleeping with me got him the social coin he needed, so there was no need for us to pretend to date anymore. I would've been more excited about it if people would have stopped asking me for the details, or if I didn't still have to sleep in his bed. We stayed as far apart from each other as physically possible, which was difficult considering it was only full-sized; he stayed up late every night, typing to one of the popular girls on AIM—the one with the worst teeth, to be fair—probably trying to convince her that I was back in Butchie's room. I wished I was, but he was still icing me out.

I don't know how long things went on like this for. All I know is, I put my things into my backpack one afternoon and walked out the door.

It was completely dark by the time I got to the banyan tree. Everyone from Naples knows which one I'm talking about; just a block from the pier, gnarled, old, looming. My dad always parked his truck underneath it when I was little, and the two of us came down to fish.

There was nobody beneath it as I stood in its shadow, yanking a dirty sweatshirt and pair of sweatpants over my clothes. It was a hot night, but the air was colder by the beach, and even colder on the shore, and I knew that by morning, all of the heat would be gone from the sand, and I would wake up cold and stiff, clothes damp and nose stuffed. I found an old pair of Butchie's socks and shoved my sore feet into my flip-flops, pulled my hood tightly over my head, and walked quietly towards the beach, moths and gnats swarming above. Security patrolled the parks at night, and if they saw me, they'd send me away. And if that happened…I hadn't got that far yet.

Planning like this always made me think of my mom, barking orders in her coach voice, and thinking about my mom was especially hard for me that night. We hadn't spoken since she broke my wrist, and so much had happened since then that sometimes, I caught myself wondering if I could ever catch her up.

Shit, did we even catch up after she left the first time?

I sighed, turning towards the beachfront houses. I didn't know which one was his, exactly, but I knew that somewhere over there, Michael was sleeping. I pushed up a mound of sand like a pillow, and listened to the waves until I was, too.

Normally, drama was one of the only classes that I actually stayed awake for, but since I'd started sleeping under the pier, I was just like everyone else in the back of the classroom, using my folded arms as a pillow. Generally, drama class was fun; it was wild and unstructured, and unlike the others on my schedule, was filled with social cliques I otherwise wouldn't see, like marching band, theater, and art geeks. The whole class was basically an extension of lunch, except air conditioned. A great place to sleep, unless you're being poked in the ribs.

"*Hey.*"

"What?" I snapped, lifting my head, ready to stomp on whoever it was, especially if they mentioned Derek, Butchie, or the sand in my hair. But it wasn't about any of that. It was Kaitlyn, a girl with a thumb-shaped face, and she was smiling at me.

"Do you want to go to the mall after school?"

"Today?" I asked, hesitant.

"Yeah, today. Is that cool?"

I didn't know what she was talking to me for, but I had nothing to lose. She was nice, the type of person who would hand you her paper to copy without you having to ask. We never really hung out outside of the classes we shared—she spent too much time getting high off weird things in the back of the art room, as evidenced by the beaded wrap in her hair.

"Sure. I go to the mall like, every single day," I yawned. Still confused, but relieved to have an afternoon potentially different from the rest.

"Sweet," she nodded. "I'll meet you in the parking lot."

When we met in the parking lot, Kaitlyn had a girl with her. I recognized her as one of the girls I'd seen standing around with the hacky-sack crew, guys in tie dye shirts who listened to Ska but preferred the trumpet parts to the punk music. She had teakwood skin and a pile of curly black hair on top of her head, her body comforting and soft like a Cinnabon, but with an attitude that was meant to evoke anything but. When she saw me approaching, she elbowed Kaitlyn in the side, narrowing her big, brown eyes.

"Who's *this*?"

"Liz, this is Rachael—from drama class? I told you about her," Kaitlyn said, eyeing a group of guys as they walked past us.

"I don't remember anything about a Rachael."

"Well, it's me!" I said with an awkward laugh. Liz rolled her eyes.

Fuck, this is going to suck, Maybe I should have stuck with myself.

"Can we get going already? I'm fucking starving."

Liz sped past me and stood next to Kaitlyn, leaving no room for me on the sidewalk. I walked behind the two of them, wondering why I agreed to this, watching Liz's curls bob and sway, those big eyes glancing back at me. Her pride made her hard to digest, but more than that, she was impossible to dissect.

As we got inside and rounded the corner near the cookie counter, I saw Josh's backpack propped up against it, and another I didn't recognize. I stifled a laugh.

"What's so funny?" Liz's brow was knit together. I couldn't tell if she was confused or disgusted—Liz looks at everything she's confused by like it's gross.

"Oh, nothing. My, uh, friend Josh works over there—I just thought of something. Something he said the other day."

"Josh? Tall Josh?" Her fearsome stare softened.

"Yeah. We're, like, good friends." Or, I *hoped* we were still good friends.

Liz didn't say anything. Kaitlyn led us to the spot-lit entrance of Abercrombie & Fitch, but when she saw someone that she knew folding shirts inside, she stopped us.

"I'm gonna go say hi. You guys go ahead without me."

"Whatever," Liz said.

We watched her until her back disappeared into the dark store and Liz snorted.

"Fuck Abercrombie," she sneered.

"Seriously."

"Right? All the clothes are, like—" Liz held up her hands, leaving a few inches of space between her palms, "—this big."

I laughed and Liz cracked her first smile. Then, she reassessed me. Maybe Liz had seen my white face and straight mousy hair and assumed I was one of those types of girls, the ones who had money for tiny tank tops that left her friends behind when she saw a hot guy. I mean, I didn't think I looked like them, but to Liz, I did more than I didn't. I got the feeling that Liz, like me, hadn't known many girls that she could trust. Now that it was just the two of us, Liz was funny, easy to talk to.

"That guy's perfect for Kaitlyn. She fried her brain sniffing Sharpies and he never had one to begin with."

The more we talked, the more I understood Liz. Her humor was self-deprecating, the way people get when they're uncomfortable in their skin. Like my baggy clothes that told people not to look in my direction, the oversized Screeching Weasel t-shirt that she wore was her armor too.

We rounded back towards the food court for free honey pretzel samples before going outside to meet Liz's mom in the parking lot. She pulled up in a shiny, new white Mercedes and rolled down her window, smiling curiously at me. Liz must not have introduced her to many girlfriends.

"Rachael, this is my mom, Isabel."

"Hey, honey. How are you?" Isabel smiled, the lilt of her accent, warm and friendly. She had Liz's doe-like eyes but traced them in double thick black eyeliner, her jet-black hair freshly blown out, Sotheby's nametag pinned to the blazer of her pantsuit.

80

"I'm good," I said. It was a reflex, at that point.

"Is your mom coming to get you soon?"

I dragged the toe of my sneaker on the curb, tightening my grip around the straps of my backpack. I could feel the air conditioning blasting through the open window; the air outside, hot and humid. In a few hours, I'd be back under the pier.

"Yeah, she'll, um, be here later."

Liz climbed into the passenger side door, but her mom craned her neck around her, still talking.

"How much later?" Isabel asked, trying to get a better look in case a lie tried to slip down my tongue past my teeth.

I shrugged. Maybe it was the beat-up skate shoes, or the oversized clothes that were very clearly not my own, or the eye contact that I was avoiding, cheeks blushing, staring down at the concrete. Or, the combination of it all. But Isabel didn't just seem unconvinced—she seemed to know my exact situation. Her intensity was bossy like Liz, but she wasn't hiding behind it. She was commanding it.

"Later, like, when the mall closes?"

"Um..."

"Why don't you come over? You can call your mom from our house and she can pick you up there." Isabel was a busy woman, but she couldn't help inserting herself. Not in cases like these.

Liz reached behind her and unlocked the back door. As I climbed in, I looked over towards the skatepark. I noticed a few familiar moppy heads, but not the one I was looking for.

Liz's house was like an operating room. It smelled like three different types of disinfectant, all competing to be majority scent. Every room was spotless and sterile, with floors so clean that you could see your reflection standing below you, stretched out from the bottoms of your shoes.

Isabel entered ahead of us, shooting her daughter a look; Liz muttered to me to take my shoes and backpack off and leave them by the door. I did as I was told, shoving my hands deep into my pockets, scared to touch anything. Isabel marched down the hallway to her home office, leaving Liz and I in the kitchen, but before she closed the door, she gave Liz another look.

"Don't forget to do your cleaning."

I spun around, trying to find a spot in the kitchen or living room that Isabel could possibly be referring to. Liz rolled her eyes and walked to the fridge.

"Hungry?" She asked. I stood behind her, peering in.

The fridge was full, mostly stacked with Tupperware containers of Spanish rice. Isabel prided herself on her mastery of rice from all regions, in all colors and variations. It was the most beautiful thing I had ever seen. The only rice I knew was -a-Roni, and the variants were with or without garlic. Liz pulled one container out and put it into the microwave, punching the buttons before reaching for a roll of paper towels. She

81

grabbed one and began wiping down the already shimmering countertops. When the food was done, she brought two plates over to the sink.

"Careful not to drop anything," she said sarcastically, scooping rice out onto the plates.

Liz poked fun at her environment but she would never outwardly defy her mom; she rebelled by drawing in Sharpie on her jeans, painting her nails black and letting them chip, sneaking out of her bedroom window at night. She made space for me over the sink and we stood there in silence, the warm, aromatic rice filling the air between us. When we were done, Liz took our plates and forks and washed them with a sponge, then put them all into the dishwasher. I lingered behind her, waiting to be told what to do.

"Let's go to my room," Liz said, having given the immaculate kitchen another once-over.

I followed her upstairs, trying not to seem too excited. I'd seen afternoons like this so many times, played out on T.V. Teen girls go to the mall, talk about boys, have a dance party in their super-teen rooms, covered in posters. But Liz's room was *not* a teen dream. Like the rest of the house, it was painstakingly organized, with carpet that had been vacuumed with the grain so that when we walked, our footsteps left soft imprints. I fought off the impulse to brush them away, and wondered if she vacuumed before school that morning or just jumped from her bed to the tile outside her door. She plopped down at her computer, flicking on the screen. I stood in the center of the room, hands in my pockets again.

"What's your screen name?" I asked, trying not to think about whether Michael was online.

"It's SqueakyChlorine," she said with a laugh.

"Is that a song?"

"Naw, it's just a nickname my guy friends gave me."

I could see the smile on her face as she said it—maybe one of them came by her house and smelled the bleach for themselves. But as she started to tell me the story, talking about their stoner antics, I had to fight off the urge to interrupt her. I mean, white dudes with dreadlocks? They were soft, edgeless, *and* they reeked of weed in a skunky, un-showered way.

"Are you dating any of them?"

"Not yet," she said, spinning in her desk chair. "They all like me, though."

"You should come with me to the skatepark sometime," I suggested.

"Really? You go there?" Her mouth hung open, half surprised at *how*, half wondering *why*.

"I haven't for a while, but I go almost every day. Then I hang out with the guys on the weekends."

"That's cool," Liz said, trying to play off the nervousness she felt around unfamiliar crowds.

"We can go there tomorrow," I said, casually.

"Yeah, maybe." Liz grinned, spinning her chair back and forth. Just as she opened her mouth to say something, Isabel knocked on the door. Liz

82

paused the music on her computer while her mom looked between us, at the smiles frozen on our faces.

"Do you want to stay the night with us, Rachael?" She asked, and I looked to Liz, who nodded.

"Definitely."

Changing It

I might have thought Michael would be the one to rescue me from Derek's bedroom (*and* my mind), but Liz turned out to be the real hero. The minute I showed up to the skatepark with another girl, my brothers forgot all about the 'sides' they were supposed to be taking, and we went from hanging in the bleachers to riding in Josh's car to a Perry party. It hurt me that Butchie still wouldn't look in my direction, but it was fun to be back with everyone again, and especially fun to have Liz in the mix. At the end of the night, Josh drove us back to Liz's house, both of their mouths red and swollen from making out.

When we got there, it was empty; Liz's mom had gone out dancing with her fifth husband, Rinaldo. We took off our shoes, and Liz ran upstairs to get on AIM, waiting for Josh as if he wasn't still driving home. I lagged behind.

"I gotta call someone," I said. "I'll be right up."

"Okay!"

I dialed the new number for the trailer. The phone rang, which meant that the power wasn't shut off, or that Mom hadn't left the phone off the hook. A little tension left my neck. The call went to the answering machine, and I listened to the sound of her voice—it was the same message that we'd had back at the Big House. It was her old radio voice, big and sultry.

"*Hi, you've reached Donna Finley,*" she sang. "*Leave us your name and number and I'll get right back to you.*"

I'd always thought it was funny that she never said my name on the answering machine, but still said "us" even though I was the only one that ever answered the phone.

"Hey, Mom. It's me. I'm staying at my friend Liz's house. It's in one of the developments over by Foxfire."

I rattled off Liz's phone number, staring out the un-smudged kitchen window, at the meticulous palms planted along the fence in the backyard. I could hear their leaves rustling gently in the midnight breeze.

"I miss you and I love you. Bye."

"*Michael is online.*"

"What?" Liz asked me from her bed. I pointed to the screen, practically lost for words, unable to process what I was seeing.

84

It was his away message. Changed, for the first time in ages, from 'unavailable' to online.

"*Michael!* He's—oh my god—" *Ping.* The chatbox opened.

madmoneyposse: *Hey rach*

Stardust781: *Hey! Long time no see.*

madmoneyposse: *For real.*

"What do I even say to that? Like, what do I *say*?" I whispered to Liz hurriedly, like Michael was on the other end of the phone, rather than on the computer.

"You should say something like...*let's change that.*" She raised a suggestive eyebrow and we giggled stupidly. I turned back to the keyboard.

Stardust871: *Let's change that*

madmoneyposse: *Ya we have to.*

Stardust871: *I'm staying w my friend*

I added this part in feverishly, wanting him to know that I was a new person. One with a friend, and one who was no longer staying in Derek's room.

madmoneyposse: *Liz?*

Stardust871: *How'd u know?*

madmoneyposse: *Josh told me. U guys can all come over this weekend if that's cool.*

I turned to look at Liz, who was jumping up and down. Josh was talking about her, and Michael was talking about *me*?

Stardust871: *See u then*

"Put a smiley!" Liz shouted, pounding my arm. "Put a smiley!"

Stardust871:☺

Liz and I were dressed in new six-dollar flip-flops when Josh picked us up, doused in body spray from Victoria's Secret (Liz smelled moonlighty, like a floral slut, while I was a citrusy one), lips glossed from free makeup samples, doing our best to look perfectly imperfect, hot but *cool.* It was a delicate balance, and when we got into the car, Liz got her reward.

"You smell good," Josh said, turning down the music so that his soft voice could be heard over the stereo struggling to play 105.5 'The Beat.'

"Thanks," she said, looking up at me in the rearview mirror. I shot her a nervous smile.

The drive from the mall to the beach block was short. We passed houses surrounded by columns, bougainvillea climbing gated driveways, brand new sports cars and Hummers glinting behind the iron bars. Celebrity sightings were a known fact around this part of town, but only the kinds of celebrities your parents knew or cared about, which was why it was generally the area where the rich tourist types hung out, or the wealthy families that had been a part of Naples since the town was first founded. I had only come down here with my dad to park under the town's oldest banyan tree and walk over to the Naples pier, carrying fishing rods.

Josh drove up to a large driveway and pressed a button, and I heard a muffled version of Michael's voice echo through the intercom.

"Yo," he said.

"*Yo,*" replied Josh.

Michael's house was the largest I'd ever seen but equally matched to those on its street. In two years, a cop will pull me over because my truck "doesn't belong in this neighborhood." I won't even have to read between the lines, the way he says it. The sweeping stone driveway opened up to a massive limestone porch, hemmed by two giant royal palms. My dad always pointed royal palms out to me, reminding me that they weren't native to Florida, and that anyone that planted one in their yard had to be rich because they were expensive, especially if you bought them when they were fully grown. Next to one of the palms was an octagonal bay window, each of the panes of glass marred by giant gray jester stickers. It was weird, seeing such a beautiful house plastered with stickers, and as we got out of the car, I noticed a few other strange things, like dirt caked into the glass and a weather-beaten brown rocking chair on the front porch, its dark wooden stain melted into the limestone in a sundried puddle. Michael opened the door before we could knock, and we were all hit with a thick wall of cigarette stench, layered over a sour smell that was unidentifiable but stomach-churning. I resisted the urge to look over at Liz, and smiled up at Michael. He looked excited to see me.

"'Sup?" He said, standing back to let us in.

The doorway was taller than both Michael and Josh, and when Michael closed the door, the only light that came in was from the windows. I could see that there was a second building behind this one, and beyond that, a private beach. The shimmering afternoon sun bounced along the waves and into the living room, illuminating the rest of the house in a faded glow. Everything looked clean, but the floors felt sticky and thick below my flip-flops. Cigarette ash rolled like tumbleweeds around our feet

"Sup, Mikey?" Josh said, and they slapped their hands together, pulling each other in for a bro-y half hug. Liz and I stood next to each other, both of us trying to telepathically communicate how strange this place was.

"Come on," Michael said. "I'll show my room."

Cats—maybe that was the smell? We walked past a large bowl of cat kibble, half of it strewn across the marble floors, and walked in the direction of the Juggalo side of the house. I knew it was Michael's room because of the rap music pulsing behind the closed door; when he opened it, the clowns stared down at us from the bay window, looming over his twin-sized bed, his bean bag chairs, and his massive T.V. with the backside of their twisted smiles. But the only other people I'd seen with Juggalo paraphernalia were the kids in wide leg jeans, tees, and jackets in every shade of black, hanging outside of Spencer's with yesterday's eyeliner caked in a stream down their cheeks. Friendly, but definitely different from me and Michael, which was why it was so shocking to see those faces in the glass.

"The music is about how it makes you feel, you know?" Michael

86

said, reading my mind as I glared up at the clowns. His words went from teenager to audiophile. "It's not about the clothes, not even about the lyrics. They say a lot of stuff just to be funny."

I nodded my head.

"You don't have to dress any type of way to *feel* a way. Ya *feel* me?"

It had felt like a challenge. And my god, did I want to feel him.

Still, looking around his bedroom, I couldn't imagine what kind of mom would let their kid put stickers on their mansion windows, but I also couldn't picture Michael's mom, not based on the night I'd seen her in the parking lot in her Lexus, or what little information I had heard about her through AIM—and *definitely* not now that I'd walked through her house. Maybe messiness was just a perk of wealth? I also couldn't picture Michael, all six-foot-four of him, laying in a twin bed. I felt my stomach grow hot, and started to wish that we didn't have to go back to Liz's house, that I could just curl up in this smoggy mansion, in Michael's tiny twin-sized bed, and never leave.

Here in Your Bedroom

"Aren't you going to say hello to me?"

Michael hadn't even switched on the kitchen lights yet, but his mom's voice sounded angry, like I'd snubbed her dozens of times before.

My throat tightened as I looked over at her. The oven light illuminated her ultra-tanned brown skin, the whites of her tired eyes narrowing as she looked me up and down.

"I'm Rachael," I said, giving her a tiny wave.

"Nice to meet you," she said, changing her tone as little as she had to in order to make the statement true. When she looked at Michael, her face softened, voice suddenly gentle. "Mikey, will you watch T.V. in your room? I've got a headache."

"Sure," he said.

She gave me another look down the center of her nose before teetering back to her bedroom and slamming the door. When she was gone, Michael didn't say anything. He put the pizzas in the oven and twisted the cap off his Mountain Dew, taking a swig.

"I'll come get these when they're ready," he said, tilting his head towards the oven. We grabbed our stuff and he took my hand in his down the hallway, back to his bedroom. In a way, it was kind of nice knowing there was chaos outside of the door—hearing someone yell or stomp their feet was nothing to stare at. They were the things that told me I was home. So, I kept coming back.

Everything around us was burning, falling, flaking like the ashes from the long-drawn cigarettes that Michael held between his lips. But I had him and he had me, nestled in his narrow bed, our knobby hips and knees interlocking like the knotted branches of a banyan tree. He was long and thin, the branchlike protrusions of his arms and legs jutting like footholds. I liked the way that my knees perfectly fit inside the bend of his, the way his collarbone dipped to hide my head, the gentle knock of hipbone against hipbone as we shifted in our sleep. We were so intertwined that it was impossible to tell who, on any given day, was the supporter or the supported, the prop root or the host—who needed protection from their mom on that day, who would need it next.

Besides, avoiding Mary was easier than hiding from *or* finding my mom ever was. Mary was like an animal running in its cage—an animal with an entire mansion at its disposal, but who favored one corner.

She ran the same route, crashed the same cupboards, hissed the same expletives. We could avoid her as easily as she could us.

Which was probably why she didn't care that the entire house was literally falling apart. Sequestering herself to the space between her kitchen and bedroom, Mary didn't see that on the other side of the courtyard, part of the roof had caved in during a storm. Or, that raccoons ran freely in and out of the house, feasting on cat food. Michael and I could hear them fighting when we snuck out to heat up our pizza, had even seen a few running past the fountain, but like everything else that went on in his life, Michael had no comment. And out of solidarity, I didn't either. But as long as Mary's corner was in order, as long as her feet still followed the trail, she could go on living in the chaos, and so could we. It wasn't like I was completely content with staying inside all day at Michael's, though. Some days—usually after a stretch of five or six absences from school—I'd shuffle out of his bedroom while he was still asleep and bring myself there, mainly to see Liz, but out of slight concern that I might get held back a year. I knew I wouldn't come back if that happened. Which would leave Michael and I in the same position: two high school dropouts sleeping in a twin bed in his mom's crumbling castle. Some people might have been okay with that, considering the castle and all, but there was a surge that coursed through my body whenever I thought about that kind of future. If that's all I wanted for myself, why even leave the trailer at all?

Royal blue furniture and Tweety Bird-yellow walls. I knew it had been a while since I'd been over to see Mom, but had it really been *this* long? The color combination was as disorienting as the paint fumes trapped in the trailer, and I staggered into the kitchen, looking, like always, for signs of life.

"Mom? Hello? It's Rachael."

The paint was everywhere, dripping down the walls. There were more pill bottles on the kitchen counter than there were cups stacked in the sink. Some opened and topless, some still sealed up and child-proofed.

"Mom?" I called again.

Still silent. Was it the pills, or...?

I crossed the few steps from the kitchen to her bedroom with my heart thumping in my ears.

Thankfully, the lump on the mattress was rising and falling. Breathing. I walked over to her bedside and could see that she'd tried to color her roots, red and gray fighting for their stake on her scalp, the only thing visible above the bedsheets. I pulled the blankets a little lower to look at her face. Her skin was waxy, and the bags under her eyes looked like bruises, creased with blue and purple. I grabbed the glass from her bedside and walked to the foot of the bed, lifting up the blankets. Once I pulled her socks and shoes off, I went back into the kitchen to wash the dishes. And maybe make sense of the pill museum that had exploded on the counter.

I pushed them into groups. Morning, afternoon, evening. Take as needed, take with food. The two things they had in common: her name on the label, and a wine glass with an 'X' through it. No drinking alcohol. Once that was done, I called Liz.

"Hello?" I could hear crunching and the sound of *The Golden Girls* theme song in the background.

"Hey, it's me," I said.

"What's up? You bailing on me?"

"No, not bailing, but do you think you could come over here tonight?"

I had never invited anyone over before, not inside. But I wasn't sure enough of the situation to leave Mom, and definitely didn't want to be there alone.

"The trailer? Uh, yeah, sure."

"Okay, cool. My mom's here and she's, like—"

"Is everything good?" Liz turned the volume down on the T.V.

"Yeah, it's fine. She's just passed out."

"Sleeping or passed out?"

"Sleeping. Probably won't wake up 'til tomorrow though."

"Alright, as long as you're good."

"I am. See you in a bit."

I hung up the phone and went back to the pills; under one of the bottles, stuck to a sticky ring, was a doctor's note that accounted for about half of the medications on the counter. Within it was a diagnosis: schizoaffective disorder. *Sounds intense,* I thought to myself.

I was at the door before Liz could knock.

"Hey—"

I quickly peered past her shoulder and waved at Isabel's shadowy Mercedes. Then, I yanked her arm inside.

"Jesus!" She cried. Then, looking around, "What the *fuck* happened in here?"

"It was like this when I came home," I hurried, waving my hand. "But then I found this doctor's note."

"Okay? What kind of doctor's note?"

"I don't know what kind, but I think it means my mom is insane? I dunno, dude."

Liz followed me into the kitchen and pointed to the wall of pills.

"And they gave her all those?"

"I guess so! I mean, at least some of them. I don't know what they're all for. And it's not like I can ask her."

"Why can't you?"

"You don't hear the snoring?" I asked, sarcastic.

"Well, when she wakes up. Can't you just wait and ask?"

"What if she needs to take some of them now? There's all these evening pills—she could've gone to sleep after we talked last night and missed a bunch already."

"True," Liz nodded. "You should wake her up."

"Okay," I said slowly. "But you should wait here. Just in case."

I went into Mom's bedroom and turned on the light. She rolled over, but didn't wake up, so I went to her bedside and flicked on the lamp. I could see movement behind her eyelids and gave her a gentle nudge.

"Mom. Mom, wake up."

She flipped again, but her eyes stayed closed.

"Mom, you need to wake up."

Nothing.

"MOM."

I heard Liz come up behind me.

"Any luck?"

"No. But I know what *will* get her up."

"What—what are you gonna do?" Liz asked, eyebrows raised.

"Get out of the doorway," I warned her. Then, turning back towards the bed. "MOM! MICE! YOU ARE COVERED IN MICE!"

It was like I'd struck her with a cattle prod. Liz screamed in surprise as Mom shot out of her bed, tearing at her clothes. Her eyes were open but unaware, spinning dizzily in their sockets. Words spilled from her mouth like syrup, unsticking from her dry lips, groggy and anxious.

"G'IM OFF! G'IM OFF!"

I grabbed for her hands and held them in mine, feeling the stab of her long nails as they pressed into my palms.

"I got them, Mom. I got them off."

It took a few minutes to get her to stop jumping around, but once she did, I walked her into the kitchen. She had torn one of the buttons off of her shirt and lost an earring in the scuffle. Her hair was matted and disheveled, and the intense bags under her eyes looked far worse under the yellow glare of the lights bouncing off the walls.

"It's Rachael, Mom. Rachael and Liz. We got rid of all the mice for you."

Liz nodded slowly. Her wide eyes were full of surprise and her lips curled inward, like she'd just watched somebody puke. Her home life wasn't perfect, but I was fairly sure she'd never seen a mental breakdown before.

"Okay, okay," Mom muttered, turning her arms over as if to check for tiny footprints on her skin.

"Do you want something to eat?"

"No."

"How about some water?"

"Nuh-uh."

"You've got to have something," I said. "You can't take your medicine on an empty stomach."

"I already took it," she said, yawning.

"When?"

"Before work."

"When?"

She hadn't been able to find work in the district for almost two years.

"Before—uhm, before you got here," she stammered, scratching intently at her neck.

"Well, I think you missed a few. Because you've been asleep for a long time."

I walked past Liz to the kitchen and filled up a glass with water. Then, I counted out all of the evening pills and opened the freezer. There was nothing inside.

"I'm going to order a pizza," I said. "And I want you to have some."

Mom ate one slice of pizza and a handful of pills before falling asleep on the couch. Liz and I sat around her, T.V. light shining down on the greasy pepperoni left in front of us, occasionally turning to each other to comment on the show.

"Fuck this bitch, man. She's always doing the dumbest shit," Liz whispered, tilting her head towards the screen.

I laughed, nodding.

"You don't have to whisper," I told her. "There's no chance in hell she's waking up."

Liz looked down at Mom's slumped body, at the uncomfortable angle of her head bent against the back of the couch. I asked the obvious question.

"Should we move her to her bed?"

"And do the mouse shit again? No way," Liz said, reaching for another slice of pizza.

"It's a *little* funny though, right? The mice?" I smiled sheepishly.

Liz opened her mouth, then closed it.

"What?" I asked.

"I just...was it, like, always this way?"

"What do you mean?"

"Your mom. Has she always been like this?"

I looked up at the ceiling. When you look back and reflect, that's when things become the good and the bad, the big and the small. When you're living in it, living it *out*, it's just your life.

"Yeah," I said, finally. "We've always been like this."

"Everyone Who's Anyone Smokes Menthols."

"You know, some moms bond with their daughters over, like, makeup," Liz smirked.

"Shut up," I replied, voice muffled as I pulled on a sweatshirt.

"What? Bro, I'm complimenting you. This shit is *way* cooler."

I grabbed two cartons of Doral menthols and tucked them into the elastic waist of my sweatpants, pulling the hem of my hoodie down.

"Can you tell they're in there?"

Liz stared at the very obvious lump underneath my clothes with red eyes, lids drooping.

"Uhhhh…"

"*Fuck.*"

Here's a thing about rehab: they have strict contraband rules. I mean, of *course* they do. But Mom didn't tell me this when she asked me to bring cigarettes to treatment—she didn't even tell me who the cigarettes were for. She didn't smoke. Not only that, but she didn't give me money for them. So, Liz and I stole them.

I marched through the front door, hopeful that the security guard wouldn't notice them this time. But, once again, I was met with a firm hand to the sternum, stopped in my tracks. Sort of how the guard's belt stopped his beige-uniformed belly from spilling onto the floor.

"I can still see them under there," he said, annoyed.

My mom was looking at me through the wire-bound windowpane of the industrial door, eyes were wide as she mimed to me, shaking her head. There was a fire behind her eyes, and even though she hadn't correctly orchestrated this mini contraband crime by giving me the details I needed to succeed, I realized for the first time that my mom had some spice to her. The same kind of spice my dad had when it came to sneaking by and committing petty crimes, a quality she detested and yet here she was, relying on me, and that same spice, to carry out her mission. She knew it was in my DNA.

"See what?" I asked with a blank face, ready to lie my way through the situation.

Every successful lie depends on one thing: disrespect. The more caricatured, the more likely the opposition is to buckle—either so they don't have to deal with it, or because they've convinced themselves it was all a misunderstanding, since no one would dare lie so blatantly and think they could get away with it. It was something I'd learned from my brothers; one time, they lit a fire in a trashcan in the food court and security came running up to us. But Butchie, Josh, and Brett just stood there, backs to the flames, and asked, "What fire?"

I was hoping for the same result, but it wasn't going that way.

"The cigarettes," the beige man said. "Can you tell me which patient asked you to bring them in?"

"No, I cannot," I said, mimicking his serious tone.

"Look kid, I don't wanna do this but if you don't stop trying to bring contraband items into my building"—he paused for a breath, waiting to see if someone was going to correct him on whose building this actually was—"I'm going to have to call up the police station."

I blinked up at him, mouth sealed. Playing dumb was my last hope.

"Which means you're going to be in trouble, and whoever sold these to you, and told you to bring them in here, is going to be in trouble, too."

"Alright fine!" I grumbled. "How many can I bring in at once?"

"One pack for personal use."

I opened the bottom of my sweatshirt and let the cartons smack loudly onto the lobby floor, stone-faced and still, staring at the lumpy dough of flesh between his dust-colored eyes. Then, I kicked them under the chair and scribbled my name sloppy and huge on the clipboard.

Back in the car, I turned to Liz.

"Let's sell the rest of these."

Steal and sell. Scheme and sell.

Or, on one very lucky occasion, obtain gallon bags of weed for *free* and sell.

Liz and I were known businesswomen at Naples High, and we used our independent studies periods to collect and move products from clique to clique, scene to scene. Skatepark, band room, parking lots. What we sold depended on what we needed; Liz was on stoner time, late to nearly every class, so she made it her mission to collect tardy slips from teachers' desks, forging their signatures. I was spending half my class time either fishing at the pier, working at the mall, or tucked into one of Michael's bean bag chairs, so I gathered validation passes, trying to excuse my absences. When we both got detention for missing school—a teacher once came down to the pier and told me to get to class—we sat in silence, not wanting to indicate to anyone that we were an operation. On a good day, we could leave campus with $200 in our pockets. Bad, and we'd smoke half our Doral menthols, picking up the habit when nobody wanted our bottom-tier tobacco.

By the time we graduated, I was 16, driving my own truck. The whole thing was bittersweet; we finally got our freedom, sure, but it didn't feel like the accomplishment we'd imagined. Liz and I were bummed to have lost our side hustle, and when my diploma came in the mail, I was disappointed. For one, I'd expected it to be heavy, important, like the ones my mom had in frames on her desk at the Big House. Instead, it was printed on lightweight paper, a photocopy of a photocopy. And the name on it? Rachael Finley-Weissberg. Not Rachael *Finley*. I was confused, annoyed. My dad hadn't been present for any of this shit, any of the chaos, the good and the bad. I'd been my own parent, my mom's parent. I didn't want his name involved, but there I was, just now finding out my legal name. And my mom? She was about as interested in this piece of information as she was my actual graduation.

"Oh, right," she said on the phone. She sounded tired. I could hear a T.V. in the background, the sound of other patients talking. She was back in treatment again.

"'Oh right' I graduated, or 'oh right' you forgot my name?" I said, tense.

"Whichever you want, sweetheart."

In my twenties, I'd feel the sting of regret for never getting a single yearbook, never doing the graduation walk, wearing a cap and gown. Never feeling a hint of pride. Kids don't know enough to think about the sentimental stuff, to step back and look around them, see where they are and where they've been. You have to tell them what's important, remind them to save their memories even if they scoff at you, ready to move on. And more than I wanted any card or congratulations, more than I'd ever want that memorabilia, I wanted Mom to acknowledge that I'd done it. All by myself. But then, nobody ever told me anything. Especially not when I wanted to hear it.

The One That Got Away

I was standing by the car, smoking one of the Dorals, when Mom came outside. It took me a second to recognize her, and when I did, I flung the cigarette, stamping it out. Not quickly enough, though.

"That's a dirty habit," she smirked. It was hard not to point out that we were standing in front of a rehab facility, but then again, it was hard to even look at her. She was nothing like herself.

Mom was drained. Flat. She looked like she had been deflated and blown back up again one too many times. Her porcelain face was spattered with big brown dots, blue blood hanging low and loose below her eyes. I walked over to her for a hug, felt her loose, pillowy arms surround me. I didn't fit in them the way that I used to, but the usual fix floated in my mind, and I fell back into a time when sleep was the cure for everything, when sleeping next to her was all that I ever needed.

"Maybe it's time to look up Harry," Mom said staring out the window as I drove her home.

"Harry? Really?"

For as long as I'd been listening to Mom's stories, I'd heard about Harry. He had been her first love back when she was just in high school, but his family had been poorer than hers, so her parents never approved; when she went off to Cornell, he joined the Army. She'd float his name whenever things were looking up, as if to say, *Okay, things are good now. You're ready for Harry.*

"He might be married, might be divorced like me," she chuckled a little, folding her yellow hands across her chest. "You never know."

"You never know," I repeated

"Do you think you could look him up for me?"

I hunched over the keyboard with Mom sitting on my bed. Her slow voice wove in and out of different summer nights, humid and huddled with Harry in Chicago—sneaking out of her window, kissing him in the back of his dad's car. I plugged everything we knew about him into the search engine, finally tacking on the last details 'army, Vietnam.'

Then, his name came up. Along with thousands of others. All of whom died in battle.

I nudged Mom's leg. "Hey. I found him."

"You did? What's it say?"

For a moment, she wasn't sallow. She was glowing like a little girl, surging with optimism, the culmination of all of those years spent thinking about him, waiting to be rescued. I swallowed, looking hard into her blue eyes, hoping she'd understand my silence. She didn't.

"He died in Vietnam."

I crawled over; the thin mattress buckled. Her cries lifted my arms as I wrapped myself around her, curling into the back of her body as tightly as our separate skins would allow, knowing that no amount of closeness could replace hope.

One month after the loss of Harry, Mom was vomiting blood into the toilet. I don't think she would have thought anything of it if she hadn't been sober; my childhood was spattered with scenes of Mom kicking the car door open at a red light, throwing up into the street. Walking over to the couch and wiping her hand on the back of her mouth, informing me that she'd just puked up blood. And every time, she'd jerk the car back into gear, or slide down against the cushions with her hands folded over her big t-shirt, and act like nothing was wrong. She once sat on a glass that she'd left in the driver's seat of the station wagon, the whole thing shattering into her ass. She hardly cried out—just reached behind her and yanked the shards out. Then, walked to the trunk of the car and tied an old sweater around her rear, which she kept on when we got home. I watched it soak with blood while she slept facedown on the floor, fibers caking into the wound. But this time, there was no pink cocktail to blame for the color, no benders to dull the pain. She couldn't run anymore.

I drove her to the hospital, and they told us that things weren't looking good for her. Her liver was in jeopardy, as were her kidneys. We booked a bunch of appointments, infusions and transfusions, and I drove her to all of those, too. There wasn't a lot to look forward to, not a lot of happiness in her present, so Mom spent a lot of time in the past, pulling up memories and old stories that had once been stoppered in her chest. I think Harry was the scab, and once he peeled off, she couldn't pretend to care about her present anymore.

"You know they told me I'd never have kids?"

We were sitting together in a clinic, a tissue-thin curtain separating us from the other people in the room receiving blood transfusions. I tried to focus in on Mom's voice, to cut out the weird beeping and buzzing sounds of all of the machines.

"They said there was no chance, not in patients with uterine cancer." She looked up at the speckled ceiling tiles. "You were my little miracle baby."

I remembered those words, how she used to tell them to me on my birthday when I was very small. I always wished that she would spend more time on the miracle aspect, rather than the dozens of ways that I wasn't supposed to be here—she'd had half her uterus removed after her cancer, had only one ovary "on the opposite side," as she liked to say.

"You had to jump in order to make it in there," she sighed, crossing

97

and uncrossing her arms, trying to get comfortable under her tangle of infusion tubes. I nodded along, back aching in the plastic chair one of the nurses scrounged up for me. Even though I was uncomfortable, I felt a brief pang of longing, the glow that comes with knowing that she fought for me.

"So, don't mind if I don't take what *they* have to say seriously."

Whenever we're in a clinic, 'they' is code for the doctors, rather than the people she used to think were spying on us. I mean, she still had her paranoia about being watched by the neighbors, but that came in second to the test results, all of the labs, and the many hospital stays she endured since getting out of rehab. Plus, there was little chance of anyone questioning whether she belonged in the trailer park; no one was asking for her skincare secrets anymore.

"Let's just wait and see," I replied. She shivered and I parted the curtain, looking out for a nurse.

"Now, look at you," Mom mumbled, drifting off. "Signed up for college."

"It's just one community college class," I told her, but she was already asleep. A nurse passed, and I called out. "Can we get another blanket?"

State-run facilities are all the same, all bleached and stale, with holes in the upholstery and stains on the walls. When I was little, if Mom's symptoms ever got worse than just puke or blood, she would go to the hospital on her own, leaving me at home from the time that I was six, sometimes for several days. I wonder if she ever came here; the transfusion center looks a lot like the DMV, only people are moaning from the discomfort of having their blood separated, not waiting in long lines. I'm anxious about how Mom is going to feel when we go home, worried that I'm going to fuck things up, stressed that we'll miss an appointment. I try to find that little shred of hope, the knowledge that Mom once battled the odds for me. I take a deep breath, willing myself to do the same for her.

It might have been easier if Michael was around. But I told myself that hoping for that was more pointless than hoping Mom's liver would miraculously heal itself; I didn't have that kind of power, and I definitely didn't have that kind of time. There was no magic cure for his agoraphobia, just as there wasn't one for the lifetime of abuse Mom put her body through.

A few weeks into my class at Edison Community College, I knew it wasn't for me. Being there, around all of those people that seemed to have their lives mapped out, felt restrictive. It felt like every other girl was going to become a bank teller, and every other guy was planning to do real estate, the same kind of desolate, hopelessly domestic, empty future that staying here in Naples was laying out for me. It all made my skin itch, and I started to daydream about working on the docks like my dad did, repelled by the idea of becoming an office drone, knuckles white around my pencil.

The day I dropped my class, I pulled up to Butchie's house.

The garage was open, and people were piled in the scrappy armchairs and torn couches strewn around the space, pushed out into the driveway to make room for more seats. I held a cigarette between my lips, smiling when I saw Richie shooting pool with Butchie. I beelined for them both, arms open for a hug.

"Rachey!" Richie said, sweeping me towards him, resting his cold can of Budweiser on top of my head. Today, he smelled like tobacco and whiskey. I missed his hugs. "The little college star."

"Not anymore," I said with a shrug. "I dropped."

"Derek always said you were smart," he muttered to me, putting down his pool cue to give me a light.

"So that means it must be true, right?" Butchie said, rolling his eyes. He made another shot, then another, clearing the table.

"Hey, nobody's better than you at pool, Butch," his dad said, clapping him on the back. "Except maybe me, you know, *before* I start in on the liquor."

I leaned against the wall, watching everybody mingle. I'd thought the party would've been a good distraction for me, but it, like everything else, was giving me the nagging itchy feeling in the back of my brain.

"What's next, then, Rachey?" Richie asked. He was the only person that called me that and I let him.

"I think I'll go to New York."

Why did I say that? I wondered, reaching for an ashtray. But now that I'd said the lie, I felt kind of stuck to it, and not in a bad way. New York *had* been on my mind; I'd been chatting with some guys up there online, Friendster friends, distant acquaintances—nothing flirty or interesting, just chatter about music—and I realized I could probably couch surf until I found a place to live. The decision was as quick and sloppy as flipping an egg, but now that it was done, I felt relief. The unknown felt so much more promising than the known. All that was left to do was tell Michael before—

"You're leaving?" Butchie asked.

I shrugged, getting used to the idea with every passing second.

"Good for you," Richie boomed. "It's good to step out on your own."

Butchie turned back to the pool table, setting up for another game. I sat behind him and watched as the game began, watched it end. Looked on as another two people came up to play, stared after their backs as they turned to leave the table. That's what staying was, wasn't it? Looking on as people came and went, won and lost? The garage was loud with music and conversation, cloudy with smoke, but I didn't hear anything. There was nothing left for me. And just like that, I no longer felt strangled by the itch. A breeze came through the garage screen.

Consolation Prize

Not talking about the future was what kept Michael feeling sane, what kept him afloat, but I needed something to dream about, hope for, work towards.

I took twenty extra turns along the drive to his, hands shaking, scared that if I spoke up for myself and told him what I was thinking, I'd lose something very important to me. I wanted him to profess his love for me, his devotion, to tell me that if I left, he'd have nothing. That he would come with or even just leave his porch. Michael was the first person I'd ever been in love with, and he was a person as fragile as our love itself. For years, I had lived solely for Michael's quiet movements, his whispers. And while we slept in the back room of his mother's house, so close to the beach you could hear the waves, I had found calm. Not in the place, but his presence. His being next to me was so big and so real and so *mine*. Until one day, like young love does, we grew differently. Our teenage love grew from nubile bliss to what felt like a teenager itself, angry and confused, ready to leave its hometown and never look back. Looking around us, I saw us for what we were, what we'd be. He'd never get help, and I'd just be here, a hitchhiker, stuck to the cuff of his pants. Work, life, friends. And then I'd come back and we'd chain smoke on our hamster wheel until it rusted to a stop.

"I'm moving. To New York."

Here was his moment. *No, stay, I love you. I am going to fix this. I'm going to get help. I'll start leaving the house. I want to take care of myself, to take care of you. I want to build a future together. You and me forever.* Instead, he stood up and walked over to his nightstand, digging around for a new pack of cigarettes. He opened the pack and pushed one between his lips. The first ones I'd ever kissed, the only ones I ever wanted to.

"You have to do what's right for you," he said.

"Where did you say you were going?"

"New York, Mom."

"Don't tell her *anything* about us," Mom had said, dropping her voice, eyes snapping away from the T.V. to stare at me, wide-eyed and serious.

"I'm not staying with Grandma. I'm staying with friends."

"Be careful, Rachael. You can't trust her."

I was leaving in an hour. Michael was maybe going to say goodbye.

"Mom, can I take this pillow?"

I didn't even know if there would be a mattress for me up North—I hadn't even mapped out the pitstops I was going to take. If there was a time in her life for my mom to be motherly, this was it: her 17-year-old daughter was driving up the country by herself to stay with a house full of men she knew from the internet this was probably the time.

"Huh?"

"Can I take this pillow?" I hold up the pillow, looking at the feathers that are poking out of its old, stained seams. We might've had it since the Big House, which probably violated the health codes of even the worst motel, but that thought was bottom tier compared to the carousel spinning in my mind.

I hope he shows. Don't get your hopes up. But what if he shows? Don't be disappointed. But you're leaving. But if he wants me to stay?

"Sure."

She doesn't even look away from her show. I tuck the pillow under my arm and go outside, throwing my small bag of shit into the backseat of the truck. I have one threadbare suitcase and a drawstring bag. I have my beat-up flip-flops and a pair of skate shoes that resemble Swiss cheese. I stare at my reflection in the side of the truck, the contorted way my arms appear to stretch the entire length of the trailer. For a brief moment, I feel big, strong. In control.

"Hey."

A car door shuts behind me. It's Michael, a teddy bear in his arms, standing in front of his mom's SUV. I wonder whether a car this nice has ever driven through the trailer park before, but the idea gets pushed from my mind because this is the *first time* Michael has ever driven for as long as I've known him. And he's here, with a teddy bear from CVS? I try not to imagine what our relationship would've been like if his driving was a normal occurrence.

"Hi," I say, mouth dry, throat suddenly itchy. He hands me the bear and I put it behind the wheel, turning to face him.

"It's not so bad here," he says, pointing to the trailer.

I shrug. He continues talking.

"All packed?"

"Yeah."

"Have a map?"

"Yeah."

Michael can't stand still. He's swaying in the breeze, shuffling his feet, uncrossing his arms and moving his hands from his pockets then crossing back up again.

"Thanks for the bear," I say, taking a step towards him. He shoves his hands back into his pockets.

"It's cheesy," he says. His eyes are on the ground. I can't tell whether he's sad or angry or worried or tired. Or nothing at all.

"I like it," I say, reaching out a hand. His bony shoulder fits perfectly underneath my fingers. He doesn't move away, but I can tell that he wants to.

"Well…"

"Well."

"I'll be seeing you." He straightens up, and my hand falls off his shoulder. He puts his arms out stiffly for a hug.

"Bye, Michael."

"Bye, Rach."

The hug is short. So is the kiss. He lopes over to the bright white SUV without turning back around. I watch him get into the car, start it, choose a station on the radio. No eye contact, no final wave. He drives away, and I hold up a hand to shield my eyes from the sun, waiting for the car to round the man-made lake, until I can't see the glossy white paint shine between the trailers, until the hum of the engine is replaced by the buzz of flies divebombing my skin. The itch is replaced with a burn in my throat, the corners of my eyes. I take a deep breath and turn on my heels.

"Mom?" My eyes adjust to the dark trailer slowly. I look at the blue painted furniture, the yellow walls. The single cup and plate on the counter. Mom is standing in the kitchen, holding a pill bottle at arm's length, squinting down at the label.

"Yeah?" She asks.

"I'm leaving."

"Alrighty, then." She uncaps the bottle and pours a few into her hand, turning them over with a long, unpainted fingernail. She tucks one under her tongue and dumps the rest back in.

"I'm going to New York," I remind her.

"I *know*," she says impatiently.

"Okay. Just checking."

Western New York, Age 18

It was midday by the time I made it to Rochester. Teeth gritty from energy drinks, eyes salty from staring at the road. I'd slept in rest stop parking lots, ate bags of chips for dinner, splashed water on my face in gas station bathrooms to stay awake. Every detour was a step further from my destination, and it felt like the longer I was on the road, the longer I argued with Michael and my mom in my head. They'd been so casual about me leaving, and that made me think that they didn't believe I was capable of staying away—the sooner I got to Rochester, the sooner I could prove them wrong.

Every house on the street was built in the same Victorian style, each in varying shades of disrepair. Some looked like family homes, with a tire swing or plastic slide growing moss in the shade, while others looked more like crash houses, the kinds of places Arielle took me to meet up with her friends out by the swamp. Everywhere I looked was gray: gray smoke coming from gray stone chimneys, their clouds amassing in an endless gray sky. I crept up to an old house with a wide front porch, a chipped yellow door, and a buckling roof. One of the house numbers had fallen off the exterior wall and had been replaced with a hand-painted '6' instead, black paint dripping ominously next to a windowpane taped up with a garbage bag. There was a hole in the front lawn that looked like it had either been used to smoke a pig, or someone tried to bury a body and got tired halfway through the process. The mailbox was on the ground rather than standing on its post on the sidewalk, and there were beer cans spilling out of a recycling bin to the side of the house that looked like it had missed collections for two months straight—that, or it was evidence of a weekend bender.

I killed the engine, ogling the house from underneath a massive oak tree. *Here we go,* I thought to myself as I opened my door. I felt my flip-flops sink down several inches into the mush below, sliding on waterlogged leaves as I staggered to the porch, feeling icy water seep under the soles of my feet, backpack slung over my shoulder. I got to the door and quickly patted down my hair, wishing I'd thought to look at myself in the mirror when I'd been in the truck, but also grateful that I hadn't because I didn't have anything to correct the situation with, anyway. I held my breath as I raised my fist to the cracked yellow paint.

"We don't have your *jacket*, Amy!" A muffled voice yelled from behind the door.

I paused, wondering if someone was looking out of one of the windows that hadn't been taped up with plastic. Then, I knocked again.

"We've looked a HUNDRED times! GO HOME."

The voice was louder, closer. I took a small breath, readying myself.

This was it, the kind of moment that sat in front of you like a top spinning on a table. I could either swipe my hand out and seize it, or I could wait for it to lose momentum and fall sadly on the floor, allowing myself to be the kind of girl that sat timidly behind a busted door while some asshole screamed at her. Was this how I wanted to make myself known? I thought about my friends back home, the acceptance that was won by letting my proverbial 'nuts hang.' I swallowed, standing tall.

"I'm NOT Amy!"

"*What?*"

"THIS. IS. NOT. AMY," I roared, voice splitting like a woman down to her last straw.

"*Huh?*"

"Come to the FUCKING door and see who it is."

Footsteps. Then, the door swung open on its rusty hinges. A squishy guy in a Bills t-shirt, sweats, and a backwards hat stood there, balancing on one filthy sock while using the other to scratch his leg.

"Oh. You're not Amy," he muttered stupidly, scratching at his neck beard.

"*Correct,*" I sneered, pushing past him.

The floorboards creaked beneath me. I craned my neck down the hallway, peering over the back of one of the ratty, mismatched couches parked in front of the T.V., an episode of *South Park* jabbering into the half-lit room. I turned on my heels, following the other hallway towards what I assumed was the kitchen, only to land at the foot of a steep, winding staircase.

"Who are you look—"

"Is Kyle here?" I asked, marching back towards Neck Beard.

"Kyle? *Oh!*" Realization colored his face. Then, he raised his voice. "KYLE?"

I heard the house shift as someone got to their feet above us. Then, the squeak of the spiral staircase I'd just discovered.

"*Rachael!*" Kyle crossed the room on spidery limbs, arms open wide. "You made it!"

"Oh fuck. This is the girl?"

"*Yes,* Spencer. For the thousandth fucking time. This is *Rachael.*"

I pulled away from our hug and raised an eyebrow at Spencer. He held out his fist, giving me an awkward bump.

"Sorry 'bout that, dude."

"It's cool," I nodded, laughing, relieved that my show of force actually worked. I felt a draft seeping in through the floorboards, cooling my wet feet.

"Is that all you brought?" Kyle asked.

"Oh! No," I replied quickly, holding up the backpack. "I've got more in the car."

"Need help getting it?"

"No, thanks," I replied, shaking my head. I didn't want anyone to see how little I had, and especially didn't want anyone discovering the drugstore bear seat-belted in the back of the truck. "This is good for now."

"Well, follow me. I'll show you around!"

We left Spencer and climbed up the spiral stairs. Once we got to the top, there was another long hallway with several rooms. Kyle pushed open the first door and stood in the doorway.

"This is my room," he said proudly. "Go ahead. Check it out."

Kyle's room was plastered wall-to-wall with posters, ranging from semi-pornographic to fully pornographic, including advertisements for flavored vodka and creased and wrinkled posters from tours and concerts. There was a Bills pennant mounted on the ceiling next to a picture of two girls kissing in their underwear, and I tried not to linger on the fact that these were the last things Kyle saw before he fell asleep at night. I cleared my throat.

"Nice room," I lied. Then, I spotted his teal Mac in the corner, propped on top of a nightstand so that he could type while sitting in bed. "And computer."

"The computer that made it happen!" He joked. I gave him a small smile and he blushed. "That was corny. Sorry."

"So, who else lives on this floor?" I asked, changing the subject.

"Nick and Nate. But they're both at work."

"Where do they work?"

"The Cheesecake Factory. All of us work there."

"Wait, *all* of you work there?"

"Yeah, everyone except Wes."

"And where does he work?" I asked, following Kyle down the hall. We walked past a cluttered bathroom that smelled strongly of Axe body spray and mildew, chilling my spine.

"He has a few different jobs," Kyle shrugged. He opened an arm and gestured up another set of stairs, even steeper than the first. "Here we are. Your room."

I crossed in front of him, feeling the temperature drop as I marched upwards, Kyle close behind, practically pressing in on me. I held onto the banister and hurried up the final few steps, nearly knocking my skull into a low-hanging beam.

It was less of a room and more of a somewhat finished attic. There were windows on three sides, two of which didn't have wood covering the old insulation beneath them, all of them allowing a cross breeze to sweep the room. The front window was wider than the others, its smudged glass level with the last remaining leaves clinging to the maple tree in the front yard, wide branches perilously close to the house. I could see my truck down the street, and imagined that, come summer, the smell of the explosive trash cans in the yard would easily make its way through the seams of the wood. Kyle stood hunched near the stairs while I shuffled around with my head ducked, checking out the old mattress laying directly on the floor, the one outlet covered in cobwebs in the corner. The steeply pitched ceiling prevented me from standing fully upright anywhere except directly in the center of the room, and when I did, my head hit the chain dangling from the single lightbulb mounted above.

"It's probably better suited for Nate than you, height-wise, but don't tell him I said that."

"I like the windows," I blurted out, trying to find something positive to say about the space.

"You might want to cover them with something if you like sleeping in."

"Good point." I dropped my backpack on top of the mattress, wondering whether the guys brought it or if it came with the house.

"Did you bring any blankets? It gets kind of cold up here."

"Yeah, I've got a couple."

"Some of us use space heaters, but I'm not sure that outlet can handle it."

A space heater seemed like a good idea—as did sheets, curtains, and half a dozen mouse traps. I turned to Kyle. "Do you know if the Cheesecake Factory is hiring?"

"They don't hire our friends anymore," he sighed, rolling his eyes. "It's a long story. But the girls that work at the bar might know of a place. I'll ask when I go in later."

"Sweet."

"You'll probably get to meet them tomorrow, actually."

"What's tomorrow?" I asked, following him back downstairs with my eyes on my feet, praying that I wouldn't land on my ass.

"Tomorrow?" Kyle laughed. "Tomorrow's a *Friday*."

In 24 hours, I would find out that the parties at this house were different than the ones back home, that nobody here got their kicks by throwing swollen grapefruits at people rowing on the canal, or putting fireworks in people's mailboxes. There would be sex and tension, powdery drugs instead of stupid pranks, actual fist fights instead of wrestling on the carpet in Butchie's living room. I would see bad break-ups and hormonal breakdowns, stand in a room filled with people whose relationships with each other were as stable as the stairs leading to my attic.

But not yet. After Kyle left for work, I went into his room and sat on the edge of his bed, updating my now-defunct Friendster page. Like all things people do on the internet, resetting my location to New York felt profound, like I was changing my name, becoming someone else. I mean, wasn't that why I came here, anyway? To be someone else?

Still, there were things I could leave behind but couldn't forget. I typed and re-typed a message to Michael, telling him that I'd gotten here safe, that everything was good. But when that felt like it was more for me than for him, I deleted it. Then, typed it again. *I love you.* Delete. *I'm sorry.* Delete, delete. *I wish things were different.*

Assimilation

I feel like I'm a kid again, trying to convince my mom that my favorite shirt isn't too small. I get my way, but now I have to sit uncomfortably for an entire car ride, hiking it down and ripping it at the neck, just to be right. The same goes for Rochester. I tell myself to make it work, to try to make it work—then, I hear a mouse scuttle past my head and cry, *PLEASE, for fuck's sake, let this WORK*—but it doesn't. It can't.

Wes and Dave are the only ones I like in the house. They actually talk to me and ask me how I'm doing, and I appreciate the effort. My other roommates, though, are frat boys without the Greek. Alternative in their music tastes but really just bro-y and uncomplicated, once you got under their clouds of smoke. They grew up with parents who would've taken their allowance away if they got caught high in high school, so now, they're perpetually hungover, always stoned, able to convince one of their moms or dads to front the cable bill for *Family Guy*. Besides that perk, the house was barely standing, kitchen off limits because of the stacks of rotten takeout from the Cheesecake Factory in the fridge. Everyone listened to their music so loud that the walls rattled, and there was a frigid draft in every room.

There was a new kind of pressure, too. The guys in relationships had very unfriendly girlfriends that hated me living in the house possibly more than I did. They were a little older than I was, and they made it their mission to make me feel as unwanted as possible, a pact made before we'd even said a word to each other. I don't dissect it; I know where it comes from, but it's playing out like a poorly scripted teen drama, and I have a hard time believing it's my reality.

"I thought all girls from Florida were, like, surfer babes, but you're not really a babe, are you…?"

Just like that. *That* was the diss.

??? Who is this funny for?

Pay back's a bitch, I hear Butchie smirk in my head. So, I don't respond. I slip out and find a different corner of the party to dissolve into, on the other side of the house, in a whole different climate. Dave, cutting lines for the guys around me. I watch, shake my head *no* when he holds up the dollar bill. I just want time to think. Plan. plot.

In the late afternoon the next day, Dave—I remember because it was unusual for him to be awake that early—hangs in my doorless doorway, speaking fast and frantically. He never tries to fuck me because he's a Weezer guy pining after Weezer girls, and I'm definitely not one of those. When he comes to my room at three in the morning, grinding his teeth and coked out of his mind, it's because he wants someone to talk to about how sad and fucked up everything is, and I hold space for him because he does the same for me. He's a peaceful cokehead, and we usually watch the same VHS of Ben Folds Five performing on some talk show while he breaks his own heart about the state of the world, or just the little brunette barista that doesn't look his way. It made us kind of an alliance. Plus, everyone else locked him out of their bedrooms.

"Look, dude," he says to me, shielding his eyes from the sun beaming onto my mattress. "Everyone thinks you slashed her tires. And I get it because she's a complete psycho bitch and she has been since high school and everyone knows that. But, like, they think you slashed her tires because she's mean to you."

"Dave—"

"Actually, Sean said he heard the door slam last night right around the time it would've happened, but I lied and said, 'Look, if Rachael went outside, I would've seen her.' I vouched for you, man. All I'm saying is, I need to hear you say you didn't slash her tires."

"*Dave.* I didn't slash her tires."

I slashed her tires.

Wes, on the other hand, was not a cokehead. He was warm, inviting, the only one that actually skated, and that reminded me of home; unlike the other skateboards that never moved from the pile by the door, Wes' board went where he went. Whenever he was around, I felt like I could finally breathe. We slept together my second week in the house, and within a week after that, he was my boyfriend. Which should have been a happy thing, a sign of moving on, but I hated that I had a new boyfriend. I hated that he wasn't Michael.

So, why did I keep going into his room?

Was I "creeping down the hallway" just like I did with Derek?

No, I shook my head, tugging the thought off my brain like a leech. *This isn't the same.* I am just desperate for an ally, shelter, something familiar but different.

And he was. For one, Wes sold weed. A *lot* of weed. Occasionally, he had a bag of pills on hand that he got as a trade, but since he was just a stoner, not actually interested in keeping the pills for himself, his room became the first stop for most people at our parties. People knew what he was up to, but most of them didn't know the extent—still, they knew enough not to fuck with him. It was the first time I'd trade stable guy for turbulence, but it wouldn't be the last; I liked that Wes was big figure in the house, and that people found parts of him intimidating. We went to sleep at night on a bed that had a hidden trundle packed with safes, all with different combinations, and in the back of his truck was a padlocked compartment with more drugs and a gun. Unlike Liz and I, who just scattered weed around our high school and spent the cash on bullshit, Wes and his cousin had an entire operation where they washed their money through the family laundromat. That's actually where the gun was—in the toolbox in his truck, under his folded uniform tee from Laundry Stop.

People like their weed guy, so most of the people we saw during the day were really nice. Most of the people we were around, except the bigger fish. Every city's drug network has a tiered system, and Wes was a very small piece in a much larger operation. I never knew where exactly he was on the hierarchy, but it felt kind of smaller-mid tier, since his main role was taking huge amounts of weed and distributing it to smaller players in the game. *That's* where his money came from. He might've kept a little bundle of it for himself to break up and sell at parties for petty cash, but Wes dealt with thousands of dollars-worth of weed at a time. Like, twenty-*thousand* dollars. We'd ride around in his truck to the bigger fish, guys with panic rooms packed with guns and passports. They were assholes, and made sure Wes knew where he was in the rankings. Whenever we pulled the truck into the garages, they didn't get up to help load the weed into the hidden compartment beneath the truck bed. They would watch us closely while we packed up, one scratching at his early-30's balding head, the other smoothing the kind of shitty mustache that probably meant he got chicks in high school, but rarely since. I learn a lot about the world of drug dealing through Wes, listening carefully to every conversation, memorizing the jargon, but I don't know what or who comes before these guys on the food chain.

Anyway, people liked Wes and therefore people like me, now. I don't have to talk anymore at parties, I get to just sit and be. No one pressures me for something they can disagree with, or tries to make me feel weird for living there. The other dudes in the house have mostly backed off, and their girlfriends have started talking shit behind my back instead of to my face. Being the drug dealer's girlfriend tipped the social scale in my favor, at least to where I didn't have anyone *openly* hating me.

Whenever he was out, I would I sit in Wes' room while he made drops, listening to music on his massive stereo, sorting weed.

Pass me da green, I need some weed with my Hennessey—
Sort, weigh, bag.
Pass me da green, I need some weed with my Hennessey—
I like the zip of the lip of the tiny baggies beneath my fingernail.
Green trees pack wood, make cabbage, I like to get high but it ain't a bad habit.

Occasionally, Kyle would knock on the door. And every time he did, I felt my stomach drop.

From the minute Wes and I coupled off, Kyle started acting strange. He insisted that we were best friends—that he *found* me—and to prove it, he always kept me in the loop on everyone's gossip. But once I started sleeping with Wes, a lot of his shit talking circled back to him, or reasons why I shouldn't trust him.

"I was talking to Shannon at a party the other night and, uh," Kyle raised his eyebrows, and his voice about five cartoonish octaves, "they used to fuuuuuuuck!"

He lit up a bowl he hadn't paid for and waited for me to say something. "How does that make you feel?"

"It doesn't," I responded, keeping my voice cool. I was sick of him bringing stupid shit like this up to me all of the time, but I also felt like I couldn't say anything because I was in his house. And, yes, he *had* got me here.

"Well, I'm just looking out for you." He says, breathing smoke into my face. "He could have STDs."

It's daylight, and I swat at the cloud of smoke in front of my face, wishing I could swat Kyle out of my life, too. But the STD thing is a valid point, and I make a mental note to go get checked.

What I didn't think to check was my computer.

Kyle and one of the house girlfriends had been catfishing on MySpace with photos they stole from my hard-drive. The fun must have subsided, though, because they escalated the joke, posting ads with my name, phone number, job, photos, and *address* on Craigslist, claiming that I was looking for a boyfriend. Not only that, but the ad encouraged whoever saw it to just show up wherever I was. And they did.

These men would come to the house and ask for me when the guys would get the door. They started to leave presents for me when I wasn't home, asking my roommates to deliver them to me as I stood out of sight down the hall, shaking my head. They would come to the bar and stare at me. They called my phone. They sent me messages. The hair on the back of my neck was constantly standing up, because I couldn't shake the feeling that I was being watched. It was absolutely terrifying, and I could not figure out why it was happening

Listen, I knew it was a gamble to live in a house full of strangers, but I never could have predicted the lengths some of them would go to make me feel unwanted. I went into this entire experience thinking I would meet people like my brothers, people who looked out for each other and got into the fun kind of trouble that happens when you play dumb pranks. But that's kid shit. The real world is mean and dark and twisted.

People have said things to me like, "You should have known better."

Well, I *didn't* know better. Nobody ever told me this type of vile was out here. That it disguised itself in our peers, and happened under shared roofs.

Here's something else: I changed all of the names of the guys in the Rochester house. I didn't have to do that with my brothers back home. In that old Victorian, few things were safe, including me. All of the guys in that house had been in their twenties—I wasn't even 18. And the minute they could turn on me for the Kyle thing, they did. They screamed at me for leading him on. My 'best friend.'

"Leading him on?" I asked. "I had a *boyfriend!*"

YEAH, the rest of the guys yelled at me. You totally led him on. Bad Rachael. Bad, bad, bad. Again and again, *you should've known better.*

Never mind that I hadn't done more than hugged the guy before.

Just by being there, I was doing a bad thing. Just by being around and unavailable, I was a fucking tease. A lot of men at this age will call themselves your best friend, but it can get really dark, and you have to know how to protect yourself.

And although I've tried to rewrite the history of this situation many times, in my gut and heart I always knew it was them. And I found out for sure 10 years later via Instagram DM.

I'm sorry I didn't say anything sooner, or when it happened, a mutual confessed. *They made it sound like it was no big deal.*

Whatever—I'm safe from this now. And those two people can sit with the guilt if they ever read this book, or not. It's not about that anymore. What matters is *I* know enough to warn someone else, like my daughter, to look out for this kind of violence.

Scene Queens

I move into a house full of scene girls. Bandanas, teased hair, winged eyeliner—they take me in and rebrand me as one of their own, and I'm happy for it. I'm an underage bartender with a fake I.D., no friends, newly 'single.' In a lot of ways, I've been alone since I left Florida; my new roommates were the kinds of girls who found strength in numbers, never going to so much as a pharmacy alone. They'd found a Myspace niche where guys thought they were hot, and they did their best to fit me into it, too. It was comforting.

My first night in the house, they flocked to me, painting my face like theirs, styling my hair, getting me ready for my 'debut' in their social scene.

"How did you even live there?"

"How could you *deal?*"

"Oh, you know," I shrugged, eyes closed. "Just got the fuck out."

I would have worn, said, or done whatever these girls asked me to, because as far as I was concerned, dressing like a scene girl was better than sleeping in a car. We'd only met a few times at different parties, but they threw me a lifeline in the form of a twin bed, saving my ass without making me feel like an idiot.

"Hold still," Sara said, tracing eyeliner onto my lid.

"Sorry," I muttered.

More pressure. A wing.

"Did something happen?" Another voice asked.

"No," I hurried, but hopefully not by too much.

"That's badass," Sara announced.

"She doesn't take no shit," another girl echoed.

It was an announcement of sorts, but I didn't believe in it. Or, didn't know if that's who I wanted to be in this town—I kept the story about Krista's tires to myself.

"All done. Cute, right?" Sara asked the room. I blinked my eyes open.

"Oh my god *so* cute."

"Perfect."

"I love it," I lied. It was more makeup than I'd ever worn in my entire life. "Thanks, Sara!"

Sara's name is the only one worth mentioning, because in the hours after I moved in, she established herself as the ringleader, which made her the one to please. She's sweet and sour, and not as wide-eyed as the other girls in the house.

"This top will look cute on you," someone said.

"No, don't wear that!" Sara disagreed, and everyone nodded.

"Rachael is gonna fuck someone in her twin tonight!"

After I walked out the door, Wes didn't reach out to me once. Not at all. So, just three city blocks down from the non-frat frat, I started my new life. My new cat-wing eyeliner held the door open for me at the bar. New bar, new friends, new men, boys—whatever they were. The only things that weren't new were my fake I.D. and the moral constraints I'd taken with me from Naples. I couldn't have sex without having a boyfriend.

That's the cheat code, isn't it? Just make them your boyfriend and there's nothing "dirty" about it. It feels so stupid as I type it out, but this is what you get when you base your whole sexual identity off something you overheard from a group of 13- and 15-year-old boys. Mix it with a TV show about sex crimes, and you have yourself an unhealthy relationship with, well, *relationships.*

First, there was Anthony. Or, 'Hot Anthony' as my roommates called him. He and his friends were the ringer-tees + mesh shorts + Converse to our house's bandanas + American Apparel V-necks. We smoked cigarettes behind the bar on my break. I liked his lips. His hair was dark. He was Italian or something, tan all year round. Anthony's friends liked to bring up the number of girls he'd slept with, to try to get me to squirm. Triple digits. He *loved* that, loved to wrap his arm around me and narrow his eyes at them, "Really, guys? This isn't the time." I was single digits, and he loved that even more. I practiced sitting still during these conversations, not letting the pangs show on my face, or the confusion. What did Anthony want with me?

"It's because you're new, everyone wants to taste the new thing," one of his friends' girlfriends said over her shoulder. Always over the shoulder to no one.

Sometimes, they asked why I wanted to date a playboy, but I didn't have an answer for that, either. And when I got tired of the questions, I got tired of Anthony. And that's how it went.

Then there was Hot Chris. Forgive the nicknames—there was a general lack of creativity in our group. He didn't really hang around anyone I knew for more than a drink, which is why I picked him, hoping to avoid the 'awkwardness' my roommates complained about after Anthony and I broke up. Chris wore tight jeans and boots with spurs. He literally looked like a New York cowboy, and everyone found out about us the way everyone found out about Chris' girlfriends.

"Johnny Cash, Rachael? Johnny fucking *Cash*?" Sara barely whispered as I passed her a drink.

"What's, uh, wrong with Johnny Cash?"

"You're fucking Chris. Everyone in this town who starts fucking Chris changes their Myspace song to Johnny Cash or Hank *Three*."

Shit. So, I did just change my Myspace song to Johnny Cash. I breathed in my cliché, glancing over at Chris, sitting in his usual booth. Go fucking figure. Chris was an alcoholic, an actual alcoholic, not like the rest of us who binge-drank every weekend and woke up with our hands shaking. He woke up with a beer and he sat at the bar all day, watching me walk between the tables. "I love you with my drink in your hand," he always told me. Chris died, actually. I was gone when it happened, but when I heard about it, I wasn't surprised. I was surprised when it made me sad.

18-year-old me treated men the way I had treated the food court employees.

Sounding boards.

Places to play myself out, to read the echoes, and decide what to keep.

I kept a running tab of what was 'good,' holding onto the digestible pieces of me, and subtracting whatever made my boyfriends recoil, testing new material with every new relationship, and shaping my womanhood in the process. 18 felt too young to be a woman, like I should have had the option to delay, but it wasn't up to me. It isn't up to any of us.

But once these boyfriends started expecting things out of me, from places and emotions I turned off long ago, I felt trapped. And whenever I felt trapped, I made as clean of an exit as I could, replacing them with new conversations and new beds, places without obligation. But even then, I only had so much control, and things got complicated. Messy, even.

I'd left Florida because I wanted more, because I didn't want to die in Michael's bedroom, but every new guy did less for me than the one that came before. And now that I was gone, and the newness stopped being new, I couldn't stop asking: is this all I get? Is this the more? Why did I even leave?

Once, someone answered for me. They said that I probably moved up the East Coast so that I could finally see the seasons. *Yes,* I told them. *I've been wanting to see the seasons.* I wanted to see a new season of my life. I'd had the same leaves for so long that I needed to move to a place where they'd all fall off, leaving me stark and naked and cold to the world, able to carry armloads of icy snow on my thin branches. Isn't that what you're supposed to do? It is, isn't it? Move on? So, then, why does reading this back make me feel like a bad daughter? Why does reading this back make me feel like a whore? Not the fun kind that takes what she wants and never looks back, but the other kind, the one people want to see hurt. Nobody ever told me that, to most, she is the same girl. Maybe it *wasn't* better to have boyfriends and all their expectations. Maybe it would have been better to just fuck with the repercussions. If you're damned if you do and damned if you don't, you're just damned, dammit.

No Plan Is the Plan

The more I spent time with Sara, the more I wanted to *be* Sara. Not because I liked her all that much, but because I had been doing a terrible job of figuring out who I was on my own. She wore tight babydoll dresses and bright pink blush that wouldn't work on anyone, but she forced it, so it did. It was actually pretty similar to the way that she was forcing her relationship with metal dude Jeff even though she listened to what she called "ambient Nihilist electronica." Whatever that meant, he looked good standing next to her in her slinky pastel outfits, with him all dressed in black, his jeans ripped. It babied up her baby.

"Pass it," she said, sticking out her pink-polished hand.

I took another pull off the plastic whiskey bottle before handing it back to her. We both hated whiskey, but Jeff said that cool girls drank brown liquor. More than whiskey, I hated the bombastic attitudes of strictly whiskey drinkers that gets passed down and mimicked, the way they all act like their $3.99 bottle from 7-11 is top shelf.

Sara didn't just *not* listen to metal—she actually hated Jeff's band. Whenever we went to watch his shows, we stayed for less than half the set before sitting in the alleyway behind the venue, smoking and drinking whatever we'd snuck in our winter coats. Hers was a winter coat, actually. Mine was just a denim jacket lined with flannel that got left behind at the bar one night, but the whiskey made me warm and we could talk to whoever came out to smoke, so I didn't mind sitting on a cold metal chair in the snow, ass freezing through my Forever21 leggings.

"Played your favorite song," Jeff said when he came outside, looping his arm around Sara's waist.

"I know," she lied. "I loved it."

I always wondered how he missed her in the crowd. But she made up for it when they were together, putting on a show of her own.

Maybe that's what I wanted to take from Sara, the way she turned it on when he came around.

I lit a cigarette and sat on my free hand, trying to warm my fingers. The snow hadn't fallen for days, but the old stuff hung around, crusty and black as the ash I flicked at my feet. The rest of Jeff's band came outside, and so did the guys they opened for. When they did, they were arguing.

"I'm telling you dude, we can't tour without merch," one guy said loudly, kicking open the door.

"And I'm telling *you duuuuuuude,* we have no choice," whined another, pulling a flask out of his jacket.

One of them was a caricature of a metal band bass player from the woods, dressed in black denim, a leather vest, and athletic shoes. The other was a clean-cut guy with blonde-grey hair and basketball shorts. A third—stocky, with big, frizzy hair connected to his short beard who looked like belonged to a completely different kind of metal band—slammed his hands against the side of his head.

"Oh my god, will you both just *shut* the *fuck* UP?" They all went quiet after he yelled, so I made the assumption that he was the alpha.

"What happened?" Jeff asked. Sara was telling him a story about some girl who was glaring at her in the venue (no such girl existed) and he pushed away from her mid-sentence, her slippery mouth hanging open stupidly.

"Our merch person bailed because he got in a fight with his chick," Stocky guy said, shortly.

"She literally left him for his brother, bro..."

Stocky guy huffed. Nothing could come between him and tour. It was his prom.

"Fuck, man. And you tour tomorrow?" Jeff asked.

"Literally the worst fucking timing," one of the other guys whined.

"Shit. I'm sorry, dude," Jeff said, ignoring him. Jeff, being the leader of his band, and a general prick overall, never addressed anyone but fellow pricks.

I don't know if it was the whiskey. I don't know if it was my butt cheeks freezing together in a metal chair. Maybe it was the realization that Jeff was Sara with a penis, and that becoming Sara would mean becoming Jeff. I hated the way they made everything they did seem like a weird, inaccessible, angry art form. And that made me itch, the way that I knew that no matter how long I hung around them, they would always be too cool for me, cool and hating each other, hating themselves. The heavy, vapid pit in my chest was already too full to hold that. I opened my mouth.

"I'll do it."

"*What?*" Sara said, turning sharply. The other guys might not have heard me, but they heard her icy voice cutting through the alleyway. They turned, too.

"I'll do the merch."

"Have—have you ever done merch before?" Stocky guy stood with his arms folded across his chest, eyebrows raised. Seeing me, small and stupid, for the first time.

"No," I shrugged. "But I've worked venues."

This was only half true. I'd sold tickets as a high schooler at the skatepark, and I'd *been* to venues. But how hard could it be? I'd sold everything from weed to homemade sweatshirts to cigarettes. I could sell merch.

"We can't pay you."

I shrugged. "Will you be stopping in Florida?"

"Yeah, why?" The leader asked, scratching his chin.

"You can drop me off there."

"That's not for another week, though."

"So?"

"You think you'll *want* to be living in a van with a bunch of smelly guys for a week?" Sara laughed as she looked around at the guys, waiting for them to join her.

They didn't. Instead, their stocky leader scanned my face, looking for signs I'd be difficult to be around. *Make up?* None. *Hair dryer?* No. *Hairbrush?* Possible. *Shoes?* Flat. His eyes stopped around my ankles, unable to decide if I was wearing socks or not. *That* would be insane. He scanned me again to see if I was insane.

"I think I can handle it," I cut in.

Sara pouted when I disagreed with her, and snatched the whiskey out of my hands childishly.

"It would give us time to find a new merch person," one of the guys suggested.

"True," said another.

"She'd have to sit in the *back*," said the whiner.

"That's fine," I said.

"Alright, then. We leave tomorrow morning."

"Pass it," I said to Sara, holding out a hand for the bottle. And she did.

When I showed up the next morning, I could tell by everyone's faces that they hadn't expected me to make it. These guys had no idea how little I had keeping me here; in the time it took me to get my things together, Sara and Jeff had decided to throuple, so it was actually good that the house was going to free up a little. After that, I texted around and found someone who would keep my truck in their driveway.

"You ready for this?" Paul asked.

Wanting to be prepared, I'd Google-searched the band the night before. Maybe I *was* a little nervous—throwing myself into a van filled with strange men was a little riskier than throwing myself into a short-term relationship. Paul was stocky alpha. The other three guys were Alec, Ray, and Kurt. Ray stuck his hand out to introduce himself while the other two stood with their hands in their pockets. Clearly, not everyone was on board with this new arrangement, but it was too late now.

"Yeah," I said, shrugging.

I crawled into the very back seat of the van, remembering how I used to always take the worst seat in Josh and Derek's cars to make up for my hassle, to make up for the burden of knowing me at all. And for the first time in a long time, I felt weirdly like myself. I wedged my backpack against the window like a pillow.

"All set?" Paul asked, turning around in the passenger seat.

No one answered him. Ray turned the keys into the ignition and the van coughed to life, and then we were driving out of Rochester.

Itchy

After flinging myself, naked and screaming, into the void in New York, the predictable calm of the van was a welcome relief. Plus, the work was easy: take the goods, give me the money, done. The cash in my hand gave me a feeling of purpose, and the new conversations kept things interesting. *You don't need fucking for this,* I thought to myself, every exchange tamping down the itch that would normally stir from all that quiet on the road. For seven calm nights, I watched the bands scream, and before I knew it, we hit the Florida panhandle. I felt like the same me that left, just decorated with the winged eyeliner I'd borrowed from Sara. Nothing profound in tow.

I hadn't seen my dad in two years, and because of that he happily agreed to pick me up on the side of the road a couple hours north of his house. Normally, we were able to stay in fans' houses that wrote the band on Myspace after shows—something the guys tried to portray as cool and glamorous on their page. In reality, sleeping on someone's un-vacuumed carpet floor with a blanket pulled taut from your skull to your toes, or fighting over moth-eaten spare beds and futons, is the furthest thing from cool. But after our last show, there had been a huge party at the house (people puking, nasty everywhere) and we were all so beat from driving that we decided to sleep in the van. When my dad got to us, we were still sleeping, half-dressed to avoid the steamy heat.

He rapped on the window with his middle finger, his face the same mix of cop-level stern and 'up-to-no-good/casing-the-joint' I remembered. I guess I would look stern, too, if my 18-year-old daughter was wearing a sports bra and a pair of Wal-Mart briefs, stretched long-legged across a bench in a van full of near-thirty-year-olds. I mean, 26, but still. Once I woke up, I saw our sleeping arrangement for what it really was (and smelled it, too) so I gave my dad a wave and began collecting my things.

Outside, I pulled on a pair of shorts, passing cars whipping hot air against my skin. I rubbed the sleep out of my eyes and gave him a small hug. His belly was rounder than I remembered, but he has the same red-brown skin and beat-up flip-flops. He hasn't missed a day in the sun.

"Hi."

"Hi, my kid," he replied gruffly. He stared at the van as I walked over to the passenger side of his pickup. "This how you always sleep? In the car like, like *that?*"

He might've meant half-naked, he might've meant on the side of the road. I was too tired to care.

"Sometimes," I shrugged. "It was just for the week."

"If you say so."

"I do."

"Okey doke."

The rest of the drive was spent in silence. I watched the tall grasses swaying on the side of the highway, unsure what to say, what to expect. When I'd called my dad, he asked how long I could stay, his voice almost hopeful sounding, like I'd actually give him an answer, and that answer would stretch longer than a couple of days. I'd been hesitant, initially, thinking about the dive we'd stayed in a few visits back—a grungy, swamp-side place with shag carpet and a T.V. so close to the coiled spring bed that you could feel the static of local stations zip across your skin. But he told me he had a house now, which I knew meant new girlfriend.

"I met someone," he said as we pulled off the highway.

"Oh?"

"Her name's Marva," he smiled, glancing over at me. "You two'll get along."

About that, we'd have to see. The types of women my dad went for after he'd ditched my mom usually ran the salty-dog circuit, their skin burnt and leathery, hair bleached white. Women whose smiles were always that neon shade that comes from a pattern of bad habits and teeth bleaching, but who hardly smiled at me at all; if they had wanted to be mothers, they would have been. I heard one of them spray something of that sort through her toxic teeth, once. As if I was in the market for a stepmom. No thanks, lady—definitely enough mom shit over here to last me a lifetime of therapy, thanks.

I picked at a hangnail until we slowed down, my dad's truck sliding to a stop in front of a small cream house on a quiet street.

"Here we are!" Dad said, a quiver of pride in his voice. I grabbed my backpack and slid out of my seat into the humid air, sweaty, blistered feet slipping in my ballet flats. I braced myself as he turned the key, already preparing a litany of excuses in case I needed to make a break for it.

"Marva?"

"In the guest room!"

Guest room? I walked into the entryway, my eyes scanning for signs of who this woman was. But there were no 'No Shoes, No Shirt, No Problem' signs, no lady margarita-villed out of her gourd, dancing around the living room. There was a crucifix mounted on one of the walls; they were painted beige, not Miami teal.

When Marva came to hug me, I opened my arms. I knew exactly who this woman was.

I sit in the kitchen with wet hair, pushing a cherry tomato in and out of a puddle of Italian dressing with my fork. My dad is cooking pan steaks with the T.V. on. The screen door is open to a weedless garden, filled with

119

crabgrass, and this makes me happy, just like the clothes Marva hung out for me on the line, the butterflies flapping through the flowerbeds. Marva is sitting across from me with a glass of peach iced tea, questions and conversation flowing with ease. When she asks me about tour, there's no judgment in her voice, only genuine curiosity. She softens me in the same way that she has softened my dad. Like butter left out on the counter.

"And do you like the music, Rachael?" She asks. Her eyes are bright blue and her hair is dark, her skin even, untanned and papery. She works for the city in an office building.

"It's okay," I tell her. "Mostly, I just like talking to the people that come up to the table."

I probably would have lied about this to anyone else.

"I'm sure you meet all kinds of folks," she says. She's a breath of fresh Midwestern air, cheery and polite. I'm looking for flaws—undertones, snobbiness—but there's nothing. When you say something to Marva, she unwraps every word thoughtfully, like it's a gift just for her.

"Yeah surprisingly. They all dress the same, but they come from all over."

"How exciting," Marva grins. "And what's next for you, now that you're here?"

My dad turns from the stove, his sunburnt face glowing like the steaks in the kitchen light. I swallow, unsure what to say.

"I'm playing it by ear," I tell her, and both of them nod.

After three days, my plan unfolds in front of me. I've been milling around my dad's house, sitting in the garden, walking around the neighborhood. The air is still, the streets are quiet. There's a pond at the end of the dead-end road and I watch turtles climb the rocks to sun themselves. I spend a lot of time in the guest room, sitting on top of the bedcovers, the ceiling fan blowing my hair. I'm lying there, eyes open, when my cell phone rings.

"*Rachael?*"

The voice on the other end is shouting. I can hear traffic blaring in the background, engines rumbling and cars honking.

"Yeah?"

"It's Paul!"

"Paul? Oh, hi!"

It takes me a moment to process, but then I remember that I gave Paul my phone number when we started tour. I didn't think that I'd ever hear from him again.

"We—we wanted to know if you could come back," he says. His voice sounds tired.

"Back where?"

I pictured them stuck on the side of the road in Florida somewhere.

"On tour. We haven't sold shit since you've left."

I pause, thinking. I wasn't surprised that they weren't selling anything—I knew that they'd have a hard time putting their egos aside to sell their own merch. And to the surprise of no one reading this, but somehow all of us at the time, it turns out that having a girl sell t-shirts at a show with a 10:1 male-to-female ratio ended up doubling sales. Girl power.

"Can you catch a flight to New Orleans and meet up with us? We'll book it."

"When?"

"Two days. And we'll pay you this time."

That night, I climb into a hot shower and lay down in the bathtub. I trace the white grout with my eyes, waiting for a stain. But there's nothing. There's 2-in-1 shampoo and conditioner, and I cover myself in it from head to toe and shave my entire body. The house is quiet by the time I get out, dehydrated and soft, spread out under the covers of a quilt stitched in 1989, in a South Florida guest room with the AC set to a freezing 62 degrees. The old ceiling fan is rocking against its loose screws in the otherwise quiet room.

I think about Marva's face, her expression. How happy it is, how peaceful. How quiet it must be to be that peaceful and happy. How still her life is, and Dad's, too. How they said they never go to bed later than 10. Memories begin to trickle down my back like beads of sweat—still, long nights in the Villa, the days in Michael's bedroom that dragged along before I left for Rochester—and I go from calm to chaotic. A deep sadness grows in my chest under the yellow light, and I kick my legs under the covers because they feel trapped, hot, desperate to move. I find the floor beneath my feet and blindly shoot out of the room until I'm in the kitchen; the burst of movement is a temporary relief, and I walk back to bed, to the icy air conditioning. I go back under the covers feeling calmer in my body, but only because I've made up my mind to leave.

I land in New Orleans full of mashed potatoes, discount steaks, restlessness. I feel bad that I didn't tell my mom I was in Florida, that I didn't have the time to see her. I *squuueezzzeee* my eyes and hope that she's sleeping okay, tell myself that she would have missed the call, anyway. When I open them back up, I'm ready to work. The band is waiting for me at the edge of the parking lot at the airport—they slept there that night. And while they look relieved, I can't convince myself that it's because they're glad to see me. Rather, my arrival meant that they could finally get on the road and out of the sticky swamp air, the kind outsiders always hate.

My first day back was quiet. We had only a few hours to get to East Texas, and as I crawled back to my old seat in the van, I felt good. Everyone had accepted that I was there, including me.

The droning sounds of the 10 freeway into Texas come to a stop as we pull up to a shoddy strip of storage units in an industrial park. You'd have thought we were lost if there wasn't a pack of similarly aging, rusted, dented vans and stickered trailers peeking from the back side of the parking lot. Nearly all of the vehicles are entertaining a circle of cigarette-smoking men in band tees, beer cans and half-empty bottles of sugary soda around their feet, the stage in between.

Behind a thin steel roller door, inside one of the units, the first band is already playing. The lights are dim, and the music reverberates off of the metal units, tinny. Hair moves, heads bang. The energy of the space is undeniable, and being here, doing something different, impulsive—I feel like the master of my destiny. But then I catch sight of the band, watching me work. Am I really in control, here? Or, am I like an obedient dog, desperate for just a scratch on the head? Here only because a random group of people claimed they needed me?

Paul, straight-faced and hurried, directs us to start tossing boxes out of the trailer and we do so in silence, huffing and puffing in the heat. We're playing catch up, and we don't have the luxury of setting up our equipment and tables away from the sweat-logged flesh maze of the zoned-out crowd. I know I'm paying for the tardiness in their heads, since picking me up was the first delay, but nobody argued when Kurt suggested eating inside Taco Bell for lunch so that he could wash his armpits in the sink. I pick up the heaviest boxes I can and press through the bodies with my folding table. *If I'm going to be a dog, it won't be the lap kind.*

Utilitarian

You're supposed to learn a lot when you travel—I mean, that's one thing that people *do* tell you. But this isn't one of those adventures. I feel no wanderlust, feel no freedom in being whisked down a stretch of highway. I am concentrated on being glorified for taking the last shower, for driving the longest, for being the one to take the dare, chug the beer, calculate the checks and divvy them up. I never take a cent that isn't mine—it's the only responsible thing about me. Being on the road, just like all of the other times before, taught me what I already knew: movement was medicine. Movement was survival. And survival, if you really, *truly* didn't give a fuck, could be fun.

Only the topic of girls could remind me of my womanhood in the van, and that meant that someone needed advice for dealing with their scorned girlfriend on the other end of the payphone, or help getting a group of drunk girls off the bus after a show. *That's* when my femininity was called on, used, useful. Otherwise, I hated when they noticed, scowled away questions from awkward dudes at the show that liked to ask which guy I'm fucking as an ice breaker.

The only guys I smile at are the ones that work at 7-11, and I'm only smiling because I'm shoplifting, hopeful that the cheer will throw them off from the fact that the Cup of Noodles I'm filling from the hot water tap next to the Slurpee machine was never paid for. Instead of checking my receipt, they tell me to have a nice day, and then I pull a bag of chips off the shelf on my way out because they're on to the next customer. That's my feminine duty to myself.

Being somewhere that wasn't really anywhere for only a night or two made all of us flippant, irresponsible, careless. When you're in a new town every day with new faces and people, nobody cares what you look like or what comes out of your mouth or whose property you vandalize, drunk off drink tickets. The hearts you break, the ones you lose touch with. It's all about the cheap thrills, the kind I was searching for.

Maybe this was the lifestyle I needed. Or, was it simply a craving? A response to a world where I don't fit, one that doesn't have a place for me. A lack of intimacy towards others and myself. Sexless, genderless, just a giant fuck-you finger dressed in a jersey she found on a basement floor. My scalp becomes part of the game, and we take turns coming up with the most vulgar things you can buzz onto someone's head using a cheap pair

123

of trimmers. Even as I feel the *hummm* of the blade in my ear, it doesn't feel like it's happening to my body. Afterwards, looking at myself in the dirty mirror in a stranger's bathroom, I don't feel cool, bold, brave—I feel like someone who absolutely does not care. Looking myself up and down, turning, I feel free.

All we cared about was the next stolen meal, the next story, the next couch to crash on. I went from one band to the next, living out of a backpack, pooling everyone's per diem so we could buy liquor. We stayed in fans' houses along the road with no rent to pay, pulling up bits of blanket or floor, falling into a booze-soaked sleep. I started taking little trinkets from the houses where girls lived, pocketing lipsticks I would never use, eyeliners that I'd forget about. *Maybe I'll be that kind of girl again,* I thought, slipping a perfume sample into my bra. *Desirable. Someone who gives a shit.* That 'me' was far away; there were nights when I refused to get off the couch even though two people were fucking, bumping my toes with their bodies, just so one of the other twenty people crashing at the house that night couldn't claim my space. Desensitized. Nothing was too gross, too crude.

One night, sleep-deprived and without a shred of self-regard, I found myself slumped down in a pilled red chair in the corner of an unnamed two-story motel just a few miles outside of a hyper religious Missouri town, jeans unbuttoned, head hanging low. We had been booked to play in their newly built venue, attached to the church and funded by its patrons. This is a common situation to be in, even as a metal band on a major record label: there's a ceiling to what you can make and where you can play, so until you're considered legends or when your fan base finally hits their forties, you're probably playing at random ass places off forgotten backroads. You might be at the House of Blues one night and an elks' lodge the next, or the local church's all-purpose room, booked by the town's most alternative 17-year-old promoter.

Earlier that day, we'd driven up to a church as big as a department store, its newness was stark compared to the dust we'd been driving through. The show was pretty run of the mill, unnoteworthy if it hadn't been for our lead singer, Auggie, grabbing the mic at the end of the show, yelling a very overplayed, stereotypical "HAIL SATAN" into the crowd to close our set. Considering the other options, 'Hail Satan' was pretty vanilla, and it might've flown under the radar if it hadn't been screamed into the brand-new church's brand-new microphone while standing on top of the oakwood flooring paid for by Missouri's most religious, buttoned-up conservative Christians. The wood glue hadn't even dried yet, and never would under the weight of the amps, or the cloud of humidity rising from the sweaty bodies packed into that two-and-a-half-million-dollar church in the middle of god knows where Midwest. And of course, not only do the people of this town have nothing better to do than to show up and protest our being there, but it's so goddamned desolate that the 'Hail Satan' rings through every kitchen and living room within a five-mile radius. We had only begun to load up our vans when a crowd of locals drove down to see us out of town.

"Easy! Easy!" Hollered our pimply promoter, stretching his arms and shielding us from a small pack of the angriest parents; the others had their heads bowed over their children in their Astro vans, muttering blessings upon them.

"It's just a saying!" Auggie yelled. "I didn't mean anything by it!"

In his attempt to soothe the Christians, he threw up two peace signs, oblivious to the fact devil-worshippers fell under the same category as hippies, hated for their weed-smoking, free-loving, anti-government-ness.

"Don't even THINK about staying at the motel in town!" One woman screamed.

"Yeah, you're gonna have to drive the extra fifteen minutes and take a left on Stewart Street—" Another one continued. Even their threats were laden with Midwest helpfulness.

The promoter tried to calm the crowd of fifteen but was met with a smack across the head from an uncle. We left him to clean up the mess and drove away, caravanning to the motel just outside city limits. There were 25 people on our tour package, and we were lucky to scrape together four adjoining double-queen bedrooms, ready to call it a night. If we didn't get to bed soon, we'd miss checkout in the morning, and missing checkout meant missing check-in for our next show. We drank Bud heavies while waiting for our turn to shower, grateful that the Christian mob meant that we weren't obligated to party with whoever was letting us sleep on their floor that night. No hangovers the next morning, just us, the hotel air conditioning, and some much-needed personal hygiene—a pretty chill night, all in all.

I was sitting in my armchair, sipping a beer and looking forward to getting out of the motel on time when someone knocked loudly on the door. I looked at the clock on the bedside table. Who the fuck needed us at this time of night?

"Are you in there?" A woman cried. "It's me, Diane from the church!"

Of course, Diane. The brunette with the three kids. We'd actually had a fairly mellow conversation before the rest of the crowd persuaded her to join them in the chase.

We shot wide-eyed stares around the room, looking for someone to volunteer to get the door. When no one did, I rose slowly, scowling.

"Nobody takes my spot," I growled, opening the door.

Diane was leaning sideways, standing under a gray light swarmed by moths. The neck of her shirt was stretched out and sad, her sagging breasts, braless, pushing against the front pocket of her jersey tee, tucked into the elastic waist of her cotton skirt. The look on her face told me that her three metal-loving kids gave her grief, and the slump of her body groaned with the weight of a loveless marriage with a man that had a "NO HIGH MAINTENANCE WOMEN" bumper sticker slapped on his truck. This, and she got her hair done at Walmart. I knew this because it was the exact same shape as my mom's when she got hers done there—

125

Walmart stylists only know three shapes.

Diane was drunk. I wasn't sure what her night looked like before she made it to our door, but she smelled like booze and beer.

"Hey, Diane. What's up? Do you need something?" I used my sweetest, calmest tone, as if the entire front end of the evening was part of another life.

"I'll tell you what I need," she slurred. "I need you guys not to come to our quiet town and preach that Satanic music to the youth, here. We aren't that kinda place, you know?"

Clearly, Diane had forgotten that the church was packed full of people from her town who actually liked our music. And that we were booked on the understanding that we would play that music in their church.

"Absolutely," I agreed. "And we all apologize for that. That's why we're out here at this motel—we don't want you to feel disrespected."

I stood on my tiptoes and peeked over her shoulder, curious as to how she got to us in the first place. There was no way she drove herself, but there was no car in sight.

Diane started in again, and I felt a tug on my shoulder. It was Frank; Frank generally stayed out of the nonsense. He was older than the oldest of us, and really just wanted to get through the tour dates and head home to work on his side project, a drum and bass album that used actual bass guitar. But he was the first one to start in on the Budweisers when we got into the room, and the A.C. was making him a little loose.

"I'll take it from here," he muttered, looking down at me. I stepped back, but stayed within earshot.

"Listen, lady," he said, his southern accent becoming thicker with every word. I'm not sure if this was a manipulation tactic or booze, but Diane's feathers unruffled the more he talked. "We got out of your hair and out of your town like you asked. There ain't nothing more we can do tonight."

Diane blinked up at him blankly. She seemed to have lost her train of thought.

"You want a beer or somethin'?" Frank asked.

"Please," Diane said. We gaped at Frank, unsure what his angle was. He turned his big body so that she could step inside, and kicked some merch kid out of a chair and turned it towards Diane.

"Have a seat, m'am."

"Nice place you have here," Diane said.

I tried to hide my growing confusion by taking a big swig of beer. The others did the same, watching as Diane made herself comfortable. She brought a bottle to her lips and took a long drag.

"I used to be wilder, back in my younger days."

"Oh?" Frank asked, sitting at the foot of the bed across from her.

"Oh, Lord have mercy, you should've seen me back then. I had boys on the phone all over Missouri."

Someone managed to turn a laugh into a cough, but Diane didn't notice.

"A real party girl, I was. Then I met Wayne, had the boys—things sure do change, don't they?"

"What sort of wilding did you get into?" Someone yelled from the back of the room. Our bodies were so tightly packed together that I could hear stomachs growling, digesting the malty booze.

"You wouldn't believe me, even if I told you," she said proudly.

"Tell us!"

"Yeah, tell us!"

Diane sat quietly for a moment, looking at the beer bottle in her hand. Then, she downed the whole thing.

"I'll do you one better," she whispered, eyes glimmering. "I can *show* you."

Diane stood up, flattening the shag carpet beneath her feet. The two minutes that followed would be forever burned into our brains. In the yellow glow of that motel room, while mosquitos buzzed in our ears, Diane held the beer bottle in one hand and turned in a half circle so that everyone could see it. Then, she bent her knees and brought the bottle to the hem of her skirt. She stared straight ahead, eyes on Frank as both hand and bottle disappeared beneath the fabric. Nobody moved. Mouths fell open. There was a small grunt and the sound of someone clapping a hand over their mouth; then, she righted herself and held her arms above her head. The beer bottle was...gone.

Sluts

One winter, El Niño halted the tour industry entirely. The news promised catastrophe to those of us who dared drive and considering our shifty vans often got flats from looking at them sideways, none of the bands wanted to drive on the unlit back roads and endless stretches of highway we normally took on tour. Not in snowy conditions, anyway. So, they split up and went their separate ways, crashing at home or with friends, the apartments they paid for while they were on the road. As for me, I didn't have a home. I'd only been making enough money to pay for my food, to buy a new stick of deodorant every once in a while. I went from tour to tour, spending the night in airports between gigs, waiting to be sent on my way. But this time, I had no one to buy me a plane ticket, no "next." I was stuck in Cleveland.

I used an ATM to check on my account balance: eight fucking dollars. I couldn't get anywhere with eight dollars. Thankfully, I had a life raft in the form of a backstage Betty. Real name, Ashley.

I'd met Ashley a few times before, usually outside as we loaded our equipment: she was short, curvy, and louder than the gate check intercoms, with brightly dyed, untoned blonde hair and false eyelashes that made her look half-drunk at all times. Which, given her reputation, could have easily been the case. The guys had met her on several occasions during their many stops in Cleveland where Ashley was a known venue hopper, always on the prowl for a new guy in music to sleep with. She seemed to glide between cliques and subcultures, not quite scene but not quite metal, as likely to go home with a rapper as she was a longhaired drummer. It was like her only line of work was to fuck and fight with as many performers and concertgoers as possible, and though I'd been given her number with the kind of sly half-smile that someone only shares when they're having a private laugh, I wondered if calling it meant I was just as predatory as they were. I didn't want to take advantage of anyone.

I dialed Ashley's number with a fistful of floppy french fries in my mouth, hoping they'd muffle the apprehension in my voice.

"GIRL! Get your ass in here!" Ashley screeched from the window as she pulled up to the curb. She drove a scratched black BMW with tinted windows, her round face barely peering over the steering wheel.

I opened the door to a blast of Swisher Sweets and vanilla-jasmine

128

body spray. An Italian flag embellished in Swarovski crystals swung from the rearview mirror, clacking against the windshield as she turned the steering wheel.

"How fucking dumb is this? How fucking *dumb?*"

I took this to mean that Ashley wasn't impressed that all the shows had been cancelled. There wasn't even any snow on the ground yet.

"Dumb as fuck," I said, sticking my bag between my feet.

"Like, couldn't they have waited 'til the storms actually *happened?*" She laughed, her voice raspy. From screaming or smoking, I'd never know.

"Thank you for letting me stay with you. You're such a lifesaver."

"Are you kidding? We're going to have so much fun!" She squealed, running a red light.

"As soon as the label pays me, I'll give you whatever," I told her earnestly. "I have literally zero in my account right now."

"Girl. Don't even trip," she said seriously, shaking her head.

I was surprised, initially, when we pulled up to Ashley's apartment. I didn't know what she did for work, but judging by the fancy car and the designer bag in her lap, I was expecting us to park in some ritzy high rise with a pool. Instead, we were surrounded by vacant lots, chain link fences, an overturned shopping cart spewing aluminum cans into the street. Ashley hopped out, toddling up a dirty stone staircase to the top floor, hair whipping in the wind.

Her place had all the fixings of a fancy place, but trapped inside of a dingy, poorly lit, outdated apartment. The plushy purple couch— something you'd see in a catalogue for over-priced dorm furniture— looked out of place on the stained beige carpet. The massive print of Audrey Hepburn and flat screen T.V., comical against the aged yellow wall paint. Evidence of money was everywhere *except* for the ground we stood on, and as Ashley pulled open the accordion wall that separated the sitting room from her bedroom, she explained the bizarre contradiction.

"My dad *hates* that I live here," she laughed. "Like, every time he sends the rent check, he's all, '*Ashley! This is the last month I'm paying for this shit hole!*'"

"Oh, it's not bad," I lied, staring at the cracks in the ceiling.

I'd lived in worse, but knew that Ashley hadn't; anything to appease my hostess, and maybe make her less likely to care that someone was sleeping rent-free on her sofa.

"Are you kidding? It's a dump," she said, plopping on her bed. "But pissing him off is the best part."

Within a month, I'd learn that Ashley was full of contradictions. First, and most obvious, was that she was little but very loud. There were dozens of bars in Cleveland, but Ashley was only allowed back at about half of them. Not because her fake I.D. wouldn't pass, but because she had been kicked out of them all for being too drunk, too wild, starting fights, or fucking in the bathroom. She got out of all of her legal troubles because her dad, she always pointed out when we drove under his billboards, was the biggest lawyer in the city. He'd wanted his daughter to go into the family trade, but she refused to take the job—or a job of any kind. "Never have, never will!" She would shout, whipping out her black AmEx wherever we went. She may have been a spoiled brat, but she was also very generous, buying rounds and covering tabs and dragging me to restaurants all across town, buying us mani-pedis at shiny salons. I guess it's easy to be generous when the money isn't yours, but Ashley, despite all her screaming and skimpy, unmissable outfits, was very soft. Ashley, to me, was easy to love, and in a lot of ways, she reminded me of Liz—someone with a lot of love to give, but prone to going about it the wrong way, chasing after guys. She wore everything on the outside, lived without secrets, without boundaries. The type that didn't like to be judged so they wouldn't judge you, always down for a good time, looking for the next move—it was a different kind of medicine, one that made living in the same place feel new and exciting. It was obvious that she'd had a hard time making friends growing up, but unlike most of the rich kids I knew, Ashley spread love like butter, planting kisses on everyone within reach, showering them with compliments, her big, brown eyes shimmering with admiration.

"I want you to fall in love," she would tell me, grabbing my hand. "You have the prettiest face in the world."

I missed Liz. Being around Ashley made me realize how much I liked one-on-one friendships, how easy they were compared to being in a pack. Girl groups had too many variables, and no matter where you lived, they were always the same, from Rochester to Cleveland to Naples. I'd hear the way girls talked about Ashley when they thought she couldn't hear, the way they made fun of the cellulite peeking out of her tiny shorts, and it infuriated me. They didn't know a single thing about her but felt entitled to the details of her life because she acted like an open book. I was very loyal to Ashley. Because, well, why shouldn't I be? She claimed me, wrapped her arms around me, called me her best friend. Sometimes the assholes who judged her would hide their comments in a half-whisper, but usually, they didn't. I'd stare firmly in their direction, waiting for their eyes to move from Ashley to me, hoping that I made them feel seen. Like, *I fucking see you, you stupid bitch.* I hoped it made them think about themselves, made them recognize their darkness. I wouldn't break contact, but they would. I was the gangly girl-bouncer designated for Ashley's nights out, and staring daggers at whoever was calling her a slut was the least I could do to repay her for her kindness. I mean, yeah, Ashley slept with a lot of fucking people. I could hear them through the accordion wall while I curled up on the couch, pillow smashed against my ears. If these girls had a problem with that, then why didn't they have a problem with the guys who did the same thing? I was too naïve to the complexities and how deep it ran at the time, and too unsure of myself to stand up to it with more than a glare, but the hypocrisy of it all could no longer be left open for my interpretation, the way it had in Rochester. Back then, it was all about the differences between hooking up and dating. But now? I was seeing it for what it was—what a man was allowed to do versus what a woman could, and how *we* as women enable those differences by tearing each other down—and it really made my blood boil.

My blood boiled up enough to curl my fists. Ashley and I were sitting outside of one of her favorite bars, Shelter. Shelter was yet another establishment that she wasn't allowed inside of, but she couldn't quite give the place up because her ex-boyfriend, Tony, worked as the bouncer, and she never missed an opportunity to dress up in spandex and parade around in front of an ex. Tony was actually the reason I knew Ashley in the first place; when he wasn't on tour as the singer of a metal band, his lower-paying gig was to use his big, brutish body to break up bar fights. In a way, I think he felt bad for setting me up with Ashley, so he allowed us to sit outside of Shelter, bringing us drinks from the bar and warding off her advances. I'd been in Cleveland for two months at this point, which was far and away the longest relationship Ashley had ever had with anyone, and I was getting antsy, using our many nights out as the remedy for my growing itch. Things didn't usually get interesting until the fourth or fifth drink, which Tony kindly tipped into our hands that night before stepping inside.

"Fucking *slut*," a voice barked.

Ashley and I were smoking, talking to some older guys, but I didn't need to turn to know who they were talking to. I didn't even get a chance to, because before I'd finished taking a drag, Ashley had been shoved to the ground. I handed my drink to one of the guys and whipped around.

The girl who pushed her was equal in size to me, which is to say, tall, gangly, maybe 120 pounds soaking wet. Her cheeks were red and her face was set, bathing drunk Ashley in her shadow, sprawled on the concrete with her drink splashed down her shirt.

"What do you have to say, *slut*? Don't know who I am?"

"No," Ashley said honestly, shaking her head. The girl took a step forward.

"You *fucked* my boyfriend."

Ashley tried to stand and the girl shoved her back down. At which point, I was seeing red. I stepped between the two of them, my neck stretched tall, hands balled into fists.

"Why don't you fight your fucking boyfriend, then?" I spit.

"Shut up, bitch."

I didn't take the time to think. Maybe if I had, I would've remembered what my dad told me back in elementary school whenever he recounted his childhood brawls, punches thrown in military mess halls, his many Miami street scuffles. *1-2, then I hit you.* One chance to back off, then two. Tell them to leave. And if they don't go on three, *swing.* That worked when I was small, but now? I wanted to choke her. I blacked out before I could remember the rules.

I was able to leverage my strength over her because she didn't assume anyone would stand up for Ashley. And Ashley didn't, either. There was no hair pulling, no girly slaps. My hands were around her throat. Glimpses of her face, wide-eyed and red, cut in and out before my eyes. Blackness. Blood. Blackness. The feeling of my hands colliding with bone. Anything and everything fueling my fists. Waves of anger and pain—not physical, but emotional, deeper—gushed through me, coursing through my veins, sending me in and out of consciousness. I swung and I swung and I swung, my knuckles connecting with every available inch of her body. I couldn't stop. I didn't even pause to breathe.

Then someone—someone large—came up behind me. They looped their arms around my torso and stood me on my feet; I panted, blinking down at the girl I'd just beaten into the pavement. Her nose was off-center, fucked up, and her lip was cut, blood streaming down her face, a pillow of skin already sealing up one of her eyes. I took one final look at her and spat, right in the center of her shirt—I'd actually been aiming for her face, but I cut my losses. It was only when everyone had gone quiet that I realized the bystanders had been gasping, shouting. I turned to look at them, ready to be punished: for the girl's friends to descend upon me, for judgment, someone to call the cops. But there were only empty faces, blank stares. When I turned, I walked over to the guys Ashley and I had been talking to and grabbed my drink, taking it down in one swig and tossing the plastic cup on the sidewalk like an athlete marching to the sidelines. *Why did I just do that?* I wondered. *The cup and the fight?* Then, I plopped abruptly on the ground, bracing myself for whatever came next. But there was nothing. Once I'd regained my breath, I turned to Ashley.

"Are you okay?" I asked. Her eyes were as wide as saucers. She was looking at me like I'd just grown a second head.

"Uh, yeah. I'm okay," she said, her voice shaky. Then, she grabbed my hands. "Are *you?*"

"Totally fine," I told her, and I was. I looked down at my red fingers, the split knuckles from where I think I missed the girl and just hit brick. Looking over Ashley's shoulder towards her, I could see her staggering to her feet, silent and circled by her friends with a jacket pressed to her bleeding face. They didn't look at me as they scurried away and piled into their car. Someone tapped me on the shoulder.

"Yo, that was sick." Tony said, handing me a shot of three-dollar whiskey.

Fuck. I hate whiskey.

Overnight, I had turned into a big deal in our small bar scene, and I felt it in my steps, stomping around like I was wearing a letterman's jacket. But not my boyfriend's. *Mine.* Captain of the fuck-up team. We'd go out, and I'd swing the hypothetical jacket over my thin shoulders, thinking, *This is bad,* but sauntering into the spotlight, anyway. Men who usually found Ashley annoying and tried to avoid having her over at their tables were calling us over, asking for the details, buying us drinks. She talked and I stood there smiling, watching her soak up their stares like a sponge. But it wasn't just men who wanted a piece of the story. A few other party girls, self-proclaimed sluts that we'd seen out and about in the city, started inviting us around. I didn't mind the attention, but Ashley was completely swept away—I wondered if this was the most friends Ashley had ever had

132

at any given moment in her life. I rode the high of my first fight for two weeks before the adrenaline started to wear off, and the conversations centering around it started to taper.

Ashley and the girls cashed in their attention chips in the form of men to go home with, but I hadn't made the most of my time in the spotlight. I was scared to turn back into a girl who could be chewed up and spit out like I had been in New York, different with each new man. Scared of the same old label, because sluts were bad.

I looked around at my new girl group. *But what about these sluts?* I like these sluts; I fought for one, I'd fight for the rest. What could be wrong with living like them?

We were settled into a booth one night, knocking back shots, when the topic of one-night stands came up. I sipped on my vodka cranberry, listening to the girls trade stories, one-upping each other. Coming out of a blackout mid-threesome, sneaking out of a window when someone's wife came home—I was a captive audience. Then, everyone, including Ashley, turned to look at me.

"What about you, Rachael?" One of them asked.

I gulped. "Umm…"

Do I make up a story? Maybe there's something from tour I could use… wait. Why lie?

I knew nobody here would judge me. Not really, anyway.

"…well, I've never actually had a one-night stand."

"What?" They shouted together, mouths, eyes, and hands all moving in unison.

"Like, *never* never?"

I nodded, twisting my finger around my straw.

"How?"

"Do you just not remember it? Because that's happened to me before," Ashley said, tipping a shot into her mouth.

"Never," I told them. "I've always had boyfriends."

I decided not to tell them I had been avoiding their label like the plague for the last four years. Or, that even at 19, I was still scared. That, despite my vagrancy and aggressive nature, I knew nothing about the world I was suckling onto. That I was raised on drops.

"Girl, you've *got* to lose that pattern," one of them muttered, shaking her head. "Get laid and get lost."

She's right—it is a pattern…and I want to break it.

"Tonight! It has to be tonight!" Ashley squealed, clapping.

Looking around the bar, I felt the scene before me shift, like someone had just twisted my kaleidoscope. All of the guys I would typically skip over were suddenly looking like possibilities, a way to level up my life, unlock some better understanding of it all. They were options. Had these guys always been here? Maybe I was closer to finding my place—*am I a Ashley, too? No, wait, that's scary,* I thought. But I could be like a *diet* Ashley.

"Any favorites?" Ashley asked, waving at the bartender. She could get a round of drinks in a church.

"Umm…"

I turned in our booth, looking the space up and down, scared but sure that I'd strike out. There were try-hards and punks, dudes with lip rings, tattoos, out of place preps in button-ups. I tried to scan for shoes, but it was too packed. A few tables over, two guys were sitting together. One had shaggy dark hair and a cute smile; his arms were toned, and the cut of his jaw screamed MAN, especially compared to the boys I was used to chasing. I was confused as to how I didn't see him before, but then realized I had endured months, no, *years* of training this side out of myself, and now, I actually had to force it out. And Shaggy Guy's friend was big, chubby, tattooed. *Bingo*. Ashley's type. She'd be sure to wing-woman if things got weird.

"That guy," I said, pointing to the one with shaggy hair.

"His friend is *hot*," Ashley said, blowing a kiss as our drinks were delivered. A couple of girls waiting in line at the bar glared. "I'll go over with you."

I straightened my back and webbed my fingers, running them through my four inches of grow out, but they only got three-quarters of the way through before reaching a knot. Quickly, I asked Ashley if I could borrow an elastic, and moved to tie my tangled mess into what I hoped was considered the cool-girl messy bun but looked more like I had just gone down on an electrical socket.

"Hot," Ashley approved.

I slid out of the booth, my stomach fluttering nervously. I was leaving the bench, the 'boyfriend-only' sex territory I'd grown accustomed to, but I put on a brave face. I knew that if I followed Ashley's lead, we'd be just fine.

"Hey," she said, pulling out a chair. "Do you mind if we join you?"

"Not at all!"

Shaggy guy stuck out his hand.

"I'm Caleb," he said. "And this is Vince."

"I'm Rachael," I said. "That's Ashley."

The rounds came and went easily, and so did the conversation. Before we knew it, the lights were flickering. Last call.

"Should we go back to my place?" Caleb asked. "I live just across the street."

Ashley squeezed my leg under the table and stood up to leave, waving goodbye to our girlfriends as they skipped out of the bar, winking at me. But as I waited to rise, watching Caleb's lead, I noticed that he stayed seated.

Then, he pushed his wheelchair back from the table.

Teenaged density swimming in alcohol, I had failed to notice that while we were all in bar chairs, he was in a different kind of seat. His strong arms suddenly made a lot of sense, and I felt my confidence around the whole situation rapidly disappearing. We were entering completely uncharted waters. It wasn't his wheelchair that scared me—it was that it was adding a second unknown to an already unknown experience. Sex education in the 1990s was simply "don't have it," and education surrounding disabilities was don't look and *definitely* don't ask. There was no crossover between the subjects either, not in school, not on *SVU*, not with my friends. How was I going to approach this once our pants were off? Nobody had ever told me that sex could be non-penetrative, except for that one time we'd huddled around someone's CRT monitor in rural Indiana, laughing at a screaming, over-the-top lesbian porno. Caleb and I were not lesbians.

As I watched him navigate the crowd of drunk, staggering bodies, I shot Ashley a glance, but she was too preoccupied with her guy, whose hand was in the back pocket of her tiny denim shorts. I swallowed the rest of my drink, trying my best to maintain a normal, calm expression as I followed in Caleb's wake, trying and failing to catch Ashley's attention. Finally, Ashley drunkenly leaned behind her guy and whispered to me.

"It's fine, I've done this before."

And I knew that she only meant following two random guys back to their house. And no, it didn't make me feel any more confident.

I hoped that everything I would need to know, I'd find out once our clothes were off. In a desperate bid to seem upbeat and helpful, and to make him feel safe around me, I grabbed the grips on his chair, guiding him around an un-moving clump of drunk girls. Then, my vodka legs wobbled, and we clipped a curb, nearly sending Caleb spilling into the street.

The big guy caught the handle and smiled down at me like a cop. "I've got it from here."

Caleb patted his lap, and I climbed in. He wasn't afraid for a moment, about the situation or me, and Big Vince pushed us to the door, Caleb's arms wrapped around my waist.

Across the street was a modern apartment building with a beautiful glass entrance. We all got into the elevator together and took it to the top floor, where Caleb rolled ahead and grabbed his keys. It was like he knew exactly what we were about to say.

"I won a huge settlement," he told us.

Huge was an understatement. The apartment was ultra-sleek, with stainless steel appliances and exposed brick walls. Half of the walls were floor-to-ceiling windows, while the rest were fixed with a complicated series of pullies and cords. I realized that Caleb didn't spend all of his time in the chair, that he was able to move freely without one, thanks to the cords. And Caleb was completely independent. He was a grown-ass, money-on-the-books, no guns-under-the-bed *man*, living in his own place. Just like his jaw line suggested he was.

Vince and Ashley wasted no time in settling on the couch, their lips locked, hands groping.

"Let's go upstairs," Caleb said, climbing down to the floor. He reached for one of the cords at the base of the stairs and hoisted himself up to the first step, then the second, one by one until we reached his

135

bedroom. He started climbing towards his bed, and I decided to give him space while he undressed. I went into his bathroom and stared open-mouthed at the massive shower with four heads. Then, I pulled my clothes off, taking a deep breath.

Confidence, Rachael. Confidence.

We started kissing, his hands moving along my body while I kept mine fixed on his neck. We kissed for a while, then, he looked at me, his face serious.

"This isn't going to work," he said, gesturing towards his waist.

"That's okay," I said agreeably, relieved that he'd brought it up instead of me.

"But you can suck on my nipples."

I froze. *NIPPLES?!?!* I screamed inside. *How the fuck do you suck on a man's tiny nipples?* The screaming lesbian porn flashed again in my head. Stiff-tongued and aggressive. I fixed my face, kept it calm so it didn't bring tension.

"Is that okay with you?" He seemed used to checking boundaries, but I'd never been spoken to like that. It was nice, and I had to fight to remember that I was *not* looking for another boyfriend.

After a few minutes of what I hoped felt like adequate nipple sucking, which I assumed would lead into some kind of return on my end but hoped wouldn't happen because the room was starting to spin and I was tired as fuck, Caleb rolled over.

"Goodnight," he said.

"Um, yeah. Goodnight," I croaked with relief.

We woke up the next morning to voices downstairs, happy and peaceful. My first one-night stand left me *peaceful.* Feeling victorious, I slid out of Caleb's bed and headed for the door, imagining the next time I'd wake up there—*fuck, I'm doing it again.* As I walked downstairs, I started to smell something. Vanilla? Cinnamon? My stomach growled.

My brain was still swimming with alcohol, so it was difficult for me to make a thorough assessment, but I was absolutely sure that the woman that I saw standing in the kitchen was the most beautiful person I'd ever seen. She had waist-length curls that hung, dark and shining, to her waist. Her tanned skin was smooth as silk against her white tank top, under which she wore no bra. And to top it all off, this bohemian goddess, in her flowing skirt and stacks of silver bangles and necklaces, was holding a steaming basket of muffins? I saw a vein start to tick on her forehead as she tried to make sense of the mess in her home. The mess in her home.

"Rachael was just using the bathroom upstairs," Ashley blurted out, and as soon as she completed the sentence, Caleb came down the stairs, his face gray.

What. The. Fuck. The realization hit me slow but hard. My perfect night with my best nipple sucking was on borrowed time. These were *her* nipples. She was his girlfriend.

"Yeah, uh, thanks for letting us stay on the couch!" I said, my tongue moving as quickly as my legs. At the door, I spun to shoot Caleb a small but severe glance, catching Ashley just as she plunged her hand deep into the basket.

"And thanks for the muffin!"

Loose Ends

When I finally *do* leave Cleveland, I'm relieved. I'm glad to leave.
I'm ready to go, get back on tour. Ashley kept things interesting enough
to where the itch never sent me off the rails, but living in someone else's
space, both of you unemployed—there's only so much Taco Bell a person
can eat, so many episodes of *The Real World* one can watch. When I say
goodbye to Ashley, she has tears in her eyes. She tells me to keep in touch,
to stay with her if the band ever stops for a show.

"You'll know where to find me," she says, pulling away from our hug,
sniffling.

I actually don't know where Ashley is. I lost her. Distance, time,
deleted MySpace, changed number—she's gone. But wherever you are,
Ashley, and if you're reading this, just know that I appreciate everything
you did for me. And that I have a $300 check with your name on it, ready
to pay you back for my Jack in the Box tab.

Post-Katrina New Orleans, Age 19

"Thanks for coming out tonight, everyone."

Cheers, shouts. Someone laughs in the corner at a private joke, unaware that the band has taken the stage. Someone else hushes them.

"Thank you, thanks so much. Beautiful night, isn't it?"

Big intros aren't common, but you can't rule them out. Frontmen front, don't they? I drink my free beer in the back of the crowd, one arm folded across my chest, waiting for the opener.

"You know what would make this beautiful night even better?"

The crowd whoops. Some drunk idiot screams "*WHAT?*"

"If that girl—do you see that girl back there?"

You know the sound when everyone in the classroom turns the page at the same time? How it almost isn't a sound because, one, you're not actually listening for it, and two, turning a page is something so subtle and quiet that when a room full of people does it, it doesn't actually sound like the thing that it is? Well, the same thing goes for when 100 people turn in a room at the exact same time. Turning doesn't have a sound—not really, anyway. But multiply anything times 100 and it'll blow your hair back.

In this case, there are actually 126 people; I was just doing my mental math before it happened, thinking, *Okay, so tickets are 15 bucks a pop and our guarantee is 50% of the door, meaning we have nearly a thousand bucks to get us to the next small town.* I was even starting to feel like this was going to be a pretty good night when the bearded fuck started talking again. Only then do I realize that the heads that I've counted up are facing me, gaping. The guys in the band, the tour manager. Everyone.

"She's cute, right?"

A couple of whoops, then a "*Boo.*"

"She won't fuck me though!"

I'm at the merch table, far from the reach of the stage lights, but I feel my face burning white hot, hundreds of shimmering eyeballs piercing my skin. I try to find the faces of my band, try to pool the comfort of my van, but they all look away, staring down at the floor.

"Crazy, right? I mean, she's cute. But she isn't *that* cute."

The crowd erupts with laughter.

I'm stuck to the ground like it's fly paper, realizing that, in this moment, nothing matters, and not in the fun way. I was vouched for, cross-referenced; I worked hard, shed my skin six times to make sure I didn't make waves, kept my gaze down so that I wouldn't accidentally bat my eyelashes. I did everything I was supposed to do to survive but at the end of the day, at the end of the bad joke, it didn't matter. It wasn't enough.

A lump rises in my throat.

I feel the urge to break the discomfort in the room and panic, wanting to alleviate the weirdness and prove to everyone I wasn't the joke, that I was actually *in* on it. That I belonged. I could go on stage and kiss him right on the mouth, whisper, "*My van or yours?*" into the microphone. I could make it part of the show, something we do *all* the time, except he and I would both know that we've only been touring for one month, that I don't know his real name and he doesn't know mine. He calls me "merch girl." I'm tossing my options around in my head, frozen and deadpan as I look out into the crowd, the sea of faces going blurry.

Guitar riffs. Drums. He lifts the microphone out of the stand and screams.

I run out of the venue, into the sticky hot heat of a post-Katrina New Orleans, only to see the headliners climbing down from the hood of their rental bus, which is completely engulfed in flames. It's on *fire*, a bus is on fire, but I can't react, my stomach is still twisting. I watch the flames shooting up from the windows, listen as the eastern European metal gods on speed, bent in half-laughter, half-hysteria, are cheered on by a handful of lucky fans who will have this memory forever. I see fire extinguishers coming, hear people yelling and still, no reaction. My head is swirling, the singer's voice still echoing in my ears, clanging against everything I've learned since leaving home, or tried to understand—Rochester, tour, Cleveland. They hate you when they fuck you, they hate you when you don't. You're either a slut or a tease or a bitch. And I'm tired, *so* tired, of being something. So tired of fighting to be nothing.

I watch the bus burn. This place, all of these places, feel violent. I am bathing in violence, breathing it in. Running around the country is no longer an escape. It feels less like freedom than ever before. *I'm sick of the egos,* I tell myself, but then I hear my voice say it out loud, like that's all there is to blame, because it's too scary to admit that it might be the whole world that's unsafe. Lowering myself down on the asphalt across from the charred bus, next to a tour manager who is screaming that he is also sick of egos, typing furiously into his Blackberry—he wants it to be known that this was not his fault. As he worries aloud about his paycheck, the world feels small again, tight and constricted, the band forming four walls around me. And I begin to itch. I want to wade out into the bayou and float out to the Gulf. Back to my own swamp. I roll over on the asphalt and look at the tour manager dead in his eye, his face lit by the last flame, speed caked in a white ring around his nostril.

"I want a bus ticket out of here." I say, direct and clear. My first request in 32 days.

"Yeah, me too."

Maybe This is a Fairytale

It's late afternoon by the time I get to the trailer. I crawl into bed next to Mom, completely defeated from my trip home. I push a strand of red hair back from her face.

I should be happy that she seems okay, but I'm not, because I know better.

Hope looks nice when it's written in Helvetica, plastered over a photo of a sunset on social media. But in this house, hope will fucking kill you. It will saunter in like a promise, wrapping you in its positive light, before ripping you limb from limb, as uncaring and cold as alcoholism itself. You beg for it to listen to you, to hear your pleas for salvation. Beg it to understand that your

dreams

      wants

           basic needs

make you worthy of deliverance. But the truth is, hope doesn't have a place here—it never has—and in order to survive, you need to lower your expectations to none. Be excited for when things happen in your favor but never consider that to be the new normal. It's *just* a calmer day. This is dealing with addicts, mental illness, narcissists—*Whoever The Fuck Is Trampling You 101*. There's no guide, just the end of your own emotional rope.

Anyone who has battled substance use, or loved someone who has used a substance, knows what I'm talking about. They talk about it in Al-Anon: you have to live in the present and face the facts, otherwise, you'll just end up dwelling on the person you used to know, or else living in the tomorrow you've already scripted out in your head, neither of which is the reality in front of you. Just because someone looks clear-eyed one day doesn't mean they will be the next, but if you're thinking 20-year-old-me had this type of wisdom, let me be the first to tell you that I did not. And will not for another 16 years, up until I'm pleading with my therapist to help me make a failing relationship work. Nails cracking, breaking, tearing off as I cling to everything we said we were. The same fight all over again.

Anyway, where were we?

I dart out of her bed, breathing heavy. I pull open drawers, cabinets, tip her purse upside down. *Score.* A four-year-old crumpled box of Dorals falls to the floor. I put one between my lips and another behind my ear

141

and go outside, around to the back of the trailer. I flop down beside the Azealia bush, my buzzing hands struggling to light up. I drag it to the bone, then reach for the next one. But before I can, my phone rings.

I don't have the number saved, but I take the call, anyway. Desperate for something, anything, new.

"Rachael?" A voice says. Deep. Tall. You know how a voice just sounds tall, right?

I lean in. There are people in the background on his end, the muted bump of some familiar tune playing on a stereo.

"Yeah?"

"It's Logan."

"Who?"

"Damn! Again? Really?" He sounds a little drunk, but at least he's laughing. I rack my brain. *Logan. Logan? LOGAN!*

"Oh my god, I'm so sorry!" I say, and I feel the smile pushing up my eyes, genuine.

"So you *do* remember?" He asks.

"Yes!" I say, maybe a little too quickly.

The first time we met was in a bar in upstate New York, once upon a tour. He had tried to hold my hand after I punched a vending machine that ate my dollar. Bleeding, drunk, the very picture of 18. But I still got my chips, and he helped me pull out pieces of glass from my skin, and as I looked up into his face—older, dark, white tee glowing in the bar lights. I remembered looking across the bar at my tour mates, their faces unimpressed with him and his shiny newness. They gave me the 'let's go' before we could have more of an exchange.

Then, I saw him again in Cleveland; I clumsily spilled my drink down his leg, but he didn't get mad. He just smiled down at me with his big Crest white strips teeth. I forget how he ended up there, but I remember him laughing along, and how good it felt to hear him say my name without hesitation. How special that made me feel.

"How's it—what's up?"

I stand up and start pacing around outside, hand in the pocket of my jeans. I look down at my outfit, then remind myself that he can't even see me. And that in every interaction previous, I've either been covered in blood or covering him in booze, and he's *still* calling. Good sign.

"Honestly? I was just thinking about you," he says.

"No, you weren't," I laugh.

"I called you, didn't I?"

I couldn't argue with that. But I also couldn't think of anything to say. Why was this guy—this older guy with a good job, nice eyes, clean clothes—calling *me?* He was J. Crew and Krew Jeans, I was free-merch-tee and Goodwill cutoffs. He was an adult, a real adult, and I was somehow younger and more confused than when I left Florida the first time, back in my mom's trailer. He read the silence on my end perfectly.

"My friends told me I had to call you. They're sick of hearing about 'that metal girl.'"

142

"I don't really listen to metal," I smiled. "Where are you?"

"Home, in San Diego. Well, *out* in San Diego. What about you?"

I walk around and around Mom's tiny rectangle of yard, phone pressed to my ear. The time difference, the age, upbringing—all of it melting away with every step.

"I want you to be my girlfriend," he says, and I hear cheers in the background, people egging him on.

I pause, thinking about the two times we'd been around each other. How, in that small span, I'd been impactful. *Desirable.* I imagined myself as a woman instead of a girl, tried to see what he must have seen, but couldn't bring myself to ask him what that was, or why he'd chosen to call me during a bar crawl with his friends. Instead of thinking about him, I thought about him meeting me. What I looked like those nights, what my words must have meant for him to invite me, almost a stranger, into his life. Could I still be her?

Maybe I'm capable of hope after all. Hypocrite.

"Hello?" I ask stupidly, pretending the phone disconnected to buy myself time. But one second later, I blurted out "Yes!" to all of them on the phone, not wanting to let the party down. I was feeling electric from the spontaneity of it all.

Are you asking yourself, *Why, Rachael? Why? We just learned this lesson. No more men, Rachael. We don't know this man, he's probably drunk dialing you. Get a grip!*

If you are, you're not seeing me clearly. This Rachael is begging for enlightenment and opportunity and only knows one way to get it. *Run.* And the newness of Logan is enough to get me out of the trailer door. Plus, if this were a princess story, you'd all call this phone call 'destiny,' and how do we know it's not a princess story yet? The girl in the trailer park? Come on, it practically writes itself.

143

Sure, Why Not?

I was stupid for saying yes, but I wasn't dumb. If I was going to fly to California on my last 500 bucks to meet up with a cocky team manager who thought he was in love with me based off the fact that I put my arm through the glass of a vending machine after it ate my money—

"I can't stop thinking about the night we met, you were insane. It was amazing."

—I wasn't going to do it without a back-up plan. I'd spend a few days in San Diego with Logan, then meet up with a band in Los Angeles. Then, once the tour ended in New York, fly back to Florida and???

Okay, it wasn't a full plan but at least I wouldn't be stranded again. And if cramming myself into a van for three more weeks was the only way to do it, then so be it

Logan was a team manager. He wasn't shy in telling me that athletes came to *him*, that they needed his word to make it big, and I liked that about him. Confident and cool but not aloof. Everything about him felt grown up. And he was happy; he laughed with a big, wide open mouth. Pleased with himself. I wanted that. When he picked me up at the airport, he stood outside of his vintage Datsun, blinding me with his beaming smile, and when we kissed for the first time, I felt held. Protected. We drove fast down I-5 with our hands on the center console, fingers knit together in a wet ball of stranger sweat.

"Do you want to feel the best thing in the world?" He asked, looking over at me, grinning like a little boy.

I stayed quiet, unsure what to expect while also wanting to appear like I wasn't expecting anything.

Logan took a quick turn off the freeway onto the on-ramp, then pulled hard on the emergency brake. For a moment, we were weightless. After the smoke cleared and the car stopped skidding, gravity came back to us.

"Flying," he called it.

I hadn't tried to see myself from the perspective of others before, but Logan wouldn't let me miss it. He talked about how he couldn't believe my job, my attitude, the way I travelled. How he wished everyone saw the world the way I did, even though I never told him how I saw it at all. I let his descriptions illuminate me and reflected them back to him, happy to be described.

At his place, his room is sterile. A black bedspread and gray sheets from the manly section at Target. Black-and-white prints of his photos on the walls. Nothing spoke of the exciting life I knew he had except for one corner of his computer desk, marred with stickers, the way every inch of desk was at Butchie's house. Different brands, some overlap: energy drinks, action sports networks. In his open closet were boxes of new shoes, skate shoes for a non-skater. It was the first time I'd ever seen this, but I was only hours away from the second—California is full of skate shoes on non-skaters. It's simply the 'culture.'

I stood close to his mirror and rubbed a squirt of expired foundation under my eyes, using my fingertips. Just like Mom did. I hoped it matched my complexion in the daylight as I scraped a comb through my hair. When that seemed like an adequate amount of time, I kicked my duffle bag into his closet and emerged from his dark room, never having turned on the light.

The beach by his place in Oceanside was so different from my beach, all cold and gray, even in the middle of summer.

"But you can walk here," he defended when I brought it up.

The sand was golden instead of white, with big grains you could see without holding them close to your eye. There were cigarettes between the pebbles, bottle caps, too. Something you'd never see on the beach in Naples. I had been to California so many times, but never down to the beach—it was never on our agenda, and even though it lacked the wilderness aspect that I was used to, with all of its boardwalks and litter, I sunk my feet in the ground and looked at it all, my eyes wide open. I looked at Logan, broad-shouldered and conventionally handsome, and I took him in, too. The stability, the calmness, his clean townhouse, the fact that he *had* a townhouse at all. It made me feel peaceful, which is kind of how most things with Logan were—homey, a little nostalgic for things that never were, safe. Vanilla-sweet and normal.

"Do you think you'll be on tour for much longer?" He asked, a breeze from the waves lifting his hair. "Or, do you have a larger plan?"

The way he said it, I could tell he wanted me to have one.

I made a note to myself: get a larger plan.

People Get Paid for This?

"You sure you can handle L.A.?" Arielle asks, arms folded across her chest.

I smile and pull her in for a hug. I'd felt her eyes on my back as I waved goodbye to Logan an uncool number of times, but I didn't care. I didn't want to miss his eyes looking back at me in the rearview mirror.

"Thanks for letting me crash for the night," I say.

We're sitting outside at some hip taco truck that turns vegetables into meat, and she's giving me the same 'wise punk elder' vibes that I'd experienced on our first drive to the mall together. She's exactly how I remember, just with longer hair—a carefully crafted attitude, schematically black attire. Too cool for me.

"I really don't know what the fuck I'm doing, I don't want to tour anymore."

Arielle has spent the last twenty minutes chatting my ear off about all the big-timers she's met through her job at Sony BMG, blissfully unaware that music streaming is about to kick the legs out from under record labels like hers.

"I'll ask around, see if there are any paid internships," she says.

The next morning, I'm lounging on her couch when she calls my cell. I've just come out of a very long, very hot shower, counting down the hours until I have to show up to the House of Blues and begin yet another stretch of bad sleep and even worse hygiene.

"You've got a meeting with Hydra Head tonight, but, you know, you should have done this yourself," she announces, happy to help but even happier to prove her connections. "You're very hirable with this resume. By the way, I made you a resume."

"Wow, okay—"

"And got you a meeting with Roadrunner in New York in two weeks."

"But I've got—"

"They're coming to the show," she cuts me off. "So, you know, try to be professional."

What's professional about being a merch girl? I want to ask her. Instead, I thank her for the opportunity and hang up the phone.

As far as record companies go, Roadrunner and Hydra Head were and are two of the most iconic metal labels around. I'd never toured with anyone from Hydra Head—they were boutique and had very little performances—but I'd shared stops with Roadrunner bands before.

146

Those on their tabs had tour buses instead of vans, booked better hotels, and had bigger crowds than any of the labels I'd worked with. They also had catering instead of lukewarm plates of cold cuts and pizza, so it was always a come up to get on a package with them. I'd seen firsthand what a difference it made when crowds came up to them after shows, asking for stories, glimpses into the glamour of their lives. It made the choice difficult.

But, ultimately, a new coast and proximity to Logan won out.

Don't get me wrong: the Roadrunner offices in New York had been fantastic. Loft-style, with big, high ceilings and exposed brick, staffed with run-of-the-mill guys in their mid-twenties with faux-hawks and sleeves of tattoos covered by Banana Republic button downs. I had fun imagining myself in that five-story building during our meeting, but when I painted the picture of big-city Rachael, she was alone, lonely. It was a cool place and a very tempting offer, but all in all, much like my brands to come, I couldn't see myself with big names, big bucks. I liked the artistry of Hydra Head, the aesthetic, their elitist attitude—music before money.

I was a ball of nerves as I dressed for my first day at Hydra Head: new ballet flats from Payless and my tightest pair of three-year-old jeans, gray because that seemed more office appropriate than regular denim. Unlike Roadrunner, their building was older, cluttered with floor-to-ceiling stretches of record boxes, all in the limited-edition pressings and the rare colorways they were known for. Walking through the cavern of boxes felt a little bit like Mom's trailer at the apex of her QVC shopping addiction, and I wondered if these boxes were ever moved, opened, or put to use, unlike any of her purchases.

The staff at Hydra Head was also much different from the Roadrunner crowd. They had long hair, long beards, and were all casually dressed in t-shirts and black converse. That, and only seven of us worked in the office, and of those seven, two of us were women—me, and the office admin, Anna. She was another of those babydoll-dress-types. She gave me a smile in the unusable, box-filled kitchenette, a tattoo peeking above the cup of her right breast. In two lunches, I'll learn that it says 'daddy,' and naïvely wonder what kind of person would pay homage to their father on their tit.

"We eat out, here," she said when I opened the fridge, looking for somewhere to stash last night's leftovers. Eager to mesh, I dumped them in the trash can and wandered back to where I came from, waiting to be formally acknowledged or told what to do. Finally, James, the director and sole member of the art department, popped up from behind his monitor. He was a soft-spoken man of about 5'4; subconsciously, I hunched my shoulders down as I shook his hand.

"Welcome to the crew," he smiled, pointing me to my desk. A cloud of dust rose from my keyboard when I blew across it; looking up, I saw that the ceiling tile directly above my desk was missing. Before I could ask about it, James interrupted me.

"You know how to open Facebook, right?"

A Fresh Start

A very generous person would call my place an apartment, but anybody outside of Los Angeles would call it a half-converted garage. It has no bathroom and no air conditioning, no mini fridge or microwave. It's backed behind an actual home, where Arielle and her friend live. I have to go inside the house every time I need to pee or take a shower, my only door opening wide and tall enough for—you guessed it!—a car to fit through, right onto one of the east side's busiest streets, Glendale Boulevard.

From my bed, I can almost pretend I'm living in a sleek loft, rather than a glorified parking space; Arielle told me I'd need to be making at least 900 a month to make it in L.A., so that's what she's charging me. She tells me it's a lesson in learning to hustle, but *fuck* am I tired of hustling. She raps loud on the garage door, and I click the button to let her in.

"How was your first day?" She asks, fingers hooked in her belt loops. She jingles against the doorway, her carabiner of keys rattling against the grommets of her belt clacking against the silver rings on her fingers. With Logan in San Diego, I have nothing to do but join her at stiff vegan dinner parties with punks-gone-corporate. She made the most of *her* 900-dollar lesson, whoever dealt it to her.

"It was good," I tell her. "They took me to lunch."

"Nice," she nods. "Meet anyone cool?"

"There's only seven of us in the whole building," I laugh. "But yeah, all cool people."

"What are you doing tonight?" She asks.

"Logan's coming by for dinner," I tell her, sitting up in bed.

"Ah, yes. The old man," she says, rolling her eyes.

"He's not that old," I say, defensively.

"He's older than you."

"You're older than him."

"Yeah, which is why I'm not dating a twenty-year-old," she says, sticking out her tongue. I know it comes from a good place, and that she's just got a chip on her shoulder about everything and anything, so I let it roll off my back.

"He's nice to me," I say, finally, reaching for the garage opener.

"Well, come inside if you guys want," she replies, looking around the room as the door lowers.

I'm excited to see Logan, and there's nothing Arielle can do to change

148

that. He's taking me out to sushi, our first date as California residents, and my budget and I are both happy to be fed a stress-free meal. *Should I feel bad that I can't afford this sushi without him?* I wonder. But no, Logan feels good. He doesn't complain about the drive, even if it's just for a short visit; whenever I tell him about anything crazy his voice perks up. He likes that I'm a little rough around the edges, likes to tell his friends my stories in a "you're not gonna believe this one" tone, is even happier when they don't believe it. Sometimes, my escapades become the joke of the night and I get to hold quarter with a table full of pro X-games athletes. They travel the world on small cash prizes from competitions, partying in red light districts and trusting the wrong strangers, only to wind up with their teeth knocked out. They never fix them because it's an excuse to tell the story. And the tamest ones, the Logans, have photos of it all. Most of them have fiancées, blonde and at home, some pregnant. I just like that Logan likes me, like his predictability, the way his stern voice steers the day. His stability makes me feel like I can be stable, too. He holds my face in his hands when it's time to say goodbye, peppers my skin with kisses. It's always then that I realize San Diego and L.A. aren't as close as they look on the map.

"I'll be back soon," he says. Then, accidentally, "Stay out of trouble."

The truth is, he only likes the trouble because it feels like it's behind me.

As soon as the garage door lowers to a shut, I get anxious. Belly one-quarter full on a paycheck's worth of sushi. Except for the sound of some kind of bug desperately trying to escape, the room is eerily quiet. I flip open my phone and try to call Liz to tell her that I made it, but it goes to voicemail almost instantly. Two contacts down from Liz, I see Mom and decide whatever is on the end of that line is better than being alone in this box.

"Hello?" She answers. She sounds tired, and I kick myself for not checking the clock. But at least she picked up.

"Hi, Mom. It's me. I'm just calling because I made it to Los Angeles."

"Hi sweetie, that's so good to hear. I was getting worried."

I didn't check in with her at all on the drive, but I also didn't check in when I was driving in circles around the U.S. for two years; now that she's on one of her longer sober streaks, I think she's starting to crave the normalcy of what looks like a standard mother-daughter relationship on her T.V. shows. We talk about the weather and she asks about Logan. Then, her voice changes.

"Listen Rach, I wanted to tell you before you left but I've been reading about these jobs that they have in Bahrain."

"What part of Florida is that?" I ask, sitting down on the edge of my mattress.

"It's not Florida, it's overseas. But someone I knew from writers' camp just got hired there after a six-year gap in her resume, and she's making good money. They pay for everything and give you an apartment, too."

149

"I don't understand, so you would just go there? For how long?"

"Only a year or two. I'd keep the trailer."

I think about the 17 years my mom spent on the couch, fucked out of her mind, without a partner and barely a friend. I think about her life before my dad, how she lived in Mexico and sang and ate exotic foods and was alive, really alive, not just breathing. I think about the itch she must have. Then again, maybe I'm projecting. Maybe I don't want to worry about her for a while.

"That sounds amazing, Mom. You have to do that!"

She pauses, processing the answer she got versus the one she wanted. I didn't know it, but this was the moment where she was hoping for the 'no, don't go, I'll change everything, I'll come home, we can make things right together, I love you more than I can bear.' But how was I supposed to know that? I had just started a new position in L.A., and here was this job dangling in front of her, a woman constantly worried by money. It was what I would've done, if it was me. Open door? Dart through. Done.

"..... okay, um ... great... so, yeah, I'll finish filling out the forms and then I guess I can leave in about three weeks if it all checks out." Her voice is weak, softer now, less sure.

"This is the best idea you've ever had, Mom. I'm so proud of you."

"Well, thanks, um—love you, Rachael."

"Love you too, Mom."

Fish Out of Water

Arielle was convinced that if I didn't do something outside of work, I'd end up moving to San Diego with Logan, something she personally considered a type of death. So, she introduced me to her friend Katie, who had a more flexible schedule than she did and could keep up with a 20-year-old's ability to stay out until daylight and get up in the morning for work.

Katie was a bar-hopping indie chick with friends in several pop bands—a great friend to have if you don't have much cash. We went to clubs, music venues, dives, pushing our way through V.I.P. lounges, parting seas of fucked-up fashion witches, equal parts Stevie Nicks and Mary-Kate Olsen, each on the verge of fainting or tripping or both. Everything they wore looked vintage but cost half a month's rent, their necks layered in silver, fingers covered in turquoise rings. I had a pair of knockoff American Apparel shorts and red wedges from the clearance box at Urban Outfitters, and recycled the same two tops every time Katie took me out on the town.

On Wednesdays, Katie went to Night Swim, an infamous summer party at the Hollywood Roosevelt. So, that meant I did, too. The only people swimming at Night Swim were real-life supermodels—the kinds you can recognize without a name. Their hairless, clear-skinned, tattoo-free bodies shimmered under the blue-hued string lights that flickered across the poolside dance floor. Everybody else—actors, musicians, socialites—gathered around the bar while photographers pushed through the crowd, cameras flashing. At these types of parties, you're soon to be pointed in the direction of a celebrity you don't recognize by an excited, buzzed stranger who is likely famous in their own way for something else you don't know about. *Welcome to L.A.*

Katie and I were on our way to grab a couple of vodka sodas when I saw a flash next to me, near some gaunt-looking girl's bruised knees.

"Did—did that photographer just take a picture up your skirt?" I asked, touching the girl on her wrist-sized shoulder. She wore a childlike tent-shaped dress, jerky body movements much like Fiona Apple's writhing in the 'Criminal' video.

"I hope so," she said, giggling. "He's, like, a legend."

Her eyes rolled deeply into the back of her head as the sentence trailed off. *Drugs?* I thought to myself, deciding that I must have misheard her.

151

I watched her slither back down into the cushions of the cabana sofa and take a drag from the tiny red straw poking out of her cocktail. Katie shrugged—she hadn't heard a word either of us had said over the yacht-rock digital mash up coming from the speakers next to our heads—so we moved on, scooting one step closer in line to the bar.

"It kind of sucks here!" Katie yelled over the noise.

"Yeah, it's *so* weird" I said. An honest review of all I had just taken in.

"No, I mean the drinks are like $17 each. I hate that!"

Just then, Katie's friend Bosh came up behind us. He was in a famous band, too—and no, I didn't know the name.

"No worries," he said, pulling a flask out from inside of his leather jacket and dropping it into my hand. "Just keep it low."

I ducked beneath him, tipping my head back. *More whiskey. Goddammit.* When I opened my eyes, a flash went off again. Not beside me, this time. Directly below me. The guy was still crouched on the ground with his camera lens pointed upwards when I looked down.

"Did you just take a photo of me?" I barked at the photographer, cheeks hot.

"Yeah," he said, smirking as he stood. "I did."

I didn't think twice. I swung my fist as hard as I could into his face. The entire crowd went silent as he staggered backwards, trying to catch his balance. He landed in the shallow end of the swimming pool, wet up to his waist.

"What the *fuck*?" He yelled, looking down at the water in stunned disbelief.

My knuckles ached, and I could feel everyone's eyes on me as Katie grabbed me by the arm, laughing.

"We have to go. *Now.*"

I still held my drink in my hand as we cut through the crowd, adrenaline giving way to a wild giggling fit.

I looked over my shoulder and saw the photographer climbing out of the pool; those that weren't watching him were looking after us, their mouths still open in surprise.

"Shit," I muttered, chugging my drink.

Our arms were still linked as we hurried out, pushing against people who were only just now coming into the party, a couple of right turns away from the aftermath of my sucker punch. When Katie and I finally got out of the maze and hailed a cab, a voice called out behind me.

"You fucking *bitch*."

It was the photographer, pushing through the hedges, branches snapping. His jeans were soaked and he held a cigarette between his fingers, his group of friends joining him on the sidewalk. One of them held his camera. I held up my middle finger and he took a step forward, wet shoes sloshing. Then, I felt a burn on my arm: he had flicked his butt right at me, his face pinched, furious.

"Go back to the fucking valley."

Since I've now lived in L.A. for 15 years, I know that telling someone to go back to the valley is an insult of the highest caliber, the California equivalent of calling someone white trash, cheap. But as a newly minted resident, I had no idea what he meant, no idea why his friends were *oooh*-ing behind him, chuckling. They must have all expected tears to well up in my eyes, for me to hurry into the cab with my head ducked in shame. Instead, I brushed the burn on my arm, face emotionless.

"I don't even know where the fucking valley *is*," I told him, walking towards the cab. I looked out the window as we drove away, smiling when I saw the look on his face, defeated by my ignorance, a small puddle of water pooling at his feet.

"I'm never coming back here." I announced to Katie, who agreed I should never come back. Both of us unaware that, in five years' time, I'd be hosting my fourth party at the same venue, including my birthday, where the guest list maxed out at 1,000 people.

I'm wondering if this place is for me; I feel well below the pay grade required to make friends or fit in. The traffic is maddening, and I feel stuck, impatient, bored, like I'm trapped in a perennial waiting room, drumming my fingers until my name gets called. Which I am, at the Planned Parenthood down the street from my office.

"Finley?"

I scan the waiting room as I get up. A faux pas, really, since people are usually here for the most sensitive subjects and they're often the most vulnerable bunch, but as I do, I realize it's the first time I've really been around normal people since I moved to L.A.

The last time I'd been to Planned Parenthood was in high school, but not for myself. A popular girl I barely knew had found me in the hallway one morning and pulled me aside to ask if I had a car. When I told her I did, she'd lowered her voice. "I have to get an abortion." We drove during lunch, and I'd sat in the waiting room, jangling my leg and reading magazines, blissfully unaware of what that might mean to a person.

No matter how responsible it is to get pap smears, I can't help but feel like a child, sitting ass-out on the edge of the examination table, kicking my feet. I don't know what they're going to prescribe me, but assume that's why it's taking so long for someone to come back in to see me. I've already peed in the cup, done the swabs, had some blood taken. They told me they'd be right back, but here I was, waiting again.

Finally, the door opened.

"Rachael?"

"Yeah?"

I was planning on saying something about having to be somewhere, but I changed my mind when I saw not just the nurse that performed the exam, but a *doctor* walking in. They closed the door solemnly behind them.

Oh, my god, I thought, stomach falling. *I'm pregnant.*

"Rachael, I'm Doctor_____."

I don't remember her name. I don't remember what she looked like. I just remember feeling like the walls were closing in on me. I took a deep breath.

"Am I pregnant?" I nearly whispered.

"Wha—oh, no, you're not pregnant," the doctor said, sitting in a chair. I thought she was going to smile, but she didn't. She brought her chair closer to me, until her knees nearly touched my toes.

"Thank god," I said, sighing.

"But I'm going to need to re-perform the pap smear."

Why hadn't she smiled yet? Did I have an STD or something? Had Logan lied about getting tested? My mind ran a strange circuit, trying to remember all of the shit I'd learned in sex ed, wondering if a condom could've broken somewhere along the lines, and hoping, really hoping, that this goddamned doctor would give me a smile. I put my legs up into the stirrups and waited.

"That's where I felt it," said the nurse in a quiet voice, pressing on my bladder.

"Mmm-hmm," said the doctor. She poked me with a few instruments, felt around. Then, she removed her gloves. "You can sit up now."

"What is it?" I asked.

"It could just be a cyst," she said. "But you'll need a pelvic ultrasound to be sure. We'll call you to set that up."

I couldn't shake the feeling that there was something more she wanted to say but couldn't, like she wasn't allowed to. If it wasn't a cyst, what would it be?

"Alright," I said, sitting up, tissue crinkling below me.

"We'll call you when we have an opening."

I was splashing cold water on my face, standing in Arielle's bathroom when I got the call. I had only just gotten home, and hadn't expected them to set my appointment up *that* quickly.

"Hi, is this Rachael? Rachael Finley?"

"Yeah?" I asked, wiping my face on my sleeve.

"We—some of your test results show some concerning numbers," the woman said. "We're going to be sending you a shuttle."

"Shuttle?"

"To take you to the hospital. You need further testing."

I reached a hand down and pressed near my bladder. It didn't hurt or anything, and I wondered if sending a shuttle was a big city thing or if I should be more concerned.

I wondered if I should call Logan, but he'd been in China for two weeks, and I didn't really even know what I'd say. That I was carpooling?

There was no music on in the van, only the steady whir of the A.C. The driver honked, pressing on the gas, jostling me with the brakes. When I got to the emergency room, the driver ushered me out of the bus and I jammed my hand in my pocket, searching for tip money but he pushed down on my forearm, as if to say no.

I was dripping sweat but shivering cold. I didn't have to wait this time. A space was already prepared, my name written on the whiteboard,

154

separated from the bustle of the rest of the hospital by only a thin curtain. Someone handed me a gown to change into. I flipped open my phone—no service.

There was a guy down the hall screaming for pain medication, and a woman in the bed next to me was shouting through the paper-thin curtain spread between us, fighting with her nurse, who told her that she couldn't leave. When she asked why, they told her that she was dying from HIV. Her voice rose angrily.

"Dying?" She yelled. "Dying *when?*"

Her voice was so clear, and not dying at all.

"By the end of the day," the nurse told her. "So, you better start praying."

My throat dried up, my stomach dropped. *Is this normal? Is where I'm at, what I'm hearing, okay?* I stared up at the ceiling, asking myself not to panic, to remember that I felt fine. The nurse closed the curtain next door and opened mine, the dying woman still hollering, spitting mad.

"We're going to bring you in for surgery in a couple hours," she told me, pulling on a pair of gloves.

"For what?" I asked, swallowing dryly.

In her hand was a plastic tube, liquid bobbing inside. "They need to get a better look at that growth, take a biopsy."

"O-okay."

"This should relax you," she said, moving towards my I.V.

"What is it?"

"Midazolam," she said. "Anti-anxiety."

When the medicine hit my veins, I started slipping, the room sliding away, brain warm, eyes heavy. I could still hear everything that was going on next to me—the woman shrieking, the coarseness of her words.

"What the fuck? What the FUCK?" I felt her bed rocking as she kicked out her feet below her blankets. "You gonna let me DIE in here?"

Is she talking to me?

Her voice began to fade. Not just because the medicine was working—they gave me another round—but because they were right. She *was* dying. Her anger dissolved into sadness, her sadness into exhaustion. A grief counselor came in and sat beside the woman's bed. She told her that she was there for her, that she'd stay by her side. The woman was dead before I went in for surgery.

They wheeled her body out before they wheeled mine. And when they did, my vision swam, blurred as we pushed past all of the people in scrubs, the glowing EXIT signs, the countless fluorescent lights. By the time we got into the room for surgery, I was asleep.

When I come to, I'm in a new room—an actual room, one with walls and a door and a single bed, which I'm occupying. I don't remember falling asleep, don't remember getting here. All I feel is an excruciating pain in my lower belly, like period cramps only a thousand times worse. I grit my teeth, holding back a shout. A doctor comes into the room.

155

"How are you feeling?" He asks, sitting in a chair by my bed.

"Okay," I say, wincing.

"We took out a pretty big mass from your uterus," he says. "So, you'll need to sit tight for a few days and recover."

"Mass?" I ask, tube-tangled hand clamping down on my belly.

"A tumor. Cancer."

I look at him, anesthesia still fogging up my brain. I scoot higher up on my pillows as if a better look will help me understand.

"You're lucky it wasn't closer to your lymph nodes, or it might have already spread."

I have nothing to say. On the one hand, I'm in shock, because it's impossible not to be in shock when someone reminds you of your mortality. But my brain is doing what it always has, compartmentalizing. Ready to package this whole ordeal up and tuck it away. So, I don't think I react the way he expects. The doctor pauses to make sure I heard him, so I feign what I think is a good look of shock, heartbreak, and horror until he's satisfied to move on with his sentence.

"I'll have somebody come in and walk you through your treatment plan. For now, rest up," he says, pressing his palm into my shoulder as he leaves.

When one of the oncology nurses comes to flush my I.V., she grabs my hand.

"Have you told anyone yet?"

"No," I say, feeling a chill as the cold solution rushes through my veins. Telling my boss that I would be missing work for a family emergency was the closest I'd come to talking about it.

"You don't have to tell everyone," she says, walking away. "But it helps to start with one."

I lay in bed, thinking. For how long, I'm not sure, but eventually, I reach for my phone. I don't even look at the message I'm typing or check the clock to see what time it is, don't wonder whether he's even going to see this while I'm awake. I write the words and send them away, then put my phone back under my stack of pillows. I feel wrung out like a stinking dishtowel—I'm tired. I need rest. I press the call button for the nurse and turn in the bed, trying get comfortable without ripping my I.V. out of place.

By the time someone comes in with pain medicine, I've thrown up on the floor. I'm hyperventilating. This nurse is different from the woman before, and while this might not seem like a big deal, when you're alone in a hospital with a cancer diagnosis and a puddle of puke on the floor, you want to see a familiar face. I gasp for air, feeling the panic drip down my face.

"What's going on? What's wrong?" The nurse asks, rushing to my bedside. The room is tilting. I see her glance at my vitals, then feel a gentle hand on my arm.

"Just breathe," she says. "Breathe."

My whole body buckles as I heave.

156

"Rachael, honey. Deep breaths."

Another nurse comes into the room. She looks at the whiteboard as she marches towards my bed, her voice stern, practically a bark.

"What's your pain? On a scale of one to ten?" She asks.

She has a syringe in her hands, ready to administer more pain medication. I look up at her and feel my heart slow. She has gray roots poking out against her box-dyed red hair, just like my mom. I manage to take one small, stuttering breath.

"I'm scared," I say.

Cancer was someone else, someone the doctors were talking to when they came up with the chemo schedule, booked the radiation appointments. Cancer was not me. I refused it.

By the end of the week, I was out of the hospital gown and back in the outfit I'd worn to work the week before, but I could not have felt further from that moment. And the instant that I stepped out of the automated doors at the front of the hospital, I felt my brain shove itself forward, propelling me—and the entire experience—away. It was like I was leaving the grocery store.

"Hey, where've you been?" Arielle asks when I come inside to fill my one cup with water. She's sitting at her kitchen table, typing on her laptop, nodding her head along to her music.

"It's—long story," I say, giving her a small smile.

"Alright then," she replies.

Back in the garage, I throw myself, gently, on my bed. I knew I would actually have to tell my roommate what was going on, knew that, yes, I would even have to call both of my parents at some point. There was also the fact that I was responding to one out of every ten texts Logan sent me, but everything had to wait. In that moment, I needed sleep, the only time I could enjoy being in my own head.

When Logan came back from Hong Kong, we put a plan into motion. I didn't know what treatment was going to do to me, so we both decided that it would be smarter and safer for the two of us to move in together. We'd only been dating for 6 months, but Logan was 26, at a stage in his life where living with your girlfriend was the thing that you did, the thing that all of his friends were doing. I was relieved that I wouldn't have to be in the detached garage, a backyard away from the nearest bathroom while actual poison was coursing through my veins.

I waited until mom was safely set up in Bahrain to tell her—I didn't want her to worry about me when she was getting her fresh start. I didn't want cancer to stand in her way, too.

"You'll power through," she told me. "The chemo's hell but there are worse things."

"Yeah, I'm going to keep working," I said, as if I had a choice. I was bracing myself for that first medical bill the way some people prepare for Armageddon, stashing away cash, living on as little as possible, saying yes

157

to every extra hour Hydra Head had to offer.

"Good. That'll make it go by quicker."

"Yeah, that's what I'm hoping."

"And you guys are moving in together?"

"Yeah, tomorrow. To Long Beach, though. It's halfway between both of our jobs."

"Well, don't think about it too much. Just keep your head down and get it done."

"Yep." I paused, wondering how short of an 'I'm telling my mom I have cancer' conversation was too short of a conversation.

Bring in the Love

Hallmark movies never get it right. There isn't a warm welcome at the chemo center, no apple-cheeked clinician reassuring you that normal is just a few treatments away. That everything is going to be okay, that you're finally healing. The chemo centers are sterile, stern. You fill out stacks of paperwork under fluorescent lights and hand them to an unsmiling nurse who has been there since two in the morning. You pass them your ID so you can prove that you're the sick person on the digital form on their monitor, and they pass it back, wordless. Maybe it's clinical for a reason. Maybe kindness, the show of any emotion, might buckle you. They probably know that.

When they call my name, I go to the back, down the hall to a room full of other people. Women, mostly. Wrapped in blankets, head scarves for some, a loved one sitting by holding a hand, laughing together, reading a book.

The nurse shows me to my chair—a pink leather recliner, utilitarian design—and hands me a stack of blankets. I look over my shoulder and see a few others, alone like me. One of them shoots me a quick smile with his entire face; the wrinkles around his eyes tell me that he smiles often and freely. I guess you bring the warmth with you, when you come into this place.

Sterile needle, sterilized entry point, sterile strip. It's 2007, pre-scroll. Opening a website on my flip phone costs $1.25 per megabyte, whatever that means. Someone must have decided that Judge Judy was the most neutral choice for the one T.V. on the wall. *Aggressive,* I think to myself. The ticking clock overhead grows loud as I think about the four hours I have ahead of me. I slump down in the chair until my back is flat, my uterus bubbling up over my hipbones. I think about it filling with poison. There's pressure, then my I.V. port starts to sting. And now my whole body is tingling and uncomfortable. When the tingling turns to burning, I squirm in my seat. I want to leave. *You paid to be here,* says a voice in my head. *This is what you're working for.*

Yes, I am grateful to be here. Grateful that a place like this exists, that me and the rest of the uninsured patients on medical grants have a place to go. I'm told that the 18k this will cost me is essentially charity—a charity that I'll have to pay back, $125 dollars at a time.

When my four hours is done, I walk to my car. The stereo clock says

159

3:30 and I kick myself for not taking the earlier appointment. Heading south with the rest of the commuters adds an extra hour to my 45-minute commute. The heat trapped in the car starts to press down on me. My eyes well.

Don't do it, says the voice. *Don't cry.*

And I don't.

Silver Linings

Of all of the crazy things chemo does to your body, taking away your sense of smell so that you can vomit into public trashcans without smelling sunbaked public-trashcan-trash might be the second-best gift. Six weeks into chemo, and I'd learned of and leaned into every bin, bush, and parking strip in my orbit, from the record label to the pharmacy, where I'd become something of a regular. Every time I went to the counter for my mountain of prescriptions, the people working would stare at me and I'd stare back. Daring them to say it. Daring them to ask if I was dying, or if I was just picking up for someone else. *So young*, they're thinking as they slide my crunchy paper bag towards me. I don't break the stare and eventually they dart their eyes away.

"Pussies," I mutter under my breath.

Everyone's loss of words was something I was sort of getting used to, even at work. The usual joking and banter was filled with sad-eyed sighs and pursed lips, my diagnosis hanging in the air like a black cloud.

"Rachael?"

Mark is still taking an absurd amount of uppers, but now when he screams for me, his tone is softer. Just as loud, but not as rude. It matches the new look that he puts on his face whenever I'm around, and makes me miss the way he used to be. Like the time he chased me around the office for "wasting paper" when I accidentally printed a blank page 100 times, then took us all out for drinks at 10 a.m.

"Yeah?" I ask, slumping over to his doorway.

"I want you to know that all of us are cheering you on," he begins. "And that nobody would think any less of you if you decided to cut back your hours."

He trails off into a long pause, waiting for me to agree with him, but my heart sinks.

"I'm fine," I reply robotically. It was a phrase I'd been saying so often that I was starting to feel like a Pez dispenser, tilting my head back and ejecting chalky, candy-coated lies.

I couldn't argue with him; I don't even have it in me to try. My eyelids feel like boulders, my neck aches from the effort of keeping my head up. I press my back into the cool metal doorway, hardly able to stand upright. I feel exhausted to the point of delirium, have been sleeping past my alarm and showing up to work late, driving the hour and a half to the office with my brain in a daze. Then, puking up my guts in the trashcan below my desk. As nice as Mark was about it, we both knew this couldn't go on forever.

"What's keeping you here?" He asks. Another leading question. I know what he wants me to say.

"I have to pay for treatment," I tell him, my voice low.

"If I can find you something easier, a few days a week, would you do that instead?" When he sees the look on my face, he continues. "We'll hold your job for you. You can come back when you're healthy."

If I'm ever healthy, I want to say. Instead, I nod my bobbling Pez head in response.

"Thanks," I say, turning to leave.

"Oh, and Rachael?"

"Yeah?"

"Go home. You look like hammered shit."

I spend the next few weeks rolling over on my couch, the A.C. on the leather cooling my boiling skin. I'm pretending to heal, pretending to take the time everyone wants me to. The worried texts have stopped pouring in, and all of the ones left want phone calls, something I don't have the energy for.

Finally, Mark emailed me that his new girlfriend Andrea, an assistant designer at Juicy Couture (something he was all too proud to share), was looking for a fit model. I responded, "Absolutely!!!!" although I had no idea what a fit model was.

There are jobs in L.A. that don't exist anywhere else, just like the odd couples it attracts. A place where the hairy old metal dude scores the fashion designer. And why not? Hustle is hustle. There's enough for everyone, and for every type of everyone to find love. And, if you're a hustler, a true 'make money when and where you can' hustler, you can invent a career here out of nothing but thin air and self-confidence. It's why I've never left.

The Juicy offices were a catacomb of pink; I was raced from a pink couch to a pink conference room and stood on a platform in nothing but my bra and underwear. Women with pens and clipboards sat around in a semi-circle, their chairs facing me as if I were on an amphitheater stage. Not all fittings would be like this—Juicy was a conglomerate, a global brand with many divisions and departments, all of whom needed to check things off their clipboards. And at the helm were two women, one of which sat in the center of the room. Tiny, curtained behind a wilderness of hair, was bohemian Jewess, Gela. She sat cross-legged in a tiny chair with her tiny arm extended out so that her tiny fingernails could be serviced by an on-call manicurist.

"She always has her nails done in meetings, she never wastes a minute of time," Andrea whispered to me.

I straightened my back and widened my eyes to seem alert, like I was not a waste of time, either.

A stern woman came up to me and cleared her throat. In her hand was a ruler, and around her neck was a measuring tape. My first introduction to my ruling power was abrupt.

"This model is a size four," she announced.

"Is that an L.A. four, New York four, or U.S. four?" Gela asked, looking up from her notes to catch the eye of the meeting director.

"L.A. four," she said. Driven by the desire to be an L.A. something, this was the answer I was hoping for. Even though I had no idea what that meant.

"Put the fall samples on her and we can start."

Four outfits later, someone asked me to announce my name and two of the people with clipboards asked for clarification in Spanish and Mandarin. After that, there was only the sound of the pink sewer's tape as it cracked taut around my waist, around my thigh, my bicep, and across my shoulders.

"Rachael?" Gela chirped. This was the first time she made eye contact with me, and I swallowed, unnerved. "Where are you from?"

"Long Beach," I sputtered.

"Are you available to come to the office two days a week?"

"Yes, definitely."

"Great," she said, turning in her chair. She looked down at one of her manicured hands then back up at me. "I like you. You're very...normal. Which is good, nobody does normal anymore."

Thank you, I guess? I thought to myself as Gela stood, piles of glittery silver chains hitting her chest. Then, she turned and very abnormally sauntered out of the room in the middle of someone else's sentence with a trail of assistants behind her.

"Okay, then, we're done here. Let's reconvene Thursday," said the meeting matron.

And just like that, I was alone again. Well, until an intern returned with my pile of clothes.

"Hey, is it true you have cancer?" She asked. Her tone made it feel like we were trading make out gossip, not whether or not I was dying.

"Yeah, but like, don't tell everyone. I just get tired of talking about it," I replied, trying to send her a hint. It didn't work. She stayed in the room while I changed back into my clothes, jabbering.

"You should blog about it. Then you don't have to keep telling people. I have a blog and it's like my personal newsletter. My family doesn't even call me anymore. It's like, just check the blog babe!" She smiled, flicking her wrist.

"Cool," I lied, nodding.

The walk back to my truck was long; longer, because I parked as far as possible from the white BMWs that filled the garage. It was the most I'd moved in weeks, and as I fought off a wave of nausea, my phone buzzed. It was a text from Andrea.

"Hey, thanks again for coming in. The rate for this job is only $75 an hour is that ok?"

OKAY? WHAT? It had only been two hours, plus an additional two to drive there and back. My head swam as I did the calculations. At two days a week, that would mean...

I answered back quickly, situating myself so that if it was a typo, she would feel obligated to adhere to it.

"Absolutely. See you Thursday. "

"Fab!! Also, I'm gonna give your number to a friend, she needs a fit model too. Don't lose or gain anything before next week... stay... normal!"

And there it was: the first-best gift. Thinness.

Don't Eat to Survive

I repeated the phrase that the oncologist told me as I drove to my appointment with the nutritionist. *Try to tackle this thing from all sides. Tackle this thing. Tackle.*

I should have been filled with "what if's," saddled with doubt, but nobody ever told me this whole chemo thing might not work, and when they did, they gave me another plan. The plans were easy. Follow the steps and succeed. Nobody ever told me to stop, sit down, to weigh it out, to talk about death. All they said was show up, take your meds. Tomorrow, show up somewhere else. So, I did. And today is just another day of doing what I'm told.

"I highly suggest a raw food diet," the nutritionist tells me, looking at my chart.

"Raw food?" I ask, remembering the American cheese that I'd melted on top of my egg earlier that morning, how someone once told me it was made of plastic. I hadn't thought about that again until now.

"No animal products, for one," she says, handing me a stack of papers, all decorated in colorful pictures of fruits and vegetables. "And mainly antioxidant rich foods, like blueberries and grapefruit."

"And that—that cures cancer?" I ask her, rifling through the pages.

"Treatment cures cancer. But a diet that *supports* your treatment is just as important. Give it a try."

I pick up my bag and turn to go. "Oh!" She calls after me, "Another thing. If you get nauseous from the chemo, try a little red wine. It might even help you with those hunger pangs—raw food isn't easy."

I drive to work, feeling the trial vitamins jangling around my empty stomach as I make my way into the parking garage. The elevator is out. I swallow some air and take the stairs, though every movement feels barbaric; I have sandpaper skin, knots for knees. They touch together as I climb the stairs, sending shockwaves of pain up my spine. When I get up to the third flight, I'm completely winded, and can feel a bubble of acid rise up into my mouth. Sweat beads on my upper lip. Two more flights to go. I pause to catch my breath but it's too late: I vomit all over the stairs.

It takes me a moment to realize what is happening. And when I do, it's hard to believe I'm here, trying to wipe the puddle away with the three Starbucks napkins I have in my bag. I'm *this* sick. *This*, right here, a pool of sick. It's then that I realize, *I need this diet to work.* And then, before I can regain my composure, *I need to work to pay for this diet, this nutritionist.* I wipe the cold perspiration off my brow, unfold the last napkin and place it gently and neatly over the mess. Then, I go up the remaining flights of stairs to work. And when I'm up, they applaud me for all my hard work. Skinny Rachael. Normal Rachael.

I have been training my whole life for this eating disorder. The long days without food, without money, the energy to sneak down the grass alley to the store. I was born with the willingness to eat the same thing every day, to cook the same flavor of boxed rice for months on end because it's all you know how to do. Microwave the same pizza bagels. Go to sleep on an empty stomach. Conditioned by the desire to leave the tiniest trace of existence, to not burden anyone by announcing my hunger, to never be labeled 'too much.' Too much to hang around, too much to love, too much to house. Now, I'm just another woman in body-obsessed Los Angeles whose livelihood—and, arguably, her *life*—is so entangled within thinness that it obscures all other truths.

And here am I with a prescriptive diet that promises health. Here I am with a plan. *Stick to the plan,* the nutritionist said, and I do. And then I get this body, from cancer and diet and discipline, and there's a paycheck at the end. The promise of wealth. In starving my most obvious appetite, I am satisfying my craving for structure; the order of counting each vitamin, each calorie, gives me balance. The rigidity of restriction gives me strength. *The rule of success is to follow the rules,* Mom always said. *Keep safe, follow the plan.*

And to my greatest relief, my sickness made me impenetrable: I was skinny from cancer. My relationship with food was not the problem. Did I know exactly how much water I could drink in order to avoid bloating? Yes. Did I know the calories in every Tic Tac I popped before my go-sees? Absolutely. I was 119.1 pounds when I woke up in the morning, 121.6 when I went to sleep.

I'm a monster and I know it. A monster of control. And it feels good, it feels *so* fucking good. I say aloud, "I feel so *fucking* good."

Maybe it's Okay

In a matter of weeks, I am down to one head of broccoli and three heaping spoons of pureed pumpkin twice a day.

I keep a pink sewer's tape under the sink in my bathroom. I take my measurements every morning—chest, waist, hips, biceps, thighs. If I'm happy with that, I drink coffee. If I'm not, just water and laxatives. I look at Logan's apples on the counter, his pack of muffins. *Gross*, I think, shivering. I get dressed—skinny jeans that are bagging around my legs, a black tank that keeps slipping off my shoulders—and walk past the patches of yellow sticky notes pasted to my cupboards, my countertops. Some say things like *18, 60, 100, 5*. Others, *egg replacer 44, cucumber?* When people come over, I hurry to throw them away. When I'm home alone, I stare at them with a strange half-smile on my lips. My trophies.

I like to be alone, with the trophies stacked around me, passing time writing the blog the ditzy intern told me to, because she was right, and you should never blow someone off because of their ditz.

The blog becomes my refuge, a place where I can type things out to digest them for maybe the first time at all. I post about my fittings, post the doodles I scrawl during chemo, write about rap that I'm listening to, which skater we saw at the coffee shop over the weekend. I'm just writing everything in my head, writing for me.

But I deeply underestimated the value of internet content at a time when "regular" people were becoming deeply online. RSS feeds were delivering subscribe-able content for the first time ever to our inboxes, and thanks to some algorithm I'll never understand, Steak Tooth grew to a following of 3,000 people, but that would remain unknown to me for another year because the page counter on word press cost $25, and I didn't have money to spare.

So, there were 3,000 people reading about where I would vomit next while wearing a rare form of prototypical vegan leather that had yet to be released to the public. And, also about my cat.

The other thing I deeply underestimated was the power of the city I lived in. It was like the minute I swore it wasn't for me, Los Angeles began to make space.

When I got the email from Podium Distribution, I had to check it three times to be sure that my eyes were not playing games on me, and that my chemo brain was interpreting things right.

Rachael/ Steaktooth,
Hi there! I'm the head of the graphic design team for DVS/Lakai, and we
saw the illustrations on your blog. We were wondering if you've ever done
graphics before? Your stuff would look awesome on a deck or maybe some
shirts.
Let me know if you're interested in this kind of work,
Sincerely, _____

The email hadn't even turned a minute old before I sent a hurried reply—one word and too many exclamation marks, the kind that many people would call unprofessional but never once got in my way.
"Absolutely!!!!!!!!!"
Here I was, making a promise to deliver on something I'd never done before. Digitizing graphics. As the excitement gave way to panic, I sent another email. This time, to my number one deep-internet guy, Michael.
M,
Hey, can you tell me how to get that free Photoshop again? Ok miss you!!!
-Rach

You see, Michael didn't just know where to get rare music before rare music or even Limewire was a thing. In my opinion, he knew everything there was to know about being online. We might have spent countless hours hovering states of depression and deep love, but we also used a lot of those late nights and days shut in together to develop a skill I had never realized was more than a hobby. At 15, we'd learned how to use the entire Adobe suite on pirated copies, just so we could convincingly punk our friend group by photoshopping pepperonis on the nipples of their shirtless bodies, or make album art for the "band" that Michael and Josh had, 'Dragons R Cool, Seriously.' Which was just the two of them screaming into a tinny sounding $9 mic from his video game headset in his bathroom, but it begged for epic album art. Not only was I unaware that this skill was an entire major in school, but I had no idea that thousands of people moved to Los Angeles to pursue it.
Up until now, just thinking about learning the Adobe suite made me feel sick with guilt, because the computer I learned it on was a computer I always felt I should have returned; my mom bought it for me back in the trailer, during a particularly terrible manic episode that also saw her purchase seven satellite dishes from QVC. I returned the dishes while she slept, fearful that if she didn't, she'd lose her car or something. But the one thing I didn't return was the computer, all $1,500 of it. It glowed in its white box next to the front door of the trailer under a pile of clothes for weeks before I could bring myself to open it up. And it was on that struggling, six-year-old computer that I attempted to scan and digitize my first skateboard graphic in Long Beach.
Which, I realize now, means that my mom helped make my career possible. That the computer was a gift, a gift that I'm thankful for, and

that I would have been able to be more thankful for if I hadn't buried the memory of it in yucky feelings for so long.

So, I guess in a way, like the early days of the blog, I am still writing for myself. To process.

A Familiar Face

"Sister!"

"SISTER!"

Liz is in my arms. My little bao bun. I am so happy to have her in Long Beach that I can hardly breathe. She gives me a giant squeeze and pulls back, sizing me up and down.

"Damn, girl. You're looking like a model."

"Oh, stop," I say, but I don't want her to. The praise pushes the hunger away.

"Seriously. What's your secret?" She gushes, plopping down on the couch.

"Cancer." I shrug. "Are you all moved in?"

"Yeah, bro! The place is nice but Stephanie's annoying me already."

Stephanie, Liz's new roommate, is an older girl we knew in Naples. A friend of a friend, someone who wanted to mix up her life by moving across the country without a real plan, the same way that Liz did.

"Where's Logan?" Liz asks, nodding towards the coordinated furniture in our apartment.

"He's traveling—he won't be back for a couple weeks. You want wine or something?" I shout over my shoulder, walking to the fridge.

As I do, I glance over at today's sticky note. *50, 30, 42.*

"Alright, classy!"

When Logan comes back, he does not come back to his usual big-tee-wearing, messy-haired couch potato, or his little stay-at-home-but-also-work-multiple-jobs-wifey. He comes back to a Florida girl—two of them—sipping wine and scream-laughing over some story about some person from some place that he's never heard of. And he doesn't like it.

He doesn't show it right away, of course. It's a slow process, sort of like how it took him a year and a half before he finally told me he didn't like my tattoos. It starts with him being annoyed that I don't answer every single one of his phone calls, his texts, in the way that I did before. It leads to his irritation that, when he is home, I'm not waiting in the kitchen like I used to be. Liz is here and we're having movie night, and he can join if he wants to. But he doesn't want to. Ever. The stability I found in Logan's rigidity, like the way he only really commented on things when he wanted them corrected, had made him seem like an adult. But these 'adult' things don't mix well with Liz. And Liz reminds him of our six-year age gap, and that reminds him of the wildness he thought he trained out of me. The wildness I thought was gone, too.

Sure, I'd stayed behind the picket fence he built around me for years, pretending that it fit, pretending that I fit into the future we were heading towards—marriage, kids, family car—but I wasn't the only one. He was pretending, too. That becomes clear to me as I'm checking my emails one day; at the top, there's a message from an address I've never seen, the name of a girl I've never met.

"Hey, this is awkward, but…"

The message is a mess of typos and misspelled words, but it's clear enough: Logan cheated on me, and this girl found out that I existed and was kind enough to look me up.

"I saw ur email on ur blog. I'm sorry about ur cancer. I never would've done this if I knew he had a gf."

I stare at the computer screen, my mouth dry. I want to say my world crumbled but instead, it settled into a knot right at the base of my neck.

I try to make sense of the mind-fuck—this was the person who told me he loved me before I went to sleep. The person who held my face in his hands every time he said goodbye. A person who made me feel precious, safe. Who wanted to take care of me, tame me—*me,* the wild girl from tour that he spent two years thinking about? He did this to *that* girl, his 'wild child,' while she was getting fucking chemo.

The only reason I didn't pack up and leave that very instant was that I didn't want to move out. I didn't want another thing on my plate. I was hurting, but I didn't know how to tell him that, or know how to have the conversation.

Thankfully, he was gone, and I had some time to figure it out.

My lips are tight when Logan comes home, when he kisses me. I say nothing. We celebrate me going into remission. We celebrate my 24th birthday. We celebrate four years together and all of his friends ask when we're getting married. He talks about kids, about moving to San Diego to the things he loves. I nod along, smiling on the outside; inside, there's a swarm of mosquitos feasting on my throat. Every inch of my being, itching.

We have a big fight before he leaves for the weekend, like we always do before he goes. He's mad that I'm going out with Liz when he's not there, is even madder when I make the obvious point that he never comes with us, even when he's home. He complains loudly about Liz when she's in our place, and she, in turn, calls him a control freak, my 'weird, lame dad.' I tell him to stop and he doesn't listen, and when I tell Liz to stop, it's with half the effort because I know she's right. When the car comes to take him to the airport, he turns to Liz.

"Don't eat any of my apples when I'm gone."

"I don't want your weird Costco apples, *bro.*" She says, middle finger raised.

Liz hasn't been eating lately either, and it has carved out her curves like a marble statue. She's not a soft hug, anymore, and more than a little bit mean.

When Logan's out the door, we line up shots on the countertop, talking.

"You're not happy, dude," she says, shaking her head. "In all the time I've been here, you've been unhappy."

"I'm not always unhappy," I mumble, tossing back a shot, wiping my mouth on the back of my hand. *100 calories*, I think. Then, "I'm just tired of fighting."

"What's the difference?" She asks.

I sigh. I know she's right.

"What am I gonna do?" I ask, gesturing around the living room. "Leave?"

Liz shrugs. "He's gone, isn't he?"

It's immature, I know, but the more we talk about it, and the more I drink, packing up my shit and leaving while he's gone seems like the right thing to do. No confrontation, no conversation. We take another shot. *100.* Then, we pour another. I lift the glass to my lips, then lower it.

"He cheated on me."

Liz coughs, choking on her tequila. When she catches her breath, she's screaming.

"What the FUCK? WHAT THE ACTUAL FUCK?"

I wait for her to calm down. It takes a minute.

"You're kidding. You're fucking kidding."

"No, I'm not."

"When did you find out?! Why didn't you tell me?" Liz was pacing up and down, a chewed-up lime wedge in her hand. I tell her that the girl emailed me a month ago and she hurls it at the refrigerator.

"We're getting you the fuck out of here. *We're* getting out of here, right now. Then you're leaving. Tomorrow."

"How are we gonna move all my stuff?"

"Don't worry about that. Tonight, we're going to have us a good time. Fuck Logan."

'Fuck Logan' was the anthem of the evening, the phrase that followed every drink, every interaction. Liz was fuming, and feeling her anger, and knowing that it was on my behalf, fueled me. A group of guys came over to our table and Liz introduced me.

"This is Rachael, she's hot and her dumbass boyfriend cheated on her."

The guys laughed, offered me sympathy, drinks. I'm feeling the tequila shots, feeling good about my decision. *Maybe I'll be single for a while*, I think, looking at the crowd in the bar.

One of the guys pulls his chair close to mine so that our knees touch. I turn to look at him. He's familiar, but not.

"It was that tall sorta skinny guy, wasn't it?" He asks.

There was something nice about the smell of his aftershave mixing with the whiskey and beer in front of him, and what I was pretty sure was weed in his pocket.

"Huh?" I blink. *Focus, Rachael.*

"The asshole that cheated on you," he continues. "He's skinny. Tall."

"Oh! Yeah, he is," I shake my head, reaching for some water. "Do you know him?"

"No, I don't—I've just seen him out with you before."

"You have?" I ask.

"Well, yeah," he replies, smirking. "But I wasn't looking at *him*."

I roll my eyes, but the compliment feels good. Men like him are predictable, they lay it on thick and cheesy because they know it works. It's a recipe and I know it, so why am I falling for it? He looks like the kind of guy who enjoys making an impression, and not the good kind.

"I'm X," he says, sticking out a hand. When I take it, he hangs on. "We should hang out."

There's something wild in his eyes that is a little unsettling, but when he focuses on me, they soften. I like that. I also like the space he takes up—Logan had been tall, but he never really made me feel small or delicate. Next to X, I feel like a doll. But I also feel bigger, somehow. More dangerous.

"Follow me outside, then," I say, and he does. Which I like even more.

I light a cigarette and sit on the curb, my dress inching up my thighs— *another thing Logan would have told me to fix,* I think to myself. X lowers himself down next to me, pulling a bag of weed from inside of his pocket.

"I knew that was you," I smile.

"You smoke?" X asks, crumbling some into a blunt.

"No. Liz does."

"Well..." He trails off, lighting up and taking a couple puffs. Then, he picks up the bag and drops it into my lap. "For Liz."

"Oh, you don't have to—"

"I've got more, trust me."

I put my cigarette out on the curb and turn my body towards him. It's dark outside, and the streetlights overhead stretch his shape into an enormous shadow. His hair is almost the exact shade as the night sky, which is just distracting enough for me not to care about the handgun I'm pretty sure I see in his waistband. It's like that look in his eyes—it makes me feel bold. I reach my hand out for the blunt. A couple puffs and I feel my vision slow.

"Can you help me move out of my house tomorrow?" I ask, coughing.

"Absolutely."

Logan didn't turn up at Liz's for two days. When I met him outside, I told him I knew that he cheated. He argued with me, but not much. Not enough.

"Look, just come back, we can talk about this." He sighed, sounding annoyed, like he was trying to reason with me, like I was making a big deal out of nothing. That made me even angrier.

"Why should I?" I asked. He hung his head, looking down at his shoes, searching for an excuse. Nothing. "You don't know a fucking thing about me."

"Rach, come on."

I didn't want to cry, but I couldn't help it. I'd been going through so much inside, so much alone, that the tears were welling, pooling, spilling down my face. Anxiety about money, about our relationship, the stress of starving myself—we were here, and I had to say my piece.

"I have an eating disorder. Can't you see that? Haven't you *noticed*?"

"What? No, you don't." He looked so certain as he said it that it made me laugh.

"Oh my *god*. I am so done with you. Don't ever talk to me again."

"You're making a huge mistake," he called out after me, and I slammed the door in his face.

The View From the Tower

Allow me to introduce my next mistake. X.

Everyone has an ex, but not everyone has an *X*.

An X is a start and a finish, a guaranteed implosion, an ex in the making. Big, Unpredictable. Unruly. But I felt safe when I was standing behind him, shielded by his hulking body, his handgun, an inner circle with a few Crips, some Boston white trash and their guns, too. The inside looking out wasn't so bad. But now, I don't like to mention that we knew each other at all because it feels a lot like playing with fire, and I try not to do that anymore.

Before I was scared, I was enchanted. He looked like the last bulldog picked in the litter; square jaw, large puppy eyes, a scowl. I didn't actually find him physically attractive, but when he fixed his gaze on me, moved his scary body close so that it could be held by mine, I lost myself. Liz said X 'Rapunzeled' me. I didn't know what she meant in the moment, but once it was out there, it followed me, and I knew she was right. Wherever we went, X stood right there to make sure that no one came close to me, but positioned himself so that they could see, so they could admire me. *His.* Shielded by the tower of his body, the tattoos climbing up his neck like poison ivy, all the way up to his temple. There was a vein there that would swell when he was angry. It filled my chest with something—was it pride?

What is it in us that wants to tame the bad boy? Is it just to prove that we can? We're fed these stories from childhood: the princess and her pet beast, the rabid monster that can only be calmed by her touch. What is the function of it all, other than to set us up for a lifetime of wanting what we shouldn't? I mean, I was the bad one once. Logan tried to tame me, and once he did, he got bored. I knew the same thing would happen with X, but I vowed to get out before that stage.

Anyways, fairytales are fucked up.

All I wanted was to feel reckless, carefree. It was obvious: I'd been stagnant all that time with Logan, and wanted to get up to no good. X was as bad as it got—all of the bartenders who saw us together told me so. They told me to stay away. All that did was bring me closer to his side and my hemlines up a few inches, daring men to hit on me because, guess what? I'm safe. You say one thing to me, and I'll sic my dog on you. He's half the remedy I've been wanting, waiting for. I'm no longer the little girl with no one to look out for her at home, or the stringy teenager

175

getting pushed around by creeps. I'm tiny princess. I'm precious slut. He compliments me constantly and I'm ingesting every word, feeling bigger, better.

I don't stop to think why it is that I allow a man to do this for me. Why his eyes do to my body what mine can't, why his words inflate my confidence while mine just seem to drag me down. Introspection is pain. I pour a full bottle of wine in a big 7-11 cup and wait for him to pick me up.

Free Market

When you fuck thugs, thugs become your social group, and in the periphery of that social group, you have your seedy, low-level hustlers, tweakers, ██████████████████████. People who swim at the heels of bigger fish, hoping for scraps they can sell on their own, but sometimes too high on too many scraps to remember to do this.

Liz and I had big plans for ourselves, and those plans didn't include staying in this circle, but we liked their hustle. Everyone was selling something, and the fact was that they all had big plans, too. Sometimes, we worried to each other that we weren't so different from them, that maybe it wouldn't be as easy to leave them behind as we thought.

In a way, we were right. We *weren't* that different.

Liz and I have been stuck on where we got the drugs for long time. So, I am going to tell the story the way I remember it.

What I remember is being in the skate bar with our crew when some small guy in an extra-large shirt gave us a big bag of cocaine. A bag large enough to send us both to jail for a while.

"What is it?" I asked, looking at the crumpled plastic.

"Coke."

The small guy shrugged, but it barely made his triple-XL shirt move "What's it for?"

He shrugged again, smiling with the remaining teeth he had.

"Whatever you want, man," he spat. He was faded, fading further, and the whole thing felt like a trap.

I opened the corner of my mouth to try and whisper to Liz, but she held a finger to her lips, gears turning. Eventually, she held out her hand. And the guy just walked away.

"*Liz!*" I nearly screamed.

The large bag was filled with medium sandwich bags filled with even smaller baggies, each one, white and measured. Nine medium bags total. Before she could make any more decisions, I obediently took the bag from Liz and walked over to X.

"Where'd you get this?" He asked, shocked but cool, leaning back in his barstool so it slightly propped against the wall.

"That guy over there," I said worriedly, motioning over to where the wiry little guy was standing with his back to us, completely moved on.

"That dude's a tweaker, it's probably just baking soda. You should get rid of it," he said.

X wasn't the type to get messed up with someone else's shit. At the time, he was trying to wash money through an online poker app, and was therefore pretty preoccupied with his own agenda.

"Well, why the fuck did he give it to us?" Liz asked, indignant.

"Liz, look at you. You both look like coke heads with your bones sticking all out. He was probably trying to buy a date."

I liked when X talked about my bones, when he validated my hard work. And I knew Liz liked it too—it was harder for her to get there.

"Okay, yeah, we should just toss it. I don't want any weird tweakers hanging around us," I said, making a move towards the door. There was a trash can in the alley that seemed like a good place to toss it, but as I stepped forward, X caught my wrist..

"Where you going?" He asked.

"To toss this in the dumpster around back."

"That guy's not going to remember you tomorrow, girls." He waited as if we were supposed to know what he was going to say next, but when our blank faces gave him nothing he said, "Look, don't you two have rent to pay?"

The cash from nine baggies of maybe-cocaine was good, but it wasn't rent. Still, we sold it off the next night to girls in the bathroom as they primped in the mirror for a price we made up, getting rid of the entire stash. No matter how long you've lived in L.A., you're rarely in a position to pass up money—I was still paying off my hospital bills, and Liz hadn't found a stable job yet. We pinkie promised each other never to do it ourselves and that it would only be until the bag ran out, but that was before we met Joe Snow—a nickname like a business card. He was a designer shoe salesman at Neiman Marcus who, of all places to deal coke, dealt right out of the store. All you had to do was ask to try on a certain pair, and you'd get back a shoebox filled with coke. Liz and I paid him a visit, and our enterprise grew just a little.

X, of course, found this hilarious. And I liked making him laugh.

Just a Little Under the Tongue

Of all of the things X loved, he loved to watch me eat. To him, I think it was a sign that I was letting loose, revealing myself. A person reserved especially for him. He knew how I clung to my calories, my cabbage soup, my cups of warm water. Getting me into a sticky booth at some cheap diner was like foreplay; I could feel his desire as I hunched over a plate of onion rings, the strap of my push-up bra slipping down my knotty shoulder. For me, it was less about making him happy and more about giving into the danger of breaking my own rules.

But after a few mornings of anxious muttering, watching the scale climb upwards mere fractions of a pound, X provided a remedy. Not for the disorder, but for our late night snacks.

For no reason at all, X was training to be an amateur MMA fighter, or whatever came closest to it. It was a very 2010 thing for people on the cusp of Orange County to do, if for no other reason than to look and act violent. X spent most of his nights with me, but when we weren't together, he was down at the gym, scabbing his knuckles.

"Here," he said to me one afternoon, a smile on his face. He held out a paper bag. "For my supermodel."

I rolled my eyes.

In the bag was A tangle of syringes. A few vials of clear liquid. What was he trying to put me on?

"What is this!?" I asked, throwing the bag back at him.

"Clenbuterol," he laughed. He brought a syringe over to me.

"Clen what?" I lifted up the vial, examining it. The label was written in Sharpie, smeared. Prescribed by a lock-doc, a back-of-the-gym steroid slinger.

"It's a weight loss drug," he explained. "A few of the guys I've been training with started to use it a week ago and they've already dropped a weight class."

I looked at him skeptically. Anything with a needle is a different caliber of drug, much more than a diet pill.

"Don't steroids give you chest hair or something?" I asked him in what I hoped was my smallest, cutest voice, hoping to make no connection to the same me who'd been plucking two black chest hairs since 1998.

"It's no big deal," he shrugged. I didn't know if he meant this about the drugs, growing chest hair, or having a few more join the two that he'd possibly already seen.

"But…it's a needle."

Even people with 'fun drug' experience know better than to fuck with needles. I was years away from sobriety, but my problems were, will be, and *are* with drinking, never drugs. I mean fine, yeah, I had broken the pinkie swear and dipped my fingernail into the small baggies but the high wasn't really for me. But needles were an absolute no.

"You don't inject," X smiled, shaking his head. "It looks scary, but if we just twist the needle off after you measure, you can squirt it under your tongue. No big deal."

I must've still looked hesitant, because he pulled me in for a hug.

"I just want you to eat onion rings with me."

A faux injection. It felt doable. And it was one of the many things that X encouraged me, whether directly or indirectly, to do. Danger wrapped in care, risk dressed in concern.

X walked me up the stairs with my hand in his, sat down on the couch. He handed me his phone.

"Have you seen this pic?"

It was a photo of two celebrity socialites, their wiry arms looped together as they left a red carpet event. Their collarbones are shadowy, etched into their bronzed skin, the hipbones jutting out of their designer gowns as much an accessory as the diamonds hanging from their ears.

"There's a rumor they're using Clen," he said. He inserted one of the needles into the vial and drew out the liquid. "A little too much but, you know, we just won't overdo it."

I stared down at their faces. Two socialites having a night out. The image is better than the one I have of a locker room drug deal in a dingy Long Beach fight gym. X showed me how to snap the needle off, then left the full syringe on the coffee table.

"I gotta go. Let me know how it feels."

"Thanks, babe."

I carried the Clen in my bag for three days before I squirted it under my tongue. By the next morning, I was feeling over the moon, high, jittery. No hunger. Two days later, I was down three pounds and was eating my first sandwich in two-and-a-half years, happily chowing down while the other Bambi-legged models snacked on their fingernails, watching me eat between go-sees with their mouths hanging open. Later that week, I sold them two syringes for what I would make in four days.

Liz and I stock up on something a little better than pickles and $3 Trader Joe's wine and sit slumped around the island at her place with Stephanie, with a plastic half-gallon of $17 vodka between us. A few of Stephanie's friends are over, and Liz is less than thrilled with their company.

"Let's take shots."

The Clen is working, but it's mixing something nasty with the egg replacer, laxatives and booze in my stomach. Laxatives are the furthest thing from a secret in the modeling world, the ugly truly disgusting side, but they are also expensive, and even though I'm booking more work than ever, I still don't have the kind of cash that could pay for Metamucil. I had been standing in CVS, weighing out the best method for shoplifting laxatives *and* Diet Coke under a t-shirt when I saw *it*. Carbonated magnesium citrate drinks, four for a dollar. In cherry *and* lemon. I was so hungry that I was actually excited to put something flavored in my body, and I'd been drinking one a day ever since.

I hike up my shorts and walk from girl to girl, handing out shots in glasses that haven't been washed since the night before.

"Do we have any chaser?" One of the girls asks.

"You've got legs, ho—" Liz starts, but I cut her off.

"I have something!"

I go into my bag and unscrew a bottle of my bubbly laxatives. Stephanie takes it from my hands.

"What is this?"

"It's technically a laxative," I tell her. "But it tastes really good. And we only need a sip, right?"

"Is it safe?" She asks, raising her eyebrows.

Stephanie was health-conscious, the kind of person who went to farmer's markets for her lettuce. But, like the rest of the girls we knew in Long Beach, she doesn't need a chapter to herself because she was as fleeting a fixture in my life as the tattoo of her name that I got on my leg. She was timid, always skirting around what she actually wanted to say. Two days after I started crashing with her and Liz, she told me it wasn't healthy to eat egg replacer instead of real egg—half the calories, zero flavor. And she was always coming up to me to ask if I was feeling okay. I only drunkenly got her name tattooed because she seemed like she needed someone in her corner.

"Worst case scenario, we shit. Right?" I ask the room.

The other girls are in. In fact, they're *too* in.

"I wish I had known about this stuff!"

"Oh my god, we're gonna be so skinny."

"Thanks, Rach!"

Stephanie grabs my wrist as I head back to the kitchen.

"You shouldn't do this again," she says, lowering her voice.

Stephanie is right. But when she and the other girls look back into their hand mirrors, I turn and mix a pinkish drink of my own: half a cup of laxatives, a few shots of vodka. I take a gulp, feeling the carbonation burn my throat, the vodka fumes rising into my nostrils. The smell is achingly familiar; my eyes water, and for a second, I consider letting them go. Letting the tears fall, leaning into the anxiety, the sadness. *What should I be doing, Stephanie?* The drink is a reminder I don't want, and it leads to all the others—I haven't thought about my mom in months. I don't want to think about my body. I don't want to be anxious about money.

"Just drink," I smile, more to me than her.

181

The Side Effects

Okay, so *yeah*. The Clen *was* making me really edgy, as speed tends to do to anyone. Between Liz and I almost getting into a physical fight in the street because she lost my purse at a dude's house, and me screaming at Stephanie in a famously L.A. restaurant that served bugs on toast, I knew I was in too deep. I would never hit Liz, so I knew I had to cut back on the Clen. And as I tapered off, I knew I had to do the same to X. There was just too much darkness there, and I knew I could do better than hanging around a trap house, wondering whose hook up brought in the MRSA everyone was afraid of getting from the couch.

But it was hard to extract myself.

"You should get a Tumblr. All the hot girls are on Tumblr."

I'm smoking weed on X's bedroom floor with my laptop in my lap, praying that I can get stoned enough to forget that he just called me his girlfriend in front of his friends. We've talked about it a thousand times, but he doesn't take the fucking hint. Or, doesn't want to.

"What's a Tumblr?" I ask, coughing.

"A blog, I guess. But with more pictures. I bet you could make money on there."

"Money?"

X shrugged. "I don't know how. But here, let's see if we can sync up your posts to a Tumblr."

X is good with computers. In a matter of minutes, he has a Steak Tooth account set up with all of my previous posts.

"What are those?" I ask him, pointing to the screen.

"Hashtags. People use them to find stuff they're into."

"So, what do I hashtag?"

"Whatever you're writing about. You could put art, cancer—anything."

I add a few hashtags to my posts, just to get a feel for the site. Then, I look at the clock on the screen.

"Shit, I should probably go."

"Where?" He asks. It's incredible how quickly his tone can change, his face can fall. His eyes look black in their sockets. Empty. It makes the ink on the side of his face stand out.

"Home. Where else?"

"Why don't you sleep here?"

"I—"

182

"You don't want to be with me, do you?"

His voice has gone cold. It makes the hairs on the back of my neck stand up, and I feel my high disappear.

"That isn't true," I say. "But I'm also not *with* you. We're not dating." I avoid looking at his face by putting my computer into my backpack.

"I'll leak your pictures," he snaps.

I pull my backpack on and cross my arms in front of my chest. Even though I'm standing and he's still in bed, he looks like a giant. My skin is prickling, but I know better.

"What fucking pictures?"

"Nudes."

"I've never sent you any."

He doesn't blink, not even once. I roll my eyes and make my way to the door, but he bounds out of bed, putting his hand on the knob before I can turn it.

"I'm sorry."

I don't reply. I'm very aware of how small my head is compared to his shoulder, which I barely reach. This is where the tiny princess charade ends. This is where his size doesn't protect me. In this room, I am defenseless.

"Say you forgive me, Rach."

I take a deep breath, hold it, and feel it stream from my nostrils.

"I forgive you."

I give myself a few days without him. To cool off, to forget. When I finally agree to meet him for lunch, he picks me up with a big smile on his face, a grocery bag in his lap. I slide into the passenger seat, the elastic waistband of my Forever21 skirt digging into my skin. X plants a kiss on my mouth, squeezing my leg.

"I missed you," he says, pulling away. He waits for me to say the same.

"Missed you," I say, quietly. Satisfied, he passes me the bag. "What's this?"

"Open it."

I do as I'm told. Inside is another stash of Clenbuterol, and a white box. I lift it up, flipping it over. There's a small apple on the front.

"It's the iPhone," he smiles. "They're brand new. I got us a plan and everything."

A phone plan seemed oddly off the radar for him.

"What? I mean, *wow*, but—this is too much."

"Do you like it?"

"I love it, but the price—"

"Don't worry about it," he says, putting the car in drive.

When we get to the restaurant we stay in the car. X helps me set up my phone, shows me where I can go to look for apps.

"Look, they have everything on here. Facebook, Tumblr—whatever you want."

I download a few, and flip open my crappy old cellphone, starting to add phone numbers.

"You don't need all those," he says, taking the iPhone.

"What? Yes I do!"

"Just me, Liz, your mom, boom," he has the contacts screen open, adds his number. Next to it, he puts a <3.

"You're corny," I say, taking the phone back. X looks out the dashboard and waves to someone, then unbuckles his seatbelt.

"We gotta get going, come on."

"Are—are we meeting someone?" I put the iPhone in my purse, confused. He doesn't respond, just tells me to hurry.

"Come on."

There, underneath the awning, is a gray-haired woman with a pair of glasses on her nose. She waves frantically, beaming as we approach.

Yes, people. He conned me into a lunch with his mother. How does this happen to a person? How? *How?!* I don't mean how did this happen to me—that part is obvious. What I'm asking is, how does a man convince himself that the girl who won't let him call her his girlfriend, who he just recently threatened with nonexistent naked blackmail, would want to go to lunch with his mother? A woman who, in just ten seconds, reveals that he has been sharing a *different* side of the story with his family.

"My baby!" She cries, and X walks over with his arms open, scooping her in for a hug. I may look like a child next to him, but she looks like a toddler. When they break away, she reaches for me, bracelets on her wrists clattering.

"And look at you, Rachael! Honey, your girlfriend is *beautiful.* Why didn't you tell me? I would've dressed nicer."

"She's kidding," he smiles, kissing me on the top of my head.

"I am, I am. It's all he ever talks about, my son," she smiles, pinching my cheek. "Lovely to meet you. Just lovely."

"It—it's nice to meet you, too."

There's no point in trying to catch X's eye. He knows that I won't be rude in front of his mother. He opens the door, shepherding us inside. And though he talks about me for almost the entire lunch, he never once looks at me. I give his mom a hug when we leave and sit silently in the car. The iPhone in my purse feels heavy.

"I knew she'd like you," he smiles as he turns on the stereo.

I don't respond. He keeps talking.

"She's already asked me what she should get you for Christmas. I told her I don't even know if you'll be here or in Florida or what but she's still going to get you something. She's so happy, like, just to have a girl she can shop for. Me and my brothers haven't exactly brought too many—"

I tune him out, let him go. He's still jabbering on as I pull out my phone; when I unlock the screen, there is a red icon floating above the Tumblr app. It says 267.

"What's this mean?" I ask, interrupting him.

"Huh?"

"The red button. What does it mean?"

"Oh, fuck! Those are your notifications!"

I open the app, scrolling through my inbox. Hundreds of responses, questions, flirtations. From posts that I made when I first got diagnosed with cancer, to my drawings, pictures of myself, pictures that I liked, playlists. *What the hell?*

"See? I was right! You're a Tumblr girl now!"

I kiss him when he drops me off, head buzzing. *267.* The ridiculous lunch is behind me and this, whatever it is, is in front of me. I feel high.

"You'll call me later?" He asks, yelling after me.

I give him a thumbs up, my head still arched over the screen in my palm.

Costco Lunch

Hey, Rachael, I just wanted to say thank you for talking about your diagnosis...

I just lost my mom to cancer and ur posts helped a lot...

Ur hot haha post more pics!

How do I get a job at a record label?

Coolest performance u saw?

What's it like to be a model?

I don't have enough time in the day. To respond, to post, to share. The questions and comments keep pouring in, and the followers are adding up every day. Unlocking my phone after an afternoon at the Juicy offices brings in a dozen new questions. By the time I go to bed at night, I have a twenty more followers than I did when I woke up.

"Bro, you're blowing *up*!" Liz says, pointing to my phone. We're sitting in the Costco parking lot, an assortment of free samples spread in front of us on the center console.

"It's so weird. I don't get it."

"It's the internet, dude. It's a weird ass place," she shrugs, trading her mini corndogs for a tray of popcorn chicken.

"No kidding. Someone asked me to send them pictures of my feet."

"Eeeew! What the fuck?!"

"I know, so gross. I just wish I knew what to do with it, you know?"

So far, X was wrong. I hadn't made any money, and we had our Costco lunch to prove it. The day after Rodger and I broke up, I realized that I still had his membership card, and with very *very* little money, an apartment with no air conditioner, and an afternoon to kill, Liz and I decided to drive over to Costco. We must have looked on the verge of collapse that day, because the first time we went in together, floating not twice but three times over to the guy with the microwave pot sticker samples, we were let in on Costco's best kept secret.

"You know, if you ask for the whole sample, I have to give it to you," the sample guy muttered.

"What?" I asked, pausing in my attempt to stab the dumpling with the dull plastic fork.

"It's Costco policy. You say you like it so much that you want the whole thing, and we give it to you. We have to. I figured you guys would be into that since you come here a lot."

Liz and I looked at each other and burst into laughter. It was either that or cry at the fact that we'd been surviving off of these little samples for weeks.

My phone buzzes in my pocket, I put down my plate and scroll.

I feel like I actually know you, someone wrote. *I swear, we'd be best friends in real life.*

I read this one loud to Liz with an egg roll sticking out of my mouth like a cigar. Giving people life advice, talking, or broadcasting at all with a sample-sized Costco lunch because that's all we can do to survive, feels fraudulent.

"Just keep talking about yourself, man," Liz says. "They love that shit."

"Why, though?"

"Why anything?" Liz shrugs, ending the conversation.

And when I look down at my phone, I see all of the people waiting for me, for my advice. My perspective. Answers to their problems. They wanted to know if their boyfriend was cheating on them. They wanted to know the weirdest experience I'd ever had on tour, the craziest sex, the biggest fight. They didn't know I was broken and broke—they just wanted some place to be heard. So, I gave that to them, because it took me all of two minutes to do so before I had to tap back into my reality.

All this heart wrenching, world crumbling, kick your knees out from under you type shit that you're going through, have gone through, will go through... has an expiration date. A time limit. Every single thing: jobs, besties, college or not?, boys..every drama that shapes your mood for the month..it won't mean a thing in a year at. all. So take them as an opportunity to figure out who you are, what you like and what you don't. You may feel stuck now..but you're not. Tomorrow(ish) you could be a completely different person if you feel like it.

Pink Starbursts

"Vegas on a weekday is a hood rich activity," Gabe says from the back seat.

We drink in the car on the ride over, passing cups, drink in the lobby of our shabby hotel, on the strip but off the map. Just me, Liz, X and one of his friends, a guy that would be shot dead in a year or two from gang violence. Liz is still affected by his death, and it reminds me I don't think about these people, or this chapter, much at all anymore. But that's jumping ahead to a time when X and I will be *done* done; tonight, we are Bonnie and Clyde, Bonnie with her ass cheeks hanging out of her dress because the cheap material is so slippery that it hikes up with every breath she takes. Clyde, with a couple thousand cash in a Supreme duffel bag, ready to spend. A lot to some, nothing to others. It was a lot to me. I'm role playing my actual life.

I swallow my free drinks and play the slots. Roll dice down a craps table. Liz and I scream 'seven!' until our throats burn, or maybe that's just the cigarettes, the cancer soaked into the carpet and chairs of the casino. SEVEN. SEVEN. SEVEN!

One more drink then strip club, someone says.

Okay, I'm gonna go to the bathroom.

I come back and find my drink still sitting at the slot machine. X hands me two rolls of quarters and says 'knock yourself out.'

Something does. It beats the money to the punch. I'm sliding off the stool, my head spinning with the numbers, drooping, slurring. *Where are you where are you where are you* I say but my lips won't move. I hit the carpet and it feels like his hoodie, soft. *Here you are! I'm in your arms.*

He lifts me up.

"What did you do to her?" Liz is yelling. "What's going on?"

"I didn't do anything. She must be drunk," he says. I hear him through his ribcage.

"No, man. No. This ain't right. Rach, can you hear me? Rachael? *Rach?*"

Blink, blink. That's all I can do.

"I'll bring her to bed."

"I'm coming, too—"

"No, man. Come on. We're having fun, right? Stay here!"

"I've got her, Liz."

188

"Text me. Text me as soon as she's up."

I'm loose, limp. Ragdoll. I feel my knees bumping together, cold skin touching cold skin, head bobbing along with my big man's strides. I can't keep my eyes open. Fucked up like this, I don't mind him touching me.

He lays me down on a mattress. Lifts my feet and takes off my shoes. Pulls my dress off over my head. The sheets are scratchy against my naked body.

"Wake me up if you need anything," he says. He kisses my head.

My head sinks into the clumpy feather pillow. My mind follows.

AND THEN I'M UP.

Where am I? What's going on? Who's here? I flap an arm around the bed but don't feel anything, don't make contact. *X? Liz? Where'd you go? Can I go, too?*

I push myself out of bed by windmilling my legs to the ground. My noodle body follows. I fight for each step as I slam into the wall, sliding along it, hoping the doorknob will catch me me. It does. It hurts.

Whoever was watching the security cameras in the hotel that night knew what I was thinking before I did. They knew where I was going. They saw a naked girl walk out of her hotel room towards one of the many elevators. Likely not the first to do this, and certainly not the last, but then, the Vegas factor hits. Sleazy hotel off the strip, naked woman hardly able to walk, alone. Something sinister, likely at play.

I smack my hand against the biggest button. CASINO. It's then that I remember the drink. *What was in that thing?* I don't like it. I want the fog to go away.

The elevator doors open. For one blinding second, I am reeling under the overhead lights, tingling with the chime of the slots, the whir of the roulette, pushing through a cloud from a chubby cigar. Then, *swoop.* Someone wraps me in one of those scratchy gray emergency blankets and I'm whisked to an office near the lobby before too many gamblers can ogle my stringy naked body.

"What is your name?"

"Rachael."

"Where is your room?"

"I don't know."

"Who are you with?"

"X."

"Last name?"

"I forget."

Questions, questions. They find X somewhere on the registry and call him downstairs. He's in basketball shorts, no shirt. He's been looking for me, and his face looks panicked. They ask me twice if I'm sure this is who I'm with—if they only knew the weight of this question for us—and he has to give them his I.D., answer a bunch of questions about me. When they're satisfied, they let me go back upstairs with him. He deadbolts the door just in case.

We drive back to L.A. at five in the morning. Half-drunk, or in my case, half-drunk-and-drugged, the spectacle of it all overshadowing the fact that someone tried to date rape me. In fact, X tells the story with a smile on his face.

"So many people must have seen you, you're out of control!" X says with pride, thinking about me with the elevator doors wide open.

Yeah, I am *out of control*, I think to myself without spending a second more examining how I feel about that. Whether it's a good thing, whether I like it or not, or even like who I am anymore. Or, if I ever have.

We get McDonald's breakfast, laughing into the drive-thru microphone. Laugh through our McMuffins and dollar coffee, laugh as we drive through the desert and into the city. And you know what? I went to work that day. Because that's what you do when trauma is your backbone.

Liquid Lunch

I see his shirt first.

"Hey!" I yell, drunk at noon. "I have that shirt."

Everyone in his booth turns; he looks up from his chicken fingers. "Yeah?"

He has big goofy hair and blue eyes. Night and day from the guy whose bed I most recently woke up in.

"Yeah. It looks better on me," I smirk. I push a strand of hair behind my ear, straightening my snapback.

"Well, yeah, I bet it does," he says. "What's your name?"

I shake my head, duck back down in my seat. This place is always crowded, and I can usually find someone like me, someone hungover or still drunk or just careless enough to spend their paycheck day drinking during the work week. It's how I've made a lot of my friends in Long Beach, and today, it's how I convinced Jeff to skip out of the Podium offices for a liquid lunch—something I learned about from him.

I'm riding a high. I told X never to talk to me again, which means there's a 50/50 chance I'll see him Friday and we'll get into a screaming bar fight and end up having sex in the bathroom, but I'm betting on myself. Single Rachael. Single Rachael has just conned her way into a made-up position called "fit and consult," which means I'm making $200 an hour to stand still but *also* talk about the clothes, making suggestions on what could be improved, asking what fabrics are being used. It's been fun to see my suggestions come together, but I daydream about the dresses I'd make if it was *my* investment money to spend. Which sounds insane when I say it out loud, but also feels strangely possible? Like, this is a city of hustlers. And I just pulled off a pretty major fake-it-til-you-make-it.

"You want another drink?" I ask Jeff. He nods, gesturing with his thumb behind him.

"That guy looks familiar."

I shrug, pushing myself out from my seat. I go to the bar and order a double gin and tonic and a Jack and coke.

"And a couple maraschino cherries," I add. "Just on a plate."

I go back to our table and pop one of the cherries into my mouth. The syrup runs down my tongue and my stomach rumbles a disgruntled "thank you" for the semi-sustenance.

"I swear, I know him from something," Jeff says again.

"Go ask him, then."

"No way. I'm not you."

"Chicken shit," I smirk.

"Asshole," he replies.

I get up on my knees so that I can see over Jeff's head. Behind him, Curly-Q and his friends are sipping sodas instead of beers, having an actual discussion over an actual meal. But as soon as my face floats above the crowd, his eyes are back on me. Very blue.

"Who are you?" I ask.

He looks surprised by me. *Aren't bar brats universal?*

"You won't tell me your name but I'm supposed to tell you mine?"

"Yep."

"I'm Blake."

"Cool," I say, sliding back down into my booth. I hear him laugh.

"He's Blake," I tell Jeff, who shrugs and stares at the T.V. behind my head, some game on the screen.

I finish my drink, twisting cherry stems around my fingers like tiny rings. My hands are shaky from either the booze or low blood sugar. Either way, another round will fix it.

Blake comes over to our table as he's leaving.

"See you around. Maybe we can match next time," he says.

I realize as he's turning that I don't want him to go. I blurt out the first thing that comes to mind.

"Follow me on Twitter!"

Unexpected Expectations

"you haven't answered any of my questions so I'm going to assume you hate me"
are they dumb? why don't you try asking again.

"how do you keep yourself going when everything you're working for seems to be falling apart around you? I don't know if you've had exactly that happen so basically...how do you motivate yourself when everything in your head is telling you to just give up? I've been having a lot of these days/moments lately and it's getting harder and harder to push through."
I call my best friend and freak the fuck out.. I usually cry...or scream or both. Then once she assures my everything is ok.. I try to remember that a (insert time frame here) ago I probably had something equally as stressful or tragic happen to me but look at me now. At the time that stress probably felt like the end of the world (it did) and now I cant even really remember it or why I stressed so much.. I feel like this happens in cycles through out life. Really you have no other choice BUT to push through .. unless you're planning on sitting in a dark room for the rest of your life? I dunno, I guess sometimes that sounds cool too.. you can sit in a darkroom for awhile.. but you've gotta come out eventually. I mean, how else will you get snacks?

"Does it take you awhile to think out your responses to questions? Because every single one of your answers is perfect and they usually always have me laughing. Teach me how to be witty :(haha."
I'm drunk :{ sometimes I edit them in the morning because I have too many typos. Are they witty? I feel like I water them down to be more real. What I type is how I actually feel about each one, but I only take about 2 minutes MAX to think and type them out. I could be funnier but it'd be less real. I'm stoked if you're laughin though. BOOM still got it. *dances*

"how do u stay so skinny?? recipes PLZ"
...These questions were harder to answer. And I avoided them by typing my raw meals out word-for-word, reading the recipes my nutritionist gave me, knowing full well that I should never share what I was *actually* doing. That is, cutting the portion size into quarters.

"you get over someone by getting under someone else?!! YAY OR

193

NAY"

AGE PLEASE. NO FUCKING IF ITS UNSAFE OK (but yeah, really thats the only way)

I'm over X. Over over over. I want to block his number but I'm scared of what he'll do, so I just respond to one out of every fifteen messages that he sends me. Some of them are sweet, filled with *I miss you*'s and *please come back*'s. Others, threats.

Fuck you you cunt bitch. I will kill the next guy u fuck.
I know where to find you and all your bitch friends
I'll be fucking your girls in a matter of time. Just wait.

The thing of it is, I know he won't do anything to me personally. But he is already fucking Stephanie—which just goes to show how much *she* actually gave a shit, and what kind of revenge-seeking-psycho X actually was. But it didn't make me feel any of the things he hoped—I mean, I didn't feel anything. I wonder if I'm lost, I wonder if I'm broken. Or, if this is strength. If I said I wanted X back he'd be over in ten seconds, eager to pretend none of those other texts ever happened, likely to take my phone while I'm sleeping and delete them so that I'll wonder if I imagined the whole thing. He's a child, a loud child. He'll take this out on someone else, maybe kick the shit out of one of his roommates. He might come for me as one of the many anons on Tumblr that like to say I'm ugly, but he won't *actually* come for me, not as himself.

It's funny how I can detach myself from the people who troll me online. Maybe I should thank Blonde Brittany for this, or maybe it's the red wine I drink out of a coffee mug while I reply. Fans of my blog love that I reply to my haters—some of them tell me it inspires them to stick up to bullies of their own.

Is that what I'm doing? Finding my power? Is this power? Am I powerful? I *am* so fucking lost.

The Other Side of the Velvet Rope

I did an interview with *Nylon* magazine back in 2014 called "Internet Girl Rachael Finley Opens Up." They ask me how my ex and I met, and I tell them. Then, I add that we went to the planetarium on our first date.

Wouldn't that have been perfect? Wholesome science geeks ogling moon mock-ups, pressing our eyes into telescopes, walking hand in hand past the euphoric purple and blue splashes of galaxies far and wide. It's the perfect backdrop for a love story. It's the perfect place to decide my baby's name (he said it, not me). I wish we had gone there first. I wish we could have stayed there for a while, perched and protected from the rest of Los Angeles, the rest of our lives.

And I'm still a bit protective. Of me, us, what went right, what went wrong. If you came here for 'the tea,' if you're this far into the book and still waiting for a tell-all, then get fucked. It isn't happening. There are details I'm keeping to myself. Details I didn't want to share in that interview (you'll find out why very soon), details I didn't even share with my ex-husband.

So, no, we did not go to the planetarium first. That was our second date. Instead, we met outside of the W Hotel in Hollywood for a S/S fashion week party.

Until this point, I've never been on a real date, and have never *actually* dated. Which is a terrible thing to realize when you're waiting for your date in a pair of sky-high platform boots that could snap even the sturdiest of ankles, eyes following every car that pulls into the valet lot across the street. I've had drunk nights that turn into relationships, relationships that bump between dive bars and dingy diners, but never dating, and definitely no first dates. And if I had the choice, I'd be wearing something a little more me, and a little less 'the only reason you're invited to the party is because no one else can walk in the shoes we're releasing.' It makes the whole night feel borrowed, like I'm just subbing in. But if the night *does* go well, my boss booked the whole team rooms at the W.

Before I can jump that far ahead, I see his hair. He steps out of his topless Jeep and hands his keys to the valet. He's wearing a cutoff Actual Pain t-shirt, shorts, a new pair of Nike sneakers. Stylistically, a cumulation of men I have known before, which feels oddly comforting. Familiar, I guess. When he walks over to me, his eyes move to the crowd in line outside the W, the flashing cameras.

"Hey," he says, his voice going up an octave.

"Hi!"

We hug, and when we pull apart, I realize his face is so much kinder than the one I had in my head.

"I'm, uh, not wearing any sleeves."

"Oh, that's okay! There's no dress code." I say this without knowing whether it's true or not; together, we look like we've coordinated this look, a sort of fashion 'fuck you.' I smooth down my $600 skirt, a gift from the reject sample pile once-upon-a-fitting.

"Cool," he nods. As we head to the front of the line, he grabs my hand.

Something happens when he does. Or, something has been happening, but I haven't realized it yet. We're talking so easily, standing close, smiling, that I'm missing the stares and the friends nudging each other, the silence when we get into the elevator. He makes a joke and I laugh, and as I do, the sound fills the small space, ringing strangely in my ears. I look over my shoulder. A dozen eyeballs, a handful of phones, all pointed at my date. He's smiling, but the grip on my hand feels tense.

"Is that your girlfriend?" Someone blurts.

"This is Raquelle," he says.

Raquelle? RAQUELLE? Oh my god. He doesn't know my name. I look into his face, hoping that my sudden shock goes unnoticed. This really *is* a first date. And we have two competing forces bashing into each other in this rectangle of space: he doesn't know my name because he's only ever seen it written online, and everybody on this elevator seems to know his.

"Do you know them?" I ask, lowering my voice.

"Oh, uh, not really."

He probably though I was an idiot for asking, but in my mind, his 100k Twitter followers didn't seem much weirder than my Tumblr followers, and I haven't had cable or television for 10 years.

We reach the top floor and I pull him out, frantically scanning the rooftop for signs of my coworkers. This isn't my first Hollywood fashion party; I've been bopping around them on random weekends with Liz in tow, but I can't for the life of me figure out why this one feels *different.* Blake is thinking that I must live at these types of events, but neither of us say what's on our minds. The pool is glowing bright blue, its edges squared off and divided by velvet ropes, separating one category of invitees from another. Top tier, all-access guests with private seating and bottomless drinks, and the rest of the crowd. Then, I see my boss's secretary standing under one of the white-curtained cabanas, looking conspicuously middle-aged and out of place—the one person I actually expected to cling to during the night, since nobody at the office ever paid much attention to either of us. Blake and I weave through the jungle of cologne and liquor, and as we do, my boss looks up from his conversation, splayed on one of the pool lounge chairs. He sits bolt upright, eyes wide.

"Rachael! *Rach!* Over here!"

We walk over to join him, each of us stunned with the other; he's never addressed me, and he never expected me to walk in with someone like my date, who I hope has heard my actual name and will make a mental note never to call me Raquelle in the future.

"Girl, this outfit! You look *amazing*. Let's grab you drinks."

I get it now. The weirdness, the newness. As my boss snaps his finger and a girl in a uniform appears at his elbow, I understand. This isn't about me—it's about my date. And walking in with him, holding his hand, has leveled me up in a way I didn't foresee.

The waitress arrives, smiling into our faces.

"What can I get you?" She asks.

We order, and when she leaves, I angle myself so that my body is pointing to Blake, edging out everyone around us. I want to get back to where we were before the stares. I want my romance. Desperately. He seems almost immune to the general buzz that follows him—a little unsettled, maybe, like he wants it to wear off—but he's focused on me. We're almost finished with our second round of drinks when my boss taps me on the shoulder.

"Come on! It's time for dinner!"

Blake takes my hand and we walk around to a private seating area on the other end of the roof, separated from the rest of the guests by walls of glass. I try not to focus on the people pressing in on the wall behind our seats; we're dining inside of a fishbowl, the exclusivity and extravagance of the event on full display for those just inches away from the top tier, a pane of glass away. When our plates are set in front of us—beautiful tiny food with sauces spread like a makeup palette left in a hot car—I think about what Liz and our friends are doing, probably passing around a jug of Carlo Rossi and playing drinking games. Would they be allowed in this room? Or, kept outside? I don't even know how I'm going to begin to explain this date. I turn and look into his smiling face.

"You want another drink?"

"Actually, I have an early call time tomorrow," he says, finishing the rest of his beer. "So I should probably get going soon."

"Oh, for sure," I say quickly, wanting to seem equally as responsible, but also wanting to secure my place in his memory. The date has to end with a kiss. "I should probably go too. Get to bed."

It's a lie—I have every intention of staying after he leaves. Nothing sounds better than crawling into my hotel bed full of fancy wine and sleeping until noon the next day in clean sheets. But I couldn't meet his responsibility with that, so I pretended I should go, too.

"No, you should stay with your friends!"

"No, really," I shake my head, feeling the wine slosh around behind my eyes, mixing with a hint of panic, my old self digging her heels in. I need a kiss, or it's like this never happened. No kiss, and no more dates. He'll be gone and I'll be alone again. I want my fucking romance. "I'll walk you out."

"You didn't have to come down with me," he says, but I can tell that he's happy that I did. He doesn't seem new to stuff like this, but he

197

doesn't seem entirely at ease, either. And I like that about him. I like that he tightens his grip on my fingers when we push past the people in the lobby.

"This was really fun," he says. "Thanks for inviting me."

"I'm glad we could finally meet up."

"Me too."

We both look at each other, smiling. Then, we lean. The kiss. My whole body relaxes.

YOU DID IT!!!! My heart screams. *A DATE! AN ALMOST NORMAL ONE!!!!*

I'm speechless, sputtering inside. And hugely relieved when he says something first.

"I'll text you tomorrow," he says, stepping back. When he does, I wish that I could leave, too. I want to go. I want to step back from the night and replay the success and normalcy of it in my head, to turn it on my tongue like candy.

Instead, I wave and watch him drive off. Then, I head back upstairs, unseen and unnoticed by the people who were staring just moments before. I am unrecognizable without him, not worth recognizing.

"Rachael, thank fucking *god* you're back." My boss says, rolling his eyes. More attitude now that my famous date is gone, but still addressing me directly. He's holding out my phone. "This thing would not stop ringing. It was, like, totally killing the vibes."

"Sorry," I say, walking over and taking it. I have multiple missed calls from a strange number, very long and unfamiliar.

"I tried to answer but I couldn't hear them. Maybe it's a scam call."

"Thanks," I tell him, walking into the corner of the room and lifting the phone to my ear. Other than *Finley,* I can't hear the message over the music. As I leave the fishbowl and walk to the emergency stairs, they call me again.

"Hello. Is this *Rachelle*?"

The voice is unfamiliar—they hurry over my name and trip on the extra letter, their accent new to me. I cup my hand around the phone, hoping that they can't hear the *bum-bum-bum* of the bass thudding behind me.

"This is Rachael. Who's calling?"

"This is Dr._____ from the Royal Hospital in the Kingdom of Bahrain, calling on behalf of Donna Finley, American teacher."

Mom? I sit down on the stairs, my legs feeling weak.

"This is her daughter. What's going on?"

"Your mother has fallen ill," says the man. "She is under a medical coma."

"Why? What happened? Is she going to be okay?"

"Allah will protect her."

"What?" I ask, loudly. "I said, *is my mom going to be okay?*"

"It is the will of Allah."

"Let me talk to someone else," I tell him. The bass is knocking into my head like a hammer, and my heart is climbing into my throat.

"The care of Donna Finley is—"

"PUT SOMEONE ELSE ON THE PHONE."

My own volume surprises me, echoing in the concrete stairwell. Another voice comes on the line, but they say the same thing. Absolutely nothing at all.

Everything is crashing down, and my heart is aching from the rebound—high-high to lowest of lows.

I don't know what I have at home that will help me, but I need to get there. Maybe I can get on my computer, find someone to email, get in touch with Mom's program or something. I think I have a letter somewhere in my inbox, a piece of paper tucked away somewhere. Whatever this is, whatever is going on with her, there's something in the way. Language, culture, religion. I barge out of the stairs into the glass room.

"Is everything okay?" My boss asks.

"No, there's—I just got a call about my mom. She's in the hospital."

"Where? Cedars?"

"No, no. She's in the Middle East. Bahrain. I have to go—"

"You can't just leave. Sit down."

He's right. I'm a little buzzed, maybe drunk. He snaps his fingers again. This time, a different waitress appears.

"She needs a shot of espresso in a cup of coffee. Got it?"

The order is filled at an impossible speed. I take a sip of the hot drink and feel it coat my throat, bitter and thick. Wine brain and caffeine jitters collide with adrenaline, and when I stand up, the room goes in and out of focus, like a camera lens closing. Pre-panic. I need to run.

"Stay the night in your room and go tomorrow—"

"Thanks for everything. Bye."

I don't know how I get to the parking garage. Stairs? Elevator? But I'm there and my feet are somehow leading me to my car, retracing my steps from hours ago. I unlock the door and find my seat. And once I do, I'm screaming. With every ounce of strength in my body, every cell bent over the steering wheel. Roaring into the black space. There's a pressure building inside of me; I grab the iced coffee left in the console and squeeze it so hard that it pops in my hand and spills cold coffee all down my lap. I want the plastic to break. I want it to slice through my hand. I scream even louder. I scream at my mom for going there, scream at myself for telling her to. I scream because she's hard to help, because nobody helps me, because nothing is ever easy or right or fair and my life is one big panic marked by smaller ones.

Then, all I have is my breath in my ears. It sounds rough, like the palms scraping Mom's old bedroom window, the only company I had when I was curled in her bed, waiting for her to come home. Now, I have to go to her. I have to bring her home.

My fingers are locked around the steering wheel. I speed through traffic, changing lanes, flooring it so I can make every yellow. Then, freeway. Everything is yellow. Then, black. Yellow, black. Headlights, no lights. Black night. I am not in my body. I am floating somewhere above the car, watching it move. I only return to myself in time to see my exit, but I'm moving too fast, so I do what I'd seen Logan do a dozen times, cruising in his old Datsun. I hear his voice.

"The best feeling in the world...Pulling the brake and flying."

I yank the emergency brake. My car jerks like it's attached to a string, and I spin haphazardly along the exit, tires squealing. It's a split second of weightlessness, and not nearly as artful as Logan's spins, but I make it, halting to a stop at the red light.

Then, blue lights. A cop car.

"Will you accept the charges?"

"FISH!"

"FUCKING BITCH!"

"SHUT THE FUCK UP, STUPID ASS FISH."

My face is encrusted with salt. Salty, thick, and rough from pleading my case. Now, I'm cold and shivering. They're telling me to stop shaking but I can't. I can't focus, can't breathe, can't speak. They lead me down a hallway, past the screaming voices, to an empty cell. Open, then closed. The lights are out, the guards are pacing, and every last freckle on my skin is frozen.

They keep it cold so that the germs can't live on any of the surfaces, and all of the surfaces are made of metal. Cold toilet, cot. You feel like a germ in here. The blanket is a sheet. I have a rash on my thighs from where I spilled the coffee, which has dried into a crust on my miniskirt. My knees are knocking into each other like teeth, chattering. When I try to cry, it rips my throat.

Jail is a pit. The bottom of a blackhole. The underside of a bruise. People are screaming because they've been here for weeks, unable to post bail, waiting to get a court date. They're screaming because they can't see anyone, but they can hear every footstep, every new entry, every door unlocking. They're cold and they're hurt and they're scared, and that does something to you. Maybe you come in broken, maybe you don't. But when you leave, you won't be whole. Jail makes sure of that.

I'm certain that my mom is dead. I have no reason to believe that she isn't. There are so many reasons a person can be in a coma, and a person like my mom, once so strong, is now fragile, alone, in a strange place with different customs where the doctors can't discuss death. I don't know that it's against their religion. I assume it's because she's already gone. And every word that's said to me, unkind and unfeeling, makes me want to go, too.

"Is that fucking *scabies*?" Shouts the female guard when the lights come on, her face pinched, repulsed. She's maybe thirty years old, but the sour air and the metallic lights make her look gray all over.

"It's a rash," I mutter. "I spilled on myself."

"Fucking scabies *trash*," she says over me.

The officers that pulled me over thought I peed myself, now I have this woman accusing me of having scabies. I wish that I had pants, but I won't get a jumpsuit for 24 more hours. I stare at my feet; they're bruised and blistered from the boots, but the concrete floor is so cold that it's better to suffer in the shoes than without. In that moment, the humor of wearing a designer outfit in a jail cell is lost on me, but every so often I see that skirt in my closet and grimace.

Breakfast is pushed under the door. Peanut butter and jelly sandwich, apple, whole milk. I turn my nose up, reaching for the apple. But then a voice echoes from somewhere down the chamber.

"No point counting calories *here.*"

My eyes grow wide. Can someone see me? Did they see me come in? Or is disordered eating just so prototypical-L.A. that even the inmates starve themselves? I feel a sob in my chest and grab the sandwich, shoving it into my mouth. When it's gone, I chug the milk and chew the apple until the core is as thin as my thumb. It's the most calories I've consumed in a single sitting in years.

When it's my turn to make calls, I dial the only number I have memorized. Liz doesn't answer calls from unknown numbers, and I kick myself for not knowing anyone else's. Then, the guards instruct me to choose a bail bonds number from the list next to the phone. I call the first name on the list, and they tell me I'll need someone to send them $3,300.

I get to call Liz again six hours later. This time, she answers. I want to cry when I hear her voice, and feel the icy phone rattling against my cheek as I tell her that I'm in jail and that my mom might be dead. I tell her about pulling the brake and the yelling and my feet in these stupid boots.

"She's all alone and it's all my fault and I have to get out of here. I have to, now," I stammer, gripping the phone so tightly that I hope she can feel me squeezing her hand.

"It's okay, Rachael. We'll figure it out." Liz is the only person I've ever believed when they say this, to this day.

But neither of us have money. Not enough, anyway. My mind reels through the list of contacts in my head, people I could tell, someone that could help. Then, I imagine telling Logan where I am and what happened. I can picture his face, the disappointment, the judgment. He seems like the only adult that can fix this, but I don't want to go there.

"We won't tell Logan," Liz says, reading my mind.

"Two more minutes," the guard shouts over my shoulder. I jump, shuddering.

"Who do we ask?"

"I think you know who we have to—"

"There's no one else?"

"I'll ask around, but I think he's the best choice."

I go back to my cell with my shoulders hunched, hugging myself to keep from shivering. I lay back down and walk through everything that happened after I got pulled over. The way the officers asked me if I'd been drinking, then saw the stain. How I lifted my skirt to the window and told them to smell it—just coffee, I swear!—and the way that they'd laughed.

"My mom is in the hospital, I'm just trying to get home to help her."

"And why did you do that? With your brakes?" One of the officers asked, pointing to the skid marks on the road just behind me.

"For, uh, fun I guess?" It sounded insane and I knew it. I've never had a logical answer, not for a single second of my life.

"You're going to the hospital to see your mom, and you pull a stunt like that for fun," he repeated.

"No, she's in Bahrain."

They exchanged a smile with one another, and for a second, I thought they might help me. That if I went down to the station with them, they could somehow use their ties with the law to get in touch with the hospital in Bahrain and spring my mom out.

They didn't.

Here's the thing about getting a DUI in California. Or, more interestingly, the way cops will try to trick you into blowing above the legal limit. When I first got pulled over, they asked if I'd been drinking. I told them that I had, just not much. When I blew, it was a .07, which is still within the legal limit. But a lot of police officers in California will suggest that there might be something wrong with the machine and ask if you wouldn't mind coming down to the station and using the breathalyzer there. I didn't know it at the time, but alcohol levels rise before they plummet. And while they said it would take a minute, it would actually buy the officers 30 minutes, which meant that there was about a 99.9% chance that the second breathalyzer test would be higher than the first. I mean, I don't know the *real* math, but you get it. This isn't to say that I shouldn't have been pulled over—I should not have been driving. I was in a serious panic, having an out-of-fucking-body experience, and taking the wheel was the wrong choice. But my rational brain left the moment I left the stairwell, and my responsibility to my mom—those ties I couldn't sever, those survival instincts we'd built around each other—kicked in. At the same time, if I *hadn't* agreed to blow a second time, they would've taken my license right then and there. I went with them to the station, and I'm glad I did, because doing so is what made the judge rule in my favor and throw out the DUI, because my first blow was legal and they should not have asked me to do it again.

I wouldn't wish my experience on anyone. Not the worry, the constant anguish of wondering whether your mom is dead, the torture of being unable to get in touch with her. Not the jail cell, the cold, harsh, inhumane way you're treated inside. None of it. I spent four nights in there feeling lower than I ever thought possible, like I'd broken a promise to every person that had every done me a kindness, every friend that had ever known me. A lifetime of disappointments screaming in my ears.

Then, I was out.

"There she is."

X. He'd been out of the state for work, but when he got back and saw Liz's message on one of his many burner phones, he drove over in 20 minutes. I shivered a new shiver, a shame shiver.

A shiver of defeat.

His arms were spread open for a hug. Behind him, a police officer printed out a form for me to sign. He collected a stack of papers for my court date; I avoided the hug by grabbing the paperwork, keeping my eyes ducked as we walked out the doors. I could feel the excitement pouring from his skin, felt the pressure of his sly smile from the corner of my eye. Outside, I turned to face him.

"Welcome to the club," he laughed, pulling me towards him. I leaned against his chest, stiff as a piece of plywood. He mistook my disgust with myself for needing him as disgust over the DUI.

"Hey, hey. Don't get so down. Come on, we'll go get Red Robin. Onion rings? I know you're hungry."

"I have to go get my car."

"You have to eat, too."

"I can't. I'm going to book a flight," I said, standing next to his car. The plan I hatched in jail, illuminated under the parking lot lights. "I'm leaving as soon as I can."

He clenched his jaw, driving to my place in silence. But my mind is loud, jumping like a song on a scratched CD, half-formed thoughts ramming into each other, tangled. I don't have the energy for anything else.

When he stopped the car, he stared at me seriously.

"Look, just come home with me."

"I'll get you the money as soon as I can," I tell him, unbuckling. "Thanks for your help."

He put his hand on mine, stopping me. It wasn't tender; it was heavy, rough. I knew that if I moved, he'd push down harder.

"I don't give a shit what you do. Okay? I don't."

Right.

"I'll get you your money," I snapped. Then, I shut the door.

Persian Gulf, Age 24

We stiffed our landlord to pay X back and pooled the rest of our money for two plane tickets. There were probably more urgent uses for that money, but I'd be damned if I could think of one better than getting him out of my life.

People glare at Liz and I on the flight. They don't like how we're dressed, how our hair and skin is exposed. Passengers push past us when we land, shoving. Now when I travel, I read up on the customs of every country, their body language, etiquette. But I didn't have the time or the foresight to do all of that—Liz and I had never traveled internationally before, had no idea what to expect. I wasn't able to get ahold of the hospital again because of time zones, but I had the first voicemail they left me telling me that Mom was in a coma, and nothing but hope that she would still be breathing by the time we arrived. The flight was a calm and sullen 16 hours, broken up by jolts of movement from when the Klonopin Liz bought from her kitchen manager wore off. Liz had dropped three in my hand as we took off, telling me to ration them however I wanted to. Right away, I chewed two with no water.

"I don't know how or why you insist on taking pills like that," Liz said to my empty head. Her voice sounds like it's coming from inside of a paper towel tube.

"Sometimes, I just like to feel every part of things. You know, before I don't," I thought I responded. Instead, I just passed out.

I'm high when we land, eyelids struggling to fight the sedation. Bahrain in 2010 was experiencing what the airport T.V.s called 'civil unrest,' so as we make our way to the terminal exit, we're met by a group of armed guards, hired by the embassy to escort us to and from Mom's apartment to the airport.

"You are not to travel without them," a private official told us. Then, he took us and our guards into a private screening room. Liz and I exchanged panicked looks, each of us wondering what my mom was actually up to, whether her job was legit. An eastern world wake-up-call for two clueless westerners. We almost reacted when they took our phones, but almost as quickly as they'd snatched them from our hands, they had placed a chip in the back. When they were done, our phones were working, able to make and take calls.

"You will call this number when you need to leave the campus, and whenever you need a ride back."

As we drove away from the airport, Liz and I stared out the windows. Seeing the blistered red and gold landscape, the Mars-like miles and miles of sand dunes and desert stretches.

There were no trees anywhere, not until we got to the gated campus, which had a green lawn and decorative palms arranged between the buildings. If there hadn't been for the armed guards poised at the entrance, the international school could've been mistaken for a campus in Florida.

When we got up to Mom's apartment building, we were taken aback. For one, it was entirely made of marble, like the most lavish suite at the Caesar's Palace hotel. Countertops, floors, walls, all the same yellow-gold marble. Marble toilets, marble camels, marble paperweights in marble bowls on marble console tables on each end of the marble hallways. It was like this country was begging its inhabitants to use the stuff in any way that they could, and while it came off as extravagant, it felt uncomfortable, and nothing like home. It could have been a palace if it weren't for Mom's trademark Rubbermaid tubs stacked on every available surface, her papers cluttered, teetering. As we walked through the apartment and put down our things, I lost count of how many boxes she'd accumulated; when she'd left Florida, she told me she only had one large suitcase. How had she amassed so much since then?

The embassy brought us food and told us to stay inside for the night, that we would be able to go to the hospital to see Mom in the morning. But shortly after they left, once the sun had fallen in the sky, we heard something erupting outside. Shouts, chants, the sound of destruction. We pressed our faces against the windows, going from room to room, but we could see nothing.

"Should we—?" Liz asked.

"Absolutely."

We ran down the stairs to the campus lawn, bolting towards the front gates. We stood there in silence, watching breathlessly from the shadows as a sea of protestors stormed down Bahrain's central street, flipping dumpsters and smashing cars in their wake. They sprayed paint on all of the surrounding windows and walls, tagging the dusty streets with black and red lettering. They marched on for some time, until all that was left behind were empty paint cans and broken glass, streets littered with garbage. And by the time we woke up the next morning, waiting for our car, their words and the walls had all been painted over. Glass windows had been replaced, and garbage swept away. As if their demonstration, and all of the feelings that fueled it, didn't exist at all. And that's how it was meant to feel. Erased.

I floated down the hospital hallway into Mom's room. She was laying there, open-eyed, looking up. I was afraid to enter, afraid she was stuck like that, but when I stepped forward, she moved her head towards me. Her face and arms were covered with liver spots, sweaty skin, a sickly yellow color, like she'd just been rubbed in olive oil. I looked at Liz standing in the doorway, and we both finally took a real breath. This had all been a misunderstanding. Our eyes agreed not to listen to anyone else in this hospital again.

I approached my mom's side, pulling up a chair. As I got closer, I could hear her voice. Weak, soft, tired.

"You're...here?"

"Mom!"

I held onto her hand to stop mine from shaking. The surface of her palm was slick, bumpy. She had raised red rashes in odd patches across her body.

"You won't believe...the craziest thing..."

"I know, Mom. Your liver, it's—"

"No, no. I fell out of a *plane*, Rach. Fell right out the bottom."

She lifted a drooping arm, miming a drop to Earth, her flat palm colliding with the scratchy hospital sheet. Liz looked at me, her eyebrows raised. She looked worried, but I felt my shoulders slope, the tightness in my stomach unraveling.

This is just like the mice, right? This is just my mom.

"Right, well, now that you're here," I turned behind us to the open door, where I could see some of the hospital staff. None of them looked in our direction, not once. Even when I'd addressed the doctor directly, he'd averted his gaze.

Mom closed her mouth. Her bulging yellow eyes started to droop.

"I hit the water," she muttered.

"I know," I smiled.

Memory. *That's* what I had to rely on. Not doctors, not the hospital. Not my family. Just memory. I knew my mom better than anyone else. Nobody knew her like I did. Nobody knew what she was capable of pushing through. She'd beat cancer by herself, hadn't she? Delivered a baby with a broken body. I was here, now. We were going to make it.

She was asleep. I leaned down to her ear.

"We're going to come back tomorrow."

Every day was the same. Wake up and have breakfast delivered. Get into the SUV with the guards, stare at their guns. Walk into the hospital, have everyone stare at us. Talk to the doctors, learn nothing. Hold Mom's hand. Awake, asleep, awake, asleep. Talk to the doctors again, still nothing. Go to the apartment, respond to Mom's family's emails with nothing. Tell myself this is normal. Have dinner delivered. Sleep. Repeat.

The hospital staff didn't ask me any questions, whether we were safe, how we felt, or even how Mom was feeling. Every word was a directive, a fact, nothing more. To this day, I'm still not entirely up to speed on the relationship between Islam and healthcare in Bahrain. But what I do know is that any time I asked what was going to happen next, or how long to expect her to be in the hospital, or whether or not I should leave or stay, the doctors told me the same thing. "It is the will of Allah."

Until, finally, on our last day in Bahrain, a nurse spoke to me. I didn't catch much of what was said, only that I needed to either sign or not sign something called a DNR.

My eyes darted over to Liz, who shrugged.

"Do I, um, do you need me to sign it?"

"It is your choice," the nurse said robotically. "But it must be done before your departure."

"What does it mean? If I sign it, what will that do?"

The way it was explained to me was that if Mom went braindead, they wouldn't keep her hooked up on a machine. And that, to me, sounded right. I looked at her in the bed; she was telling Liz what channel she wanted the T.V. turned to. Her eyes were yellow, but they were focused. She wasn't talking about falling out the sky anymore. She was, from where I stood, improving.

I nodded. "I'll sign it."

It was pages long, entirely written in Arabic. Even if there had been someone around who could translate it for me, I felt confident that I didn't need to. I didn't want my mom to be on a machine for the rest of her life. If something happened...I pushed the thought out.

"Make the plan with the doctors" Liz suggested, pushing the thought out, too.

We would wait until her systems were stable enough for her to travel, then she'd get on a flight to Miami. Mom's program director suggested I take a few things back with me from her apartment so that she'd have them after she left; the rest, she said, would be taken care of by the school.

After I signed the paper, Liz stayed back in the hallway so that I could say goodbye to my mom. The day before she'd been chatting, scolding Liz and I for not following the instructions on the face cream we'd found in her bathroom. We'd burned both of our faces because we left it on for too long, and when she narrowed her eyes at us, I could see *her* behind the yellow skin.

"Can't you two read?" She exclaimed loudly like we were the two biggest idiots she'd ever come across.

Now, Mom's eyelids were lowering as I slid onto the edge of her bed. Her body was hot; I could feel the warmth radiating from underneath her blankets before I even leaned down. I touched her arm, moved my hand up to her cheeks. Bloated and taunt from the steroids they'd been pumping her with, hard in the wrong places. Ten years earlier, she would've cringed if she'd seen herself in a mirror, the grown out gray patches, the bare nails and lips.

I remembered one time when she'd drove us both to the hospital when I was nine, and she'd looked into the rearview mirror and reapplied her lipstick before staggering out the door, dry heaving. I forced myself to smile. I told both of us that I'd get her back to that place, maybe not the picture of health, but the old picture of herself. Happier. The two of us, together. I'd try to convince her to sell the trailer and come to California. I'd try to be patient.

I'd forgive and forget.

Nobody Told Me

After I went to jail, my car never made it out of impound; like I said, there might have been better uses for the money we scrounged up, but I couldn't think of one at the time. I took the bus to all of my fit jobs, head pounding, constantly looking down at my cell phone so that I wouldn't miss a call from the hospital.

Blake—or, Bully, as I called him—had no idea about my arrest. And I kept it that way because I *needed* a good distraction, although he often wondered out loud where I went that week or so after our date.

I was desperately focused on inching back towards the normalcy. A relationship bright, shiny, and unscathed. Back towards that moment, that kiss outside the W, when we were finally alone.

It was difficult, almost impossible, to get there. I spoke on the phone with the hospital nearly every day, asking how she was, checking in. We'd plan for one flight to Miami, then have to change it a few days later when progress wasn't being made, and every time we did, I'd have more papers to fill out, more forms to sign, more calls to make with doctors, airlines, ambassadors, her program director. But the people in charge of her care never made me feel like this was abnormal, and neither did anyone else. The contact with Mom's family felt weird and distant, and though I'd wondered where they'd been and why they didn't help, I didn't want to get into it, not while I was working on getting her home. When I'd told Grandma what was going on, she didn't seem shocked. And every time I updated her, her responses were the same.

Just get it handled.
We'll wait and see.
Maybe the next flight.

My mom died on December 3rd, 2011, just two months after I'd been in Bahrain.

Southern Live Oak

One day after you died, a relative I hadn't spoken to in ten years called my phone to remind me that I shouldn't expect inheritance from Grandma because she paid thousands of dollars to cover your medical bills, to bring your ashes home. The tone in her voice was curt, just as I had always remembered it. Just as you always said she was. I was just shocked that she gave me a call at all; she wanted to remind me of the things we did, that made us difficult to love, and I listened, just to know, to get the clarity they never gave you after they froze you out.

The ashes, Mom. I'm so sorry. We've been reciting the plans for your body since I can remember. One-third of your ashes, you said, were to be buried under a big Florida oak tree. The biggest I could find. And if I couldn't find one, or, find one that I was allowed to dig beneath, you said I should plant one myself, right on top of the dust of your bones.

The other third, you said, you wanted in the ocean. You loved the ocean, but you never really saw it. So, I was to wade out into the water and spread you out in the waves, watch you float down to the bottom to become part of the silky-soft sand. That way, I could come back to you. I could feel you beneath my feet.

And the final piece of you, you said, was for me.

That's why it hurts, Mom. It hurts to say, even in my head. Even on a page, ten years later. That *they* took the ashes. That I wasn't invited to the funeral. That the funeral wasn't what you wanted. That Grandma called and all she could say to me was, "We're having a little ceremony tomorrow, but you don't have to bother coming. It's nothing, really."

I didn't think they had you, I didn't think the ashes were even stateside. But they put you in a plot, with a family name on it, like the good Catholics they are.

"I've always had this grave paid for," Grandma said. Then, about the oak, "There's a big tree close by, anyway."

A few weeks later, I got a card for the ceremony in the mail, along with a CD of photos. It looked like more than "nothing really." And more than I could have offered you.

You talked about death so easily, so frequently, that I wonder if you knew what was going on underneath your skin. I kind of hope that you did. If anyone deserved to know how they were going to die, it was you. There was so much in your life that surprised you, that you didn't know, that people didn't tell you. I wish I knew what you wanted to hear.

Nobody ever told me to go to you.

To hold you.

No one said, *take the time.*

To touch you.

To remember your face and feel the temperature of your skin.

I thought I was doing the right thing. I thought I had to handle the details. The paperwork, billing departments, organizing—nobody told me it wouldn't matter.

Nobody ever told me to call just to talk to her even though she wasn't lucid. That what she might have said wouldn't matter as much as hearing her say it. Nobody told me that I'd know nothing except pain and regret for not making that a priority, for not quitting my job to live at her bedside and just be. To make up for everything that happened. To just spend time. I didn't know I could. I didn't know. I had no one to tell me what do, seeing my mom like that.

Nobody ever told me my mom wasn't going to come home.

For all that, I'm sorry. I'm sorry and I love you.

Up and Over

"Hey!"

"Hey, how's it going?"

I'm scaling a fence, waving over my shoulder. I pull myself onto the roof. When I'm up, the neighbors give me a smile, and I give one back. Then, I jump down from the roof onto the balcony and unlatch the window. And when I leave, I go the same way.

Bully and Adam share a house. When they're gone, I sign for their packages, make appointments with the plumber, reschedule with the landscapers. I change the filter in the refrigerator and clean the lint from the dryer. I let the maids in when they get locked out. Which is funny because of the three of us, I'm the only one that doesn't have a key.

"Hey, Rach—can you make sure you let Owen in? He's coming by in two hours," Bully says, calling me from set.

For a moment, just a moment, I pause and wonder where he thinks I am, where he thinks I've been.

You never ask me to be there—I even went home this morning, just to see if you'd notice. To give you space, to see if I wanted it, too. 'Healthy space,' or whatever.

Here's my healthy space: I jumped on the bus, an hour and fifteen minutes from the east side to the Hills. And now, I'm doing it again. And once I'm there, I walk up the hill in the platform heels I wore to work because I didn't have time to switch if I was going to catch the bus. 1.8 miles up the hill, forty-five minutes walking in the sun. My calves throb; I blink away stars. At the top, I scale the mansion in three minutes, now that I've gotten the hang of it. And by the time I'm in, dabbing sweat off my cheeks, Owen is knocking. 0:00.

I don't even have the time to consider the insanity of it all, because if I did, I'd have to consider the other thoughts waiting for their moment. And I'm not doing that.

When I don't talk about it, nobody else does. Aside from Penny, Adam's mom, pulling me into a hug from the other side of the kitchen island one day, my mom's death is out of sight, mind, body.

"We weren't that close," I lie. Penny doesn't need to worry about me.

It's been a week, and my body is a cog that will rust if it freezes. Being where I have to be, and where Bully wants me to be, is a gift. Purpose.

19 Days Later

Did you know that many actors were theater kids?

I didn't. It makes total sense, though.

Think about the theater kid you went to high school with, and hold that image up side-by-side the next time you see a movie poster or red carpet. Better dressed now, thanks to the art club kids. Stylists, creatives, makeup artists—those are the people propping them up, getting the actors and actresses' clay bodies ready to be molded into whatever shape they need to be in for the industry, for the role, for the night. The most desirable hires are clay-ready and eager for a mold, excited to ditch their dorky theater days for whatever prototype—funny guy, sweetheart, heartthrob—the spotlight decides. It's even better to go in without a sticky past to pick apart, or a personality that leaves a strange mark. If you can check those boxes, then you're already every casting director, agent, and publicist's dream. Because being in the spotlight, people are going to chip away at you. And when they finally reach the center, you don't want them to find a goddamned thing. I'm not saying these theater kids don't have trauma—they've got plenty of that going around—but it's different in the way that most of them have good families, someone to call, a place to keep their stuff. They have access to college degrees and hairlessness and soft skin secrets. They are polished as they exit the kiln.

It's easy to be around people like that because nobody's issues are on display. Not in this Hollywood. I keep myself hidden behind my teeth, as hidden as I can be, so that I don't make waves.

I'm scared people will learn the darker pieces of me. More than what's on my Tumblr, anyway. Bully likes that I'm rough, wild, loud—it pairs perfectly next to him. He treats me like a black jewel, a diamond squeezed and shaped in swamp mud, under the pier with the mosquitos, in the back of a tour van, in a bar fight. I hear him say this to people at parties, and when he sees me seeing him, he rushes over and squeezes my cheeks like a fish.

"Isn't Rach cute? I love her face."

Another thing he says: he likes that I'm not fussy, because I don't ask for a drawer at his place. He doesn't know that I sourced one silently, using the hallway dresser that nobody has touched since they leased the fully furnished house. He smiles when we have parties or go to bars, likes how I take up space, how I drink, how I keep up, but I don't let it all out.

213

That's for him to do. He's the quarterback and I'm the center. A sidekick. It's the easiest role I've ever played.

Our house parties are huge. *Workaholics* cast and crew, and others from Comedy Central shows, intermingling with pro-skaters, lead singers, rappers. An Olympic athlete is beginning his relationship with an A-list model on our balcony. And Will Sasso, Will *fucking* Sasso is standing in the corner with a suit on, questioning whether he came overdressed or to the wrong address, fancy champagne bottle in his hand, Bud Lite cans at his feet. Liz is here, too, lost somewhere in the mix, telling watered-down and censored stories like I do, trying to fit in. At some point in the night, people circle around Bully and me, watching as the two of us grab catered trays of Panda Express off the counter and throw them at the wall. By the time we wake up the next morning, it will be gone; $250 and a pack of maids referred to us by someone higher on the food chain takes care of it all. Our chaos wiped away like the walls in Bahrain, the secrets of every celebrity house, scrubbed away with a sponge.

And in the middle of it all, a wild love. A want, a *need*, to stop myself by starting for him.

In our first weeks of dating, you called me your sunshine. And I called you my little black cloud, maybe because deep down I knew we were doomed, or maybe because everything was poetry then, even when you were pouty. The beginning of us. The part of a relationship where you skim past the potholes, the hiccups, the red flags. Drunk on adrenaline, drunk on $23 drinks.

We were very different from each other. It was a truth we knew but decided not to say. When someone stole the gifted Gucci wallet out of your bedroom during a party, I balled my fists in anger, stomach turning. *They came into your bedroom. Our room. Here. After drinking our beer, standing in your kitchen, talking to us.*

"They must've needed it more than I did," you said.

Innocent. I didn't fight you on it. I tried to bend my perspective, to find the positive like you did, and when I couldn't, I just stayed quiet.

Fans pushed cameras in my face when we walked together, asking for a picture. They thought you were your character, they modeled themselves after this version of 'you.' Loud, rude, fucked up. No 'please,' no 'thank you,' 'excuse me.' Just take, take, take. I'd step to the side, and the sun would shine on you. It lit up your teeth. I'd move to the back, and the lights would stay on. You couldn't say no. Your greatest fear was losing your momentum.

That's why you jumped. Drunk. Another party, five days after the last, out of hand and out of sorts. You took me to bed and kissed me on my head, told me you'd be up soon. I could hear the music thumping, the rattle of the 3 pictures on the walls. I fell asleep before you climbed up the roof, scaling the wall like I did to get in the house. But you were already on top, already the center. You just wanted to stay there, didn't you? And this was it. The big play. The wild guy from the wild show where every day is a party, every move is a dare, a middle finger. Larger than life. You leapt, and you landed on a beer pong table, directly on your spine. The whole thing filmed by a party guest, the film then sold to TMZ. Someone we trusted, someone in our house. Your pain for hire.

You got up from the table on your own. Got up and changed the fucking music. You came upstairs and went to bed, and when the light started coming through the curtains, your groans roused me from sleep. You couldn't move. I found your phone and called your dad, and he told us to go to the hospital. And after we got there, and the x-rays were taken, and the painkillers poured in, they told us that you broke your back. Centimeters away from full paralysis. My mom had been dead for 12 days, and here I was in a hospital. I tried not think of her in the same sort of room, dying alone, dying abandoned, but you made it hard.

"I hate you," you said.

It was a voice that wasn't yours. You looked at your dad.

"Get her out of here. Get her out. *Now.*"

And your dad, the salesman. He walked me out of the room and pitched me on something no one should ever buy.

"That's just the medicine talking. He doesn't mean it."

It was a side of you I hoped I'd never see again. I popped one chocolate chip cookie from the nurses' station into my mouth, then another, then sat down on the linoleum and waited until you were asleep. Only then did I crawl alongside you in that shaky bed, frozen until visiting hours were over.

Christmas Eve, I walked the three miles back to your house from Burbank and climbed a window into your empty house and ordered pizza for dinner. Pizza topped with pasta. Bingeing my way through the emotions. Liz was waiting at the door, ratty and mad from the hour-long bus ride, but insistent that I could not spend my first Christmas without my mom alone. I let her in and stared at the splintered pieces of the beer pong table that were piled up on the curb next to the trashcans.

Mars brought this up the other day while we were driving in the car. Her dad, jumping off the roof. For obvious reasons, I've kept her away from the full story, but when children retell stories about their parents— the wild kind, especially—they do it with the sort of pride that hurts to erase. I've turned it into a story about the dangers of drinking, and why you should always be careful with your body. But even as I repeated that line, I found myself thinking about those days in the hospital with him. Days after my mom died, hearing him tell his dad that he hated me. I'd blamed it on the morphine for so long that I didn't stop to think about the fear I'd felt, hearing his voice. Afraid to leave the hospital because I didn't have anywhere else to go. His dad looked away from him and back at me, and the sad, sort of flat-mouthed smile he gave me, and the feeling of being without a place, brought me back to my childhood.

I was at my grandmother's house. Young, without my mom. A trip way back, back when we still knew these people, so that she could work summer school to make our ends meet. I was squirming, anxious for her, anxious around her family because I knew how guarded she was around them, too. One night, my grandparents were talking in the living room; they thought my cousin and I were asleep, but we were whispering in the bedroom, listening to their conversation through the open door. We heard my name and both turned our heads towards them, and it was then that I heard my grandfather say that he always hated me. He hated that I was sneaky, said that I closed doors behind me because I was up to no good and couldn't be trusted. And there I was with my cousin, frozen in embarrassment because she was hearing this, too, and maybe because it was true. And before I knew it, I was crying, walking towards them, to the couch where they were talking. My grandfather refused to look up at me, and all my Grandma said was, "Bill, that's enough."

She grabbed me and took me back down the hallway, pushed me into the spare bedroom where I was supposed to be sleeping and shut off the lights. And nobody ever talked about it again.

It was then that I realized why my family hated me. My grandfather was the patriarch, and if he said something, you followed. His beloved Donna hadn't, and this is what happened to her. *This* child. And the flat smile that my grandmother gave me when I woke up the next morning was the only thing anyone was allowed to offer me, because that's what my grandfather decided—everyone else was just following suit. Which is why I was where I was when the man I loved told me the same thing, and I just dangled off the side of the hospital, placeless.

And to this day I still can't understand how anyone can hate a child, because even when Mars reminds me of something that hurts, even just by smiling her dad's smile or painting the rowdy behavior I have grown to despise with the heroism kids do when talking about their parents, she is still a child that can wait to learn what hate means, who needs us to be her superheroes, without any flaws.

The day after Christmas, you were tapering down your morphine and asked if anyone from the party had come to check on you, who had called. And not wanting to disappoint you, not wanting you to see the world for what it really was, a crowd of people willing to break into someone's room for a stupid Gucci wallet, but gone when he was down, I told you a lie.

"Yes, they came. So many of them. You were just asleep."

All Access

They didn't notice me until Coachella. Spring, 2012. Our first time going, first time photographed as a couple. It was him they were after, so I cut my walk slower when I saw the paparazzi come out, took a big step backwards. But no, they waved me forward, waving me next to him.

Bully reached out, grabbing me by the arm before whispering under his breath, "*Smile*."

Coachella has two separate entrances: one for regular concertgoers, and another for celebrities. Part of what makes Coachella so desirable is the celebrity attraction, and it cashes in on practically every attendee by forcing the lime-lit crowd to walk across the entire park in broad fucking daylight. It's why it's the only festival that gives you wristbands based on what level of celebrity you are. A-list, and you get invited to the side stage, away from the fans; every level down, more and more immersed in the crowd. Bull and I were front of ground, as far from A-list as you could get, and just as happy to be there. We walked where everyone else walked, and even as we did, even as people snapped photos of us, or clamored to get close to Bully, I could not wrap my head around the amount of wealth the festival goers had. What and who they were wearing, the places they were staying. Some of them wait their whole year just to take a pill and sweat in the Sahara tent next to some Disney star in a flower crown. The energy is magically intense for that reason alone, because in the middle of it all, you're feeling the expectations of these people, the reason they put up $1,300 for a single ticket.

That's the Coachella *experience*.

It's why there are hundreds of websites reporting the same 'who-wore-what-with-who' stories about Coachella all across the internet. I was dressed in all black and had purple hair; a little ass peeked out of my cutoffs. Every piece of clothing was a gift from a now-defunct fast fashion institution, a trade for submitting articles to their blog. I didn't think I was throwing on a 'look,' but together, I was the "perfect antithetic to his style, 'emerging comedian,' the grungy girl to his comic book boy." Or whatever it was they wrote. People reported on my black anti-Coachella-Coachella outfit for days on end, and by the time I got to the hotel that night, my Tumblr was exploding, a surge of non-Steak-Talk celeb junkies merging with my usual crowd. At the time, I couldn't pay much attention to it—swarms of festival goers were eating up the local cell data, and we had

13 after-parties to attend, all during the same time slots. But when I got home from the festival three days later, things that I'd shared on my blog were being reposted by Bully's fans, interpreted then re-interpreted in the completely bizarre internet way that filtered every celebrity relationship in 2012. And I wasn't prepared for it.

Industry Jargon

Other than my Tumblr inbox exploding with questions and insults, my life didn't change much after my first paparazzi. Bully's inbox, on the other hand, erupted with corporate party invites. We had officially entered the celebrity machine, ready or not.

I was still a little uncomfortable at the parties that we didn't host; I didn't realize that we'd be going three times a week, every week, for the next six years. So, I followed Bully around, feeling his nerves while trying to stifle mine, hoping to make a place for him, to say the right thing, offer my hand.

One night, we were at a party at a writer's house. I hated writers' parties. I hated being around them, outside of their conversations, watching their big, exclusive words build a fence around them and us—I guess they've got to use that degree somewhere, but seriously. If you've never been around this then maybe I'm the one sounding bitchy or elitist, but man, if you *have* experienced it, you know exactly what I'm talking about. They look down their noses when you try to nod along, judging you, using first names they know you don't know, laughing when you don't get the joke. I fucking *hate* people like that. But if you're an actor who wants to make big money, you need to get writers' credits, and when you're after writers' credits yourself, you have to schmooze in writers' circles.

So, there we were.

On one end, you have the poorly dressed, oddly shaped men with their necks arched high in order to look taller, squabbling about politics, censorship, media. On the other, wives and partners talk quietly about less controversial yet elitist subjects, assessing one other's status, privately ranking the group, joined by disgruntled women who *are* writers, but are never actually included in the writers' circle. Bully and I are sort of straddling the line, trying to stay as close to each other as we can without looking like outsiders, which we definitely do. The women are all suited in Wes Anderson-looking outfits and I'm in a $45 bandage dress; they're pontificating on which white wine they'll have next, while I take whatever the sever puts in front of me. *Spanish? French? Organic grapes?* I'm judging them as much as they are judging me, only I'm not vocalizing it (but I *do* feel enormous pressure to type, "okay, okay, not all writers" at the end of this paragraph).

"So, Rachael, Elisha says you're into fashion."

One of the husbands has left his circle, has his arm around his wife's childbearing waist. He's trying to invite me into the conversation, make me feel comfortable. It's a nice gesture that most people would read as human kindness, but one that his insecure bride can't handle.

"She's a *model*, Joel, I already told you."

Ding ding ding. There it was. The usual game. You might miss it if it hasn't already happened to you a dozen times before in educated circles, but me, I wait for it, now. There's tension in the air because this is the weird dance women do: veil criticism as a comment, wait for recipient to read between the lines. This comment is particularly intention, as it always is, because underneath the word is the subtext. Undereducated. Young. You know this because you hear them laugh off the other actors' model girlfriends when they leave.

"I'm actually a *fit* model," I blurt. "I work in garment construction."

"But the fit models don't talk, do they? I have friends in fashion design, and they told me—"

Elisha loves the idea that there are women who are unworthy of speaking at work, despite her work in the feminist-think-piece genre. A pigeonhole in and of itself.

"I actually do talk. I work in fit and consult."

The key is to answer quickly, with a smile so strong it'll break them in half. Otherwise, they'll think they've won the round.

Bored, Elisha turned away, pretending to look for an orange wine.

Really, what I would have liked to say was, *I read you loud and clear.* Five inches shorter than me, five years older. Not as certain as you'd like to be that your husband cares about brains more than beauty, that he wouldn't run off with a young thing if he was given the attention. Frumpy Joel. If we were in Long Beach, I'd step on her flat-haired head with the treads of my boot. Maybe Bully smelled trouble, or maybe he just got tired of the non-conversation he was having to push us both towards the bar. He doesn't like these types either, really. They don't know how to party.

I think he's going to tell me not to listen to them. That they're wrong. We get our drinks and he takes a long swig, looking at me.

"You shouldn't have worn that. It's causing too much attention."

He finishes the drink, grabs another, and leaves me by the bar. I watch the back of his head until I can't see it in the crowd. Every step he takes, takes me away from what he used to say. That he loves these things about me. The tarnished silver he wore proudly. That he swore he'd never change, never try to shine. But now?

My thoughts swirl on the car ride home: Bull's words, Elisha and her pack of hens, the ones I grew up with. I think about the way we're conditioned from such a young age to believe that there's only one castle, one throne. It reminds me so much of middle school, but instead of feeling broken up about the way I've been treated, or tearing into myself for the answers, I already have them. The truth about Frumpy Joel and his wife, the truth about marriages in Hollywood.

Wives come to the daytime events, girlfriends come to the afterparties.
Not only this, but I'd laughed with the other woman.

I wonder if this makes me a snake.

I wonder if that's what will happen to me one day.

Then, I remember that I'm the only one invited to both days and nights. Not that I know what to make of that, either.

When men get famous, the world opens up to them. The expectations shift, and so does the blame. They cheat, it ends up in tabloids, and people will chat over lunch dates, swapping gossip, sighing, "What did she expect?"

Shame on the woman for thinking he loved her. Shame on her for thinking she stood a chance against fame. How dare she not realize for a moment that this world is his, and she should be grateful for any scraps she is thrown. And if she attempts a career of her own, God forbid, her success will never be hers. She'd have nothing without him. Shame on her, really, for assuming she had worth, an identity, potential.

Don't think people say these things? Go read them for yourself. Comment sections, gossip blogs, fan pages.

Maybe Elisha already knew. Maybe that's why she acted the way she did.

Or, maybe she was just a bitch.

Studio City

Just us, and I feel safe. Loved.

Laying around, dreaming of cartoons we wish existed, decorating our house, filling it with insanity. Dreaming of insanity. Dancing circles around the real hardwood floors of our empty house, furniture not yet delivered. Dancing circles with our iguana on our heads. I like how simple we are when the lights are low. When I wake up with my hand tangled in your hair, like I couldn't bear to let you go from me, not even for a moment. Not even to dream.

I like to listen to our voices echo, Bull. Just you and me.

We go out and you paint your thumb nail to match mine. Black, gray, blue—the hues of those dark bars in Studio City where we go drinking alone, together. Two suckers with no self-esteem, afraid of going deep in case we find out we don't match at all. Remember when we jumped the gate at Universal Studios? We climbed to the top of the WaterWorld ride, just to lay there and laugh. We limped all the way home, bare feet scraping on the pavement, barely able to watch our steps because we kept turning to look at each other. You never tell me how you're feeling, but in those moments, I know you love me. I know that we match in more ways than nail polish.

Maybe this is my big romance. Imperfect, in ways, but definitely here.

But at some point, these nights stopped being enough. You wanted so much more than this, so much more than me. I keep trying to pinpoint the moment it happened, but I can't find it. I can't find the place.

You left me at the top of the ride with no way down.

Fluorescent Pink Sharpie

I'm pacing the house, trying to figure out what to wear to my first red carpet event. The Comedy Central Roast of Roseanne. Anxious, I call Bully.

"What are you wearing?"

"A pink shirt. It's got kittens on it."

"Okay, so..."

"It doesn't matter what you wear, as long as you match me," he says.

I hang up the phone with a smile. Back to playing sidekick.

I open the cardboard box where I have been keeping the gifted clothing sent specifically for me: three dresses total, and none match Bully's shirt.

I hate wearing dresses; I don't feel like myself in them.

Every dress I'll wear for the next six years will be gifted to me by brands who need help marketing their products. I keep them all in the box, because that's what you do with dress-up clothes. And when I go down to the garage to get something out, I'll be reminded that I'm just clay to be molded, too.

I decide on a white spandex dress I bought in Long Beach, back when I first started going to Hollywood parties. Two dresses for $85. I search the box for pink accessories, pink anything, but there's nothing. Brands don't send me anything soft—they send hard metal, chunky silver, black. They have made up who I am and matched me to their recipe. Grunge. It's on trend!

Next to where I'm digging through my box, there's a cup on the counter. Pens, markers, loose ends. I snatch a pink Sharpie highlighter and run to the bathroom. I soak my lips once, twice, six times around before the pink starts to show.

My lips are new lips. Slightly larger than in years before, thanks to yet another freebie—a little Juvéderm to lift them up at the ridge. I didn't think twice when the girl at the house party offered to do mine, figuring my natural face was full of flaws, and she would know what was best to fix me. No one ever mentioned they saw a difference, not even Bull, but now, the pink highlighter makes them jump off my face. I run my tongue over them to see if this idea will sustain the night, or if it will leak off when wet, or kill me dead right here from toxins.

I pause.

Nothing happens; the taste is oddly sweet.

Satisfied, I use my mom's old tube of pink and green mascara—you know, the one all moms use—that I haven't thrown away yet. It makes me feel like a woman when I carry it around. Next, one coat of CoverGirl foundation, thick enough to hide the freckles popping off my face, dark enough to match the tan I've accumulated, waiting for the bus in the sun. The tan hides some of the things I hate about myself, the things I see when I stand in front of Bull's ten mirrors. I hate the way I look in all of them; I turn, surveying my body, thinking how embarrassing it is that someone has seen me from that angle, this one, there. My legs are a battlefield of large, dark hair follicles, scars from a decade of shaving incorrectly, razor bumps from shaving incorrectly just yesterday.

Here I am, nude except for my pink highlighter lips, my made-up face. White dress balled up on the bed because I'm not ready to pull it on yet. When I do, it's my hundredth life. I have lived a hundred lives, but the girl standing in front of the mirror, going to her first red carpet event, is the one most people will remember. Getting here has been exhausting.

Still, I'll keep running. Do what Bull needs me to, smile how and when he wants. When we smuggle in friends from behind the fence—Tyler, Lee—and bring them onto the carpet with us, it feels more real. More like me. They put us directly in front of the stage, just to be sure the cameras would catch our faces when they panned the crowd.

Whatever that power means is lost on me. I'm wondering if anyone knows I'm wearing highlighter on my lips.

Brunch

HOW TO PARTY: SAY YES.

It doesn't matter if you're tired. Tired isn't invited. "Everyone" is, and "everyone" will be there, they tell you. Open bar. An invisible assistant orders the booze and it shows up, unpacks itself, forms an island on the countertop.

Outfits are out. You look fucking dumb. Pull something on; the less care, the better. If you still smell like last night's liquor, congrats. The air in the room covers your tracks, a sturdy concealer covers dark circles, lipstick brings the attention to your mouth, to wine-stained teeth. Good, because we're all reading lips. We can't hear over the speakers.

It's a good night when Liz comes. Nothing is too weird or too loud. Lines are being cut on the table, one, two, three. People we don't know, faces full of glitter. Long for her, short for him. Another one for her. They duck their heads down and rise back up, refreshed, like a bird that just dipped its beak in water. The drugs sustain others, but we don't need them. What we need is each other, and these nights together, me and Liz, sustain us. If this is the 'top' everyone talks about, I'm happy I get to do it with her.

We are sitting on the countertop, her bony shoulder bumping my twiggy arm. On paper, this party would look like the ones in Long Beach, but the booze is better, the stars are brighter, and nothing feels the same. It's fun to be small-town Florida girls at a Hollywood party—nostalgia fills your chest, pumps you up. *We're here! We did this!* When we say that, people think it's a chant, a manifestation, but really, we're just shocked we're both still alive.

A bug-eyed girl comes up to us, but we can't hear her. We can see her mouth moving like a rabid animal, up and down, open and closed. We climb down. The words spilling from her lips (lipstick fading, several drinks deep, maybe, or could just be from talking) are too fast to make out. She won't stop.

"Come on," I say, and we pull her into the bathroom. "What's going on?"

"*IjustImeanI'mnotsurehahahathispartywowthisissuchacrazynightIlove yougirlshahahaweshouldhangoutmoreandlikethis—*"

"Oh my fucking *god*, shut up!" Liz barks.

But the girl is coked out, high as fucking hell. Otherwise, she'd know

225

to be a little worried about the tone of Liz's voice. There's no telling if this person is happy or on the verge of a breakdown. But she's annoying as shit. That's for damn sure, and we can't get rid of her. We usually like it when the girls gather around us, talking and laughing, but when the fucked up ones do, you've gotta shake them. Otherwise, the other non-cokeheads will think you've gotten lost in the dust, too, and that's not a label you want here, despite what the white-nosed Disney star next to you might suggest. Liz and I left that in Long Beach—we are enough of a party as is.

Tipsy but not drunk, I don't have the patience. But I do have a remedy. She's still talking, holding onto my wrist, trying to tell me something that only a high person would think is important.

"Okay, uh, Liz will get you some water." I interrupt her, unclenching her fingers. I pass her hand to Liz, who sighs loudly. When they're out of the bathroom, I open the cabinet.

HOW TO PARTY: BE THE SOLUTION.

Tylenol P.M. I shake one into my palm, toss the bottle next to the sink, then go into the kitchen to grab a water. When Liz and the girl return, I hand her the pill. She wants to party harder, but it's the last thing she needs.

"Here," I say, "It's—"

She pops it in her mouth, grinning. I sigh. She doesn't care what it is. She opens her mouth: still blabbing, only now, she's hiccupping.

Fuck.

"*Great,*" Liz groans. "Now she's even more annoying."

"Maybe go get her more water, something to wash it down with," I suggest. "I'll stay with her."

I don't want her around us, but I don't want to completely ditch her, either. Not while her heart is thumping like a racehorse, not before the Tylenol offsets the stimulants so she can function normally again. Or, at least guide herself through this party.

Liz wades through the crowd. I'm watching people's feet, their shoes. Some Vans, mostly heels. I watch the feet navigate around each other, veering over spills, teetering on the flat floor.

Liz comes back. She hands me my drink, then leaves one on the side table for our friend, who has found someone else to engage with. She picks the cup up like she put it there herself. Liz and I lose it, and tumble away in a fit of laughter.

The night moves on, and we're slowly able to inch away from our cling-on, eventually able to pass her off to someone who accidentally showed interest in something she said. *Their loss.* We go upstairs to where a small group is circled on the couch, passing joints around. My eyes burn from the smoke; they act like we've been there the whole time. Easy, familiar. Nobody asking who you know or what you do or trying to make you feel dumb. It's all dumb. It's probably a weekday, but none of us live that way anymore.

"I can't believe she's not asleep—I gave her three of those P.M.s that were floating on the counter," I hear a guy say.

"Wait, who? Who did you give the Tylenol P.M. to?"

"I dunno, this girl who was acting crazy upstairs. Just wanted to save her from herself, you know? She just needs to sleep it off," he shrugs, smoke flowing out of his mouth.

"Wh-what did she look like?" I ask, knowing exactly how he's going to describe her. And when he does, panic hits me. But not Liz.

"*Dude*, I gave that girl a googly eye!" She cries, bursting into a fit of laughter.

"Oh my g—wait? What about a googly eye?" I nudge her in the chest.

"I dunno, I was searching around in my bag for a lighter and she asked me if I had any pills. I didn't, but I had this googly eye at the bottom of my purse and she ate it, man. It was the funniest fucking thing—"

"*Liz*," I mutter, poking her again. She looks at me with red eyes. "We gotta find that girl."

"Why? Let her bother someone else."

I lower my voice even more. "*I* gave her Tylenol P.M. Which means she's had, like, four."

"Shut the fuck up." Liz's eyes widen.

The truth was, the Tylenol wasn't going to kill her—I mean, I was pretty sure of that, anyway. But what had started out as a helpful idea was now running the risk of becoming a nail in some girl's coffin, and at the end of the day, no matter the many risks and stupid ideas we come up with, Liz and I are not the pieces of shit some people make us out to be. Well, maybe Liz was for letting her eat a toxic, plastic googly eye.

Just kidding, Liz.

HOW TO PARTY: DON'T LET ANYONE DIE.

We jump up from the floor and start opening every door in the house. A gang of girls in the bathroom, one crying. A couple making out on the stairs. Finally, we open the office door. The girl is inside, her short bob sticking to her face. She found a blanket somewhere and pulled it over herself. I bend down and put my hand above her nose. Little breaths. In and out.

"She's okay," I say.

Liz sinks down onto the floor next to me. Then, we erupt with laughs, clinging to each other, our fingers cold. When we regain control, she looks in her cup. "Do you need a refill?"

"Yeah."

We spend the rest of the night in that room, talking, getting drunk, taking turns feeling for a pulse. When the sun comes up, the girl rises from her blanket.

"You guys wanna go to brunch?"

"Why not?" Liz says.

The Cavity After Candy

There was a set of drawers in the Villa with handles shaped like
starfish. It was made of white painted wicker that chipped when you ran
your fingernails over it, and had nothing inside except a stale, scentless
lavender sachet. Every time I walked past it, I told myself I'd put
something inside, but I made a pile on the floor instead. We left the dresser
behind, but I keep it in my head: a set of drawers with handles shaped like
closed fists, places where I keep memories tucked away and locked up.
Airtight. Out of sight, out of mind. It's where I keep the old me, the me
that came before, the me that no one knew. The stench of my past, curled
up like a stinking stray cat, hiding behind the lavender pouch. So far, it's
working. I never think about the times that came before the now.

We were at the Dodgers game, waiting to see Bully and his castmates
throw out the first pitch. All week, I'd been complaining about my vision;
things would suddenly get wavy, like they were bouncing around on a
waterbed. Crazy curves, up and down. Me, dizzy, running out of Bully's
bedroom to throw up. I was sitting with his dad and the other girlfriends in
our seats, watching the three of them smile for photos, pose in the dugout.
Then, things got bouncy again. I almost passed out right there in my
impossibly tight white Dodgers spandex, my Dodger blue socks.

"Rach, honey, you just need a burger." His dad said, handing me a
water bottle.

"I...I don't think that's it," I stammered, head between my legs.

Bully said the same thing. So did Liz.

I didn't need a burger. I mean, I did, but really, I needed chemo.

When death knocks on your door twice, maybe you should give in, I typed
on my Tumblr one night, drinking red wine.

Then, delete, delete, *deleted.*

I don't want to bum anyone out.

I knew that I wasn't going to be able to work through my cancer.
The doctor told me that it had already started to spread to my lymph
nodes, and that we needed an immediate treatment plan. Aggressive
chemotherapy, intense radiation. He told me that it was going to be
worse this time. That if I wanted to beat this, we'd have to bring out the
big guns. As I'm hearing all of this, I'm still more afraid of the cost. I
have never *not* worked. Not since I got my first job at Chick-Fil-A. The
entire bus ride from the hospital to the hills, I calculated what I had in

228

my account, what I'd received from Mom's estate sale, the jobs I had left before treatment began. It was nowhere near enough. It had taken me years to pay off my cancer debts the first time.

I got to Bully's and climbed up the roof. I unlatched the window. I went into his bedroom and put on one of his t-shirts. I thought about screaming, curling up in a ball and crying, but then I remembered that Adam was getting a new T.V. delivered and that I needed to be downstairs to hear the doorbell. Then, Bully called.

"Hey!" He shouts. I hear the sound of traffic, of air whipping through his topless Jeep. "How did the appointment go?"

I think about saying what's on my mind. That I'm scared and unsure what to do. But instead, I take a deep breath and shout back. "Fine. I start treatment in two weeks."

"I've been thinking, you know, maybe we should get married."

Car horn. The passing static of a car radio. I think I must have misheard.

"What?"

"Married! I think we should get married!" He yells, and I can see the smile on his face, hear it in his voice. I shake my head. Violently. *No. No. No.*

"No. Absolutely not."

"Why? You can get on my insurance, not have to worry about working—"

"I don't want to get married for health insurance, Bull."

"It's not *just* for health insurance. You know that."

In all honesty, I did not. When someone calls you from their car while driving on the freeway with a thousand sounds whizzing in your ears and asks you to marry them two weeks before you're due to start chemotherapy, you do not know that you are being proposed to for more than just health insurance. I wanted romance. I wanted more.

"Let's talk about this later," I tell him.

"We're going to do it," he says, unphased. "It's the right thing."

I hung up the phone and felt one of the drawers pop open behind my forehead: a pile of my dad's clothes in the driveway, his surfboard cracked in half. I sunk to the floor and put my head between my knees.

We got married in the Los Angeles county courthouse on September 7, 2012. Him, smiling in a pair of jeans and an 80s printed button up. Me, trying to forget the fact that we just got in a fight five minutes earlier over the simple white sundress dress I was wearing, now covered in the blue-black circle skirt I'd worn for three days in jail. Don't ask me why I still have it.

"The white dress is too much," he'd said. "Too wedding. We could get photographed or something."

The dress wasn't very me, but it was free, fresh off the sample rack, and I thought It'd make him laugh.

Why even try to hide it? I could have just published the draft on my blog, because in 36 hours, someone we trust will have sold the story of our wedding to TMZ. And, with it, the story of my cancer. Bull and I will only speculate about who did it before we decide it was inevitable.

What a strange pill to swallow.

We'll spend the next few days navigating calls from friends, upset because they think we hid from them. Hurt that they weren't invited to the wedding. People wondering how sick I am.

Spending our time on these phone calls instead of living in these important days, not digesting any of the moments we should have.

Tabloids and bloggers will call Bull a hero, a man who truly embodied the spirit of "in sickness and in health. Tout him for the things he promised it wasn't *just* about. And I tried to cling to that promise, to my romance. The reason I said yes.

I told myself not to read them, to focus on getting healthy. But it got hard when the rumors started swirling, when the same people who applauded Bully for marrying a sick girl started picking me apart.

Does she even have cancer?

She still has all her hair.

She trapped him

Imagine being that desperate for attention…

I packed up their words and opened the drawer for fame.

Goliath Grouper

RACHAEL ANDERSON LIP INJECTIONS???
This is the title of a post on a celebrity take-down site that was
emailed to me by a fan. I read it from the comfy white corduroy couch
in our house while Bully was on set. At first, it made me laugh (*finally,
something gossip-worthy*), an escape from people publicly pondering my
death date. But it was the photo attached that sent me screaming into
my pillow: it was from the day before. My face tight, swollen, and round
from the steroids pumped into my body twice a week in the Cedars-
Sinai oncology ward. In fact, until this article, I didn't think I looked that
swollen at all.

I don't like to think of myself as fragile, or as the type of person that
could be broken by something so inconsequential, compared to everything
else going on in her life. But this post got me, and I buried a new type of
rage. Deep.

I wish I could have known on my first day as tabloid news. I wish
I could have seen it, that third wheel, hitching to our sides like a leech.
Every time someone talks about you, it grows, making some people swell
with pride, and crushing others with its weight. And you can't complain
about fame, because so many people want it. Bully did.

Me? I was just the girl he'd plucked out of bar fights, doomed to spend
the next six years trying to choke the parasite out. My worst enemy, his
best friend, seeping under our door. The dark, ugly shadow in the corner
of the screen during a movie. Blink, and it goes away.

Am I seeing things? Is it really that bad? I asked myself in the early days.

Now, I'm *sick*-sick of it. Sick of being sick. Of being bored in our new
home together, alone. I started photoshopping obscene, oversized pouts
onto every one of my pictures. When the publicist would ask which photos
I wanted to use for different releases, I'd send them grossly doctored
ones. Adding fuel to the fire and watching fame play its little game on
my laptop. Getting up to puke. Coming back to the couch. Reading the
comments.

I waited for someone in charge to say something, but no one ever did.
No one near me ever said anything at all. These images felt like control—
plus, if these were *real* fans, they'd know I got these injections a whole
eight months prior to my cancer diagnosis. I scoffed, yanking my mouse
down the sides of my mouth on each side until I looked a goliath grouper.
Then, I hit send.

That's Not True

Let me be clear: Fans are *fanatics*. They are, by definition, single-minded. Hungry, rabid, desperate. They don't care that you're a human being with wants and needs. They clamor around you like an angry mob, tearing at your being, fighting for the chance to touch you, look at you, scream into your face. They don't ask questions. They don't care how you're doing. They latch onto you, sometimes screaming a name that isn't even yours.

We had only been at SXSW for seven minutes before they saw us. Our hair tucked under hats, wrapped in hoodies in 87-degree heat.

A guy with a squirt gun came up to us. He had the glassy-eyed look of a person who'd spent his day drinking vodka instead of water, the designer clothes of Beverly Hills, the smirk of a frat boy.

"YO! WHAT'S UP? I KNOW YOU!" He couldn't place us, but we paused for a second to give him time, to get his picture so we could keep pushing through to our hotel.

I stepped back, waiting. But you gave me a look, telling me to come forward. As soon as I did, the fan pointed the squirt gun in my face, spraying me with lukewarm water.

"Stop," I said. My voice was stern. You squeezed my wrist. A hard grip telling me to soften.

He squirted me again. A stupid smirk sprawled across his face.

"Dude. Cut that shit out."

People started to gather around us; we knew we could only wait a moment or two longer before the crowd became too thick to escape. I often wonder why we didn't have security for times like these, but then remember the promise we made to never come off as too good for people, even as our stars started shooting. Not to ever place ourselves above them. But then, shit like this would happen, and I would feel like I was slipping below.

I wiped my hands on my face and saw my mascara on my palms. *Great*, I thought. *Now people are going to report about me crying at SXSW.*

"Enough," I spat.

"Relaaaaaax, bitch," he said, squirting his gun over my shoulder, inches from my head. "I just want a picture."

"Me too!" Yelled four others, excited for the moment. These people knew exactly who we were.

"Fucking stop or you're not getting anything."

"*Rach,*" you said, teeth clenched, smiling for someone else.

My ears were ringing. People like this want the same thing, the same smile. I tell myself it's the last picture. Then, I'm getting us out of here.

I held my hand out for his camera, waiting.

Squirt.

I didn't think. I swung, open palmed, upward. His goofy, drunk body swayed, the squirt gun was airborne—then, both fell. You grabbed me by the elbow and pulled me away, hopeful that the crowds of people, the other flashing cameras and famous faces, distracted from the confused man on the grass. When you decided we were far enough from my crime, you threw my arm back to my side. Your face was hot with rage.

"What the *fuck* is wrong with you? What the actual FUCK?"

You kept your voice low. Some indie band was playing in the background. A girl behind your shoulder was pointing at your back; she recognized you by the hair that made it out of your hat. We have only a few seconds before they walk over, then it's back to our roles.

"He wouldn't stop. I told him over and over—"

"It doesn't matter! You can't do that to them!"

My voice started to break as I realized that it wasn't us against them. Not at all.

"But he wouldn't listen. I told him—"

You felt them closing in on us, so you took my hand. Squeezing tight. You said, *"Leave that shit behind in Long Beach."*

But you forgot to ask if I was okay.

"Hey, Rach? Do you think you could just photoshop a Psyduck on here? I feel like I can't find anything I want."

Bull had been in a fit since we got home from SXSW, scouring the internet for t-shirt gold for his wardrobe—his *T.V.* wardrobe. He has always liked wild shirts, so his character did, too (I guess I can't entirely blame his fan base for not seeing the difference between their Bully and mine).

I looked up from the couch—he had an electric blue tee pulled up on his laptop.

The Psyduck shirt took ten minutes, but we spent the rest of the evening sitting leg-to-leg, laughing, drawing shirts. We needed this, and we both knew it. It's never just us anymore; we have a team of people around us and when we don't, our house is filled with friends. Every hour is spoken for: work, promo, parties, "mandatory, career-making events," packed houses.

I try to make the most of days on the mansion couch when I'm alone, recovering from treatment. I've never rested like this, never even pumped the brakes. Plus, the expensive fabric on the couch leaves slightly less painful indents on my skin than my Long Beach sofa had, 20 hours of laying down later. But I'm getting restless, feeling purposeless as the time ticks by.

The idea laid itself out so clearly in front of us, exactly what to do. Wardrobe needed three of each design, and the print shop minimum was 74. That meant we'd have a surplus of 71 tees...

"Bull, Bull, Bull!" I sputtered, interrupting the simmer of his creative soup. "I know exactly what to do!"

"We should sell the extras!" We smiled, in unison.

Teenage wasn't me, but it was '*us.*' The couple the fans wanted. Quirky, funky, wild. A united front. Funnyman and whatever I am. I filtered myself through him, through his audience, going with Bully's gut. We created his wardrobe and posted the extras online; by the weekend, we sold out. So, we made more. And then more.

I began to shine again. Purpose, execution, a result. *Worth.* I stacked up a bunch of designs, prepping them for the upcoming festival season, for the sea of eyes on us every year. I planned it right down to which shirts Bully would wear on which day, planning wardrobe changes for the afterparties. So that, by the time we stepped out of the celebrity gates and made our walk through the crowd, the advertising would already be done. And it was.

As the brand grew, it became my main priority. After treatment, I'd sit upstairs organizing orders; when Bull got home from set, he would go into the garage and bring orders up to the living room where the two of us would straddle over mounds of tees, packing, leaving notes for customers whose names we started to recognize. Bull loved the creativity of it, and I loved the analytics, the data, the upticks in sales and the downs, how to manipulate them both. All of this, just by being ourselves. Just by being *together.* The brand grew quickly thanks to the support of our friends, and after one year, I got us an office and a team of people.

Fanatics want to lift you up as much as they want to watch you fall— to them, it's all entertainment. It does not occur to a fan to treat you like a person, because in their eyes, you are a commodity. Something for sale. Something they can resell to their own audience for likes. Bully says we can't have anything we have without them, not our house, our careers. I tell him that's not true.

Supporters actually know what's important to you. Your values. Your character. They don't just want to see you—they want to see you *happy*. You can form a genuine connection with a supporter because they see you as a human first. When you interact, it's friendly. Gentle. A wave in a restaurant. A nice message on Instagram. The Teenage customers, my Steak Talk readers—*those* are our people. Bully says you can't have one without the other. I tell him that's not true.

234

What You Came For

We just wanted to know how viable my eggs were. What the chances would be like when that time came, when we slowed down. So, we did the hormone injections. I wince at the thought of more needles; the tiniest pin-prick reminds me of those five years of IVs, amplifying the pain 100 times. But still, I painted my stomach black and blue. Every day, twice a day. It looked like someone had broken a pen under my skin, ink blob bruises dripping down a concave page.

Usually, you were gone too early to be there for the morning poke. Sometimes, you were out too late for the night one. So, I did them myself, crying on the bathroom floor.

There was a -33% chance it would happen. I had one fucking egg. One viable egg. But the minute it did, I changed myself. No late nights. No sleeping on my stomach. No longer starving myself, because I couldn't starve baby. I went paleo—*beyond* paleo—and read every article, ingested every vitamin, that would benefit Spawn. Our little science miracle. The way I looked to you, to *them,* didn't matter anymore. Now, nothing matters except this.

Motherhood, big and bold, happened to me before I could make a decision. I'm scared about quitting cancer treatment, scared about growing a baby in a hostile body and bringing it into a hostile world, but it's already underway.

The cheap elastic from my latex dress bites at my skin whenever I exhale, so I'm keeping my breaths shallow, holding Bull's hand as we check into the V.I.P. entrance at the back of the party. I get them confused a lot—which party is which—and that annoys him. What he doesn't know is that I do it on purpose, this confusion; I shy away from details about things that he might want to share with me, because that's the stuff he's excited to tell me about. It's his whole world. It's the same reason I've only been to set twice since we met. But this is the WME Emmy's party, and that's notable enough for me to commit to memory.

Plus-one's are rare at most events, but, lucky for our codependency, we've always gotten them. Everyone shows up with their teams—an agent, a manager, someone's assistant, and usually someone from childhood who has been hired to hang around—and about one hour later, it's only the teams left emptying the open bar because the talent has hopped into an

Uber headed to whoever's house for an afterparty. But not the Emmy's. Tonight, it's a thinned-out pack of A-listers and a handful of rising stars, hand-picked by their agencies and thrown into the mix. I think that's who we are. And I know that a lot of you came to this book looking for stories like this, so here it is. I'm gonna give it to you exactly how I took it in.

We barely cross into the party before a model I know from back in the day (who I guess is doing well, because she's here on her own) finds me and drags me away from Bull, her skeletal fingers wrapped around my elbow.

"You've got to meet Charlize," she squeals. "Oh my god, you just *have* to meet her."

Yep. That's the one.

She met Charlize in some way that I can't hear over the sound of the music, but I'm making faces and noises back so that she knows I'm impressed—I mean, we haven't spoken in years. She only found me so that she could validate her success through the success of knowing a successful person. I give it to her because everyone needs that moment, and I've got time to spare.

We get to a barstool where there's a small circle of five-foot-eight-and-taller women with angel faces hunched like gargoyles around their seated queen, and my model friend squeezes past, leaning over to whisper-yell something into Charlize's ear. Like synchronized swimmers, the other models fan out to allow her to look at me directly.

"Hi, Steak!" She cries out, her melodic voice low.

Charlize is tall and golden, like you're imagining her right now. I like that she acknowledges me—it's like talking to the sun. But we have nothing more to say and we both know this, so after a few polite exchanges about the color of her dress and the loud music, I tell her to have a great night and turn my back, scanning the room for wherever Bully has gone off to.

When my back is to the circle, I take out my phone to text Liz, *Charlize called me Steak.* And even though the white-blue screen only lit up the models' dark corner for half of a second, I feel the air pressure shift around me in the way that it always does when a phone emerges at a Hollywood event, so I drop it back into my bag before anyone's eyes can narrow at me. Liz doesn't need any context, anyway, and she probably won't respond—it's just how we talk. She holds my stuff, my memories, accolades, weird interactions. Things someone might need if they were talking to their parents, getting older, or, you know, writing a book. She's my second pair of eyes and ears.

Bully is across the room, standing with his guys. Their Charlize is Vince Vaughn—he is for a lot of people—and I approach the circle slowly, smiling. Bully grabs my arm on the way in, telling me to be quiet. I am an expert at hearing what he never says, reading the shifts in his body, the grit of his teeth. His anxiety. The clenches of his jaw. Which grab says, '*stop, Rach,*' and, '*Let's get the fuck out of here.*' And, once he's finally liquid-loose enough for us to have a little fun, when it's time to cause some mischief.

That's when he slams his arm around me all silly, pulling me in, shoving me out. It's all I'm here for, waiting for the thrill that keeps us, *us*.

There haven't been many of those since I've gotten pregnant, and as soon as I start to show, I know I'm going to have to stay back while he entertains his spotlight. I mean, he's still grappling with what it means to be himself, even, and me plus a baby are ??? But tonight, I'm balancing us in six-inch heels, little Spawn tucked and hidden in a latex dress that bells out just enough to hide what can't be hidden one month into a pregnancy. All fine and good as long as I don't breathe in and bust us out of this zipper.

I can tell that Bully doesn't want me to interject, so I make an excuse that no one hears and head to the bar, happy for the line as I figure out what the best-looking and most inconspicuous non-alcoholic beverage would be. The bald head in front of me turns around.

"I think I finally got her attention, do you want me to order for you?" Larry David asks.

"Uh, yeah, I'll have a soda water. Thanks!"

"What, like a seltzer?"

I nod, and he shouts at the bartender.

"Okay, yeah, she'll have a seltzer!"

He points back at me with his thumb as he disappears into the crowd, like a scene out of a T.V. show he stars in.

I don't need to name everyone here. Just know that they *all* are. Mark Wahlberg is sitting in the only lit corner, catching the fluorescence pouring out from the event kitchen, his legs strung through a stair banister, laughing with the catering staff. Like a movie *he* stars in. Maybe that's how all actors end up looking once they've been around long enough, as comfortable as they are onscreen as off, so much so that it's hard to tell if the scene you remember from the party even happened, or if it was something that you watched on HBO. Bull, on the other hand, does not look relaxed. His pack has dispersed into semicircles, each defined by the hoped-for trajectories of their careers—A-list jocks, *writer*-writers. Which leaves Bully looking for me, but he's intercepted, as he often is, by the cloud of smoke that he always seems to find. Before Teenage, we never talked about whether he actually liked smoking weed, but at this point, it's part of our business plan, something I learned to market for both of our benefit. It's the least destructive part about his fans thinking his personal life matches the one on *Workaholics*, anyway.

I follow the fog, and as I get closer, I see Wiz Khalifa taking a long pull from a blunt before passing it to Bull.

"Yeah, so, we just wrapped the season and, I dunno, I guess I'm about to have a kid," Bull says, his pitch upbeat.

He holds the blunt between his fingers for a moment before passing it to the next person, too caught in his head to take a hit. I smirk for a minute, realizing that this is the first person I've heard him share this out loud with. Maybe because Wiz is a dad, too, or maybe because of Bud Light. I break into a full smile as I slip into the seat next to him.

"This is my wife," Bull says.

I take a deep breath, ready for my big moment.

As Wiz grabs softly for my hand, ready to make an introduction, he looks right at Bull and says, "Oh. But is she the mother?"

And somehow, that's the most normal thing that happened to me that night.

Three

As my belly got bigger and the days got different, I tried not to examine our lifestyle. The way you kept at it. Before, I'd miss the guy that ██████████████████████, the person who climbed fences with me and ██████████, who dove into pools during black-tie soirées. Sober and pregnant, I knew that *we* needed to change.

Just hide for this one, Rachael.

Stay home, Rachael.

It was a risky pregnancy—maybe hiding it *was* for the best—but there's babble in the kitchen now about how these new identities, dad/mom, might affect our careers. I stuffed our miracle baby under an XXL hoodie. I didn't speak up, because I figured management knew these things better than I did. I wish we would have come together. I wish we had been mature enough to sit down and try to see it from each other's perspectives. Instead, I feel myself detaching.

It's the first time I feel myself moving away from you, and us, instead of leaning in.

Your fame won't allow us one minute, and it won't let us have this, either. The ultrasound. It was on a FAN BLOG before it was under a magnet on our fridge.

"You can't leave anything in your car, Rach," you said at my busted-open door.

"Do you want to call the police? File a report?" Someone on our team asked.

"No, this was my fault, I shouldn't have left anything in my car," I repeated. Then, said it again, to remind myself. I worried about how they knew where we lived, and wondered if it was safe for the tiny thing inside me.

I wanted more time with that moment—the real me and you—in that small room. A little nose. A heartbeat. The balled-up fist. The way the doctor's face brightened, embarrassed, when she admitted her mistake.

"Not a boy after all."

"What?" I'd asked. Cold jelly on my growing stomach. Bruises gone, but feeling a new one form on my heart.

"It's a girl."

She left the room because I was sobbing. You looked shocked. A little ashamed. When she disappeared, you held my hand very tightly as I tried to find the words.

I can't watch a girl go through what I did.

We trade spots. You are the sunshine. I'm the clouds.

"Rachael, you were *meant* to raise a girl."

Mars, I want you to know that when they pulled you from my body, me and your dad looked at each other right in the eyes for a very long time. We were in love, and we cried.

Shock and Awe

She was the first baby I ever held—the first baby I ever touched, I think.

When she came out, they placed her on my chest and I panicked, frozen, until my body started to charley-horse from the way I was laying there. Until a nurse came in and saw that I was inept.

They get us settled, and I feel her. A little body, small and soft. Screaming, red-mad. She doesn't want to be in this world.

Hey, kid. Same, I think.

She has the same skin tone as Bully. I hope she gets that tan that he has—that kind that comes from within—but neither of our anxieties. I hope she's tall like me, with a worm's body, so I can tell her how to live in it. Everyone who sees her says she looks exactly like Bull. Everyone except Liz.

Liz hangs in the doorway, perfectly still, her mouth open. She stays there for a while, then sneaks calmly up to the little plastic tray where Mars is sleeping.

"Donna? Is that you?" She exclaims.

I laugh in a way that pains me, knowing she will never see her. She and she, her and her.

I know that they will never know each other's soft skin.

After a grueling 20 minutes of being on this side of me, Mars drifts off to sleep. Bull's phone rings, and I shoot him dagger eyes, piercing him, *mauling* him; in that moment, I realize that I won't be able to try and fight the maternal instincts. It's not even a decision I can make. The love I have for Mars is the love my mother had for me. Unavoidable.

I wrap myself in it, and it becomes so clear to me that what happened to us was a lack of support. The world chewed my mother and spit her out. It decided that she was a difficult, loud woman, too imperfect to fix. I am difficult and loud. I am imperfect. But I know, deeply, that everything is different now. It *has* to be. For Mars, for myself, and for the little Rachael I was.

Radioactive

They don't know what it's like to hold your baby in a space suit.
Once a day, a few minutes at a time. Watching her body shiver when your
crinkly-gloved hands touch her skin.

They don't know what it's like to stand at the top of the staircase and
shout down to her when she cries.

"I love you I love you I love you. I'm here, Mom's here."

I had one month with her. One month. Of feeding her, smelling her,
swaying our bodies like crab trap buoys in dark morning water, holding my
breath so I can hear hers. Living in the warm, pink space of her smooth
head on my neck. 30 days. Then, they took her downstairs and left me up.

I can't touch my baby because I'm going through radiation. No skin
to skin. No snuggles. I can't pee in the same toilet as my husband or the
nanny because the radiation could transmit to my child. I am isolated. I
am poison. It's told to me in so many ways, so many goddamned times,
that I start to embody it. I move angry. My mouth is tight. When I yank
my blankets over my head, threads snap.

Bull goes back to filming, so it's just the three of us. Mars and nanny.
Me.

"MarMar. Mar. Hi."

Here, I am soft. I spend hours a day trying to find new ways to bond
with her. Songs that I can sing from a distance. Old t-shirts that she
can nuzzle into. A squirt of my perfume on the nanny's neck. My voice,
jabbering endlessly, bouncing off the walls. The nanny sits on the bottom
step while I'm on the landing. When Mars needs a change, she walks away.
I stare down the empty stairwell. It's like looking into the curves of my
heart.

That's when I'm upstairs, locked in our bedroom, daydreaming
about murdering the nanny. My radiated, post-partum, wine-drunk brain
picturing my hands twisting her neck, plunging swords into her chest,
ripping her hair out. Every lack of maternal instinct that I had worried
over when they told me Mars was a girl, bent backwards. This was
something visceral. I had to blink it away.

Poor, innocent, Valarie looked up and smiled at me, asked if I wanted
a smoothie.

"No thanks!" I hollered, extra sweet, extra kind, to make up for what I
was doing to her in my head.

Just For Me

Non-Disclosure Agreement, Age 27

Six months into our relationship, I told you that I would love you even if you were just a pizza boy, and I meant it. You were my world. And you smiled along, pressing your mouth against my neck. "Oh, Rach," you said. Which I took as endearment, but it was actually you telling me to take a pause, step back.

Six years later, I'd scream that I wished you were just a pizza boy. That I wanted you back. And you'd scream in my face until I didn't even recognize you, lips curling around the words.

"I am SO MUCH MORE."

And both of our hearts would break.

Mine, because it was my last grand stand, fighting against the wedge your career had driven between us.

Yours, because I was failing to see your light, as bright as you made it. Failing you because I couldn't just be 'along for the ride,' because fame and I were oil and water, and that water had the power to wash us both away. The foundation we'd built, the stability I'd thought we had. I anchored down my anger, and the more I did, the more I recoiled from our lifestyle. The damage it did to my life, my family. My best friend.

Friends—I begged you to find new ones. *Real* ones. People who could just hang out with you without taking your photograph. I'd had people like that, but they'd fallen away once I had Mars. Maybe that's what you were afraid of. We have so many people at our kitchen table, in our pool, on our tab, taking percentages, but who is here for US? For me? For you?

(And *no*, I'm not talking about who you think I am. Any names I've mentioned in this book—it isn't them. So, don't go making assumptions on Twitter.)

We weren't just writing separate pages, anymore. We were on separate chapters. And those chapters would eventually become different books. When I filed for divorce, someone on our team, paid to care for us, asked me to sign an NDA so that I wouldn't "write a book." He laughed after he said it, trying to make it seem less threatening. As if I was a risk, as if I wasn't the only one protecting 'us' this entire time.

Peachy Pink

When we first moved from the Big House into the apartment off the highway after my parents' divorce, Mom brought her silk loveseat. I did not ask how we would manage it, if moving it with just the two of us was even possible. I just knew that the couch was important to my mom.

She had let go of many things—homes, husbands, family—but the loveseat persisted. It was luxurious, delicately stitched, a cool shield against the oppressive Florida heat. The silk was peachy pink, almost cream, like a vanilla orchid. She had chosen it herself. Lifting it, you could feel the weight of her expectations. We broke into a sweat, heaving and spitting as we tipped it into the truck bed, doing the same when we arrived at the apartment, all the way up the narrow flight of stairs to our door.

But it didn't fit. We flipped it, turned it, my eight-year-old arms shaking, tears welling in my eyes. No dice. We got it in as far as we could and went to sleep. Mom in her bed, me on a pile of clothes on the floor, loveseat jutting like a tongue from the open mouth of our door.

Like a scene out of a horror movie, I woke the next morning to the screeching sounds of a chainsaw.

"MOM?" I screamed, leaping back, sleepy eyes unfocused. "MOM?"

The room finally spun into view, and I saw her. Standing over the couch, lips and nails painted cherry red, the metal blade of the chainsaw shimmering in the morning sunlight. She lowered it down and tore through the silky fabric, spraying feathers like blood around the room, a smile on her face.

"Time. To. Go!" She grunted, splintering the wooden frame. Then, with a swing of one of her long legs, she kicked half of it down the stairs.

When I look back on this memory, I look back on myself.

I think I've been cutting couches the fuck in half for the last decade. And then some.

TWO

Panicked and cornered by my decisions, I fled to the only place I knew could hold me. I booked a two week stay at the large hotel where Mom would take us for holiday buffets; this hotel, like the pier, is one of my town's crown jewels, and although it's dated now, it remains the same, elegant in a Sinatra's beach type-of-way. We'd wear matching black velvet party dresses for the occasion, and I'd watch the reflection of the silverware, the tiny lobster forks, dancing in the glow of Mom's gold jewelry. A taste of 'the other half,' washed down with vodka tonics (hers) and strawberry ice cream (mine).

Mars and I pull up in the rental car: five streets down from Michael's mom's house, three miles from our skatepark. Within earshot of the pier, and the mosquitos underneath. Since packing up Mom's trailer, I've only been back once—I didn't realize how long my body has ached for home. I hold Mars to my chest and point to the lizards slipping beneath the saw palmettos, unsure of how she will react to living things. Birds land on our waterfront balcony to squawk and shit.

This is the first time I've ever spent our money. The very. First. Time.

The only finances I have ever had access to came out of the sale of my mom's trailer- spread delicately across four years, gifted clothing getting me from event to event. It's not that I haven't benefitted from the money we make—things like food and mortgage came from somewhere, some invisible piggybank that collected our webstore funds. I used the tail end of my savings to get to Florida, and it was just a coincidence that the accountant called me while I was there.

"Rachael, we need to have more of a spend on the books for the sake of taxes, so we got you some credit cards," he said. "You know, for the brand."

At that moment, I realized that I had been a squatter in your life, too. That I had nothing to show for myself. No proof I was there at all. I felt defeated and child-like. Worried that I needed to ask permission for what came next.

"Send mine to the Naples Beach Hotel," I told him, uneasily.

"Can you work from there? You can only use these for work trips."

"Absolutely."

Work and lizards are all I can think about. Small inklings of fear start to set in, and I understand that we—the new we—will be on our own soon, and I'll need to stabilize us financially.

I invited the skatepark to the resort, one last win for all of us. In the past, we'd been unable to interact with the wealth of our city as insiders, *real* insiders, not the service staff. I told them the reason for my visit was so that Mars could meet my brothers, but really, I just needed a space to think. *I might just stay here forever,* I think.

Four-and-a-half weeks later, Bully showed up beachside. Not begging. Frustrated.

"Come on. Let's just go home."

"Why? It's perfect here," I challenged.

We'd only been here together twice before, and outside of the beachside cabanas, Bully felt like a tourist, fighting with the bugs, the sap-like air. Now, I watched him move agitatedly around the room, stepping over my suitcase, peeling back the shades, ready to leave. Inconvenienced. Uncomfortable in every way. I sat back on the bed with my arms folded and remembered the last time we'd laid together in our bedroom.

"You know, Rach, I never understood you until right now," he'd sighed.

I'd propped myself up on my elbow. The tone in his voice was unfamiliar.

"All of this, everything we have—you don't care about it." He had then raised a limp hand, gesturing around the dark bedroom as if it were our own home, our life. The high ceilings, the balcony, and the ball of 800-thread-count sheets on the ground, were all blue-black and blurry. They could have belonged to anyone.

"You don't care," he'd said again. "All you want in life is to impress your 13-year-old self."

Before I could ask what he meant, my husband turned his back to me. I will never forget the look of it, the way it rose and fell as he laughed one short, dull laugh.

"They should have never taken you out of the swamp."

Wild

I am the swamp.

Dark, mucky, icky, dangerous. A force to be reckoned with. My slinky, reptilian body sways as I float down the pavement of this Pacific Northwest city.

Stay away. Don't even look.

Actually, *look if you dare.*

Sand spurs flick off the end of my tongue, slip through my fingertips. Crude and foul. Ready for a fight.

The gold bracelets, the herringbone necklaces, trinkets that say, *Yeah, I spend,* hang stupidly from my body like truck nuts. Funny, cool, disgusting all in one.

This isn't a new me. It's the full me, released for the first time. She's always been inside me—I just needed to get angry enough to let her out.

Anger swiped the card, replenishing my wardrobe with pieces from my past. Now 'Vintage' tees and tchotchkes that had fallen away, that were lost in transit, or auctioned off from the storage unit my mom lapsed in pay. I bought them all, every last thing.

Anger bought my dream truck. Five thousand bucks for a topless Bronco, while everyone around me loaded themselves into 75k Ranges.

Anger burned it all down. And when there was nothing left, well, that brought confidence.

Go ahead, hurt me. I fucking dare you.

I'm not playing those games anymore—sit back, stay quiet, wait in the wings. It's fucking rigged. I'm playing *your* game now. It's big and messy, but that's the point, right?

I don't have a chip on my shoulder. I have a crack that runs all the way down, through the soles of my feet, anchoring me in myself. Like a mangrove root, locked in murky swamp water.

And like the swamp, I don't sleep.

Dial '1' for Room Service

Mars and I are living in hotels around the city. I'm too scared to make a more permanent move, anxious to receive the call.

I'm desperate for the "come back," the "it's me and you," the refocus I need on us. But it doesn't come. We are coiled around a tray of room service, the leftovers of which I'll finish for breakfast in the morning. In a way, these nights are magic for me and Mars. I have everything together, tight and perfect, because there isn't a chance I will ever let her down. We have berries for breakfast and read books in bed, cuddled up together all day, watching all the cartoons we can watch. She likes Mom's depression because it keeps us in the bed for hours. She loves when I lay there and let her eat french fries off my head. I enjoyed this part of the sadness because it brought us closer together, but the darker side reared its head when she was gone.

In a futile attempt to shock him into fighting for us, I decided to stick him with Mars for a week at a time—one week on, one week off—while he fumbled through a production season. I wanted him to feel it, the drain, the fatigue, to chew on the rinds of everything I managed while he was at work, things he never had to think about before. I wanted him to see me. My value. What he was missing.

I thought it would work, I thought he'd realize he needed us together. Instead, it led to the darkest times of my life. Me, realizing how, in a lot of ways, his love felt like my mother's. Unspoken, flawed, surrounded by chaos. And also, seeing how it wasn't. My mom and I were alone, stranded within each other, without a community. Whereas Bull and I had everyone around us and it was still just as dark and lonely.

Thoughts like this make the room extra still when she's gone, and that stillness makes me itch. At first, I blame it on the room, the recycled air. So, I switch hotels to one nearer to her, so it's convenient. Bull doesn't ask where I'm staying, anyway. The surface level we existed in while my mother was dying is back, sparing him the questions, the answers. If he asks, then he will be forced to do something about this mess we've made. It's been two months of hotels though, and I'd really like him to come over, but I'll never ask.

When the new address does nothing to calm my itch, I start calling around, seeing where our friends are. For a while, this feels like relief. Los Angeles is an alcoholic's city. You can go to champagne brunch to liquid lunch to happy hour to exclusive event, seven nights a week, if you want. If you have an itch like me, you will. If you can't stand to be still, alone, unloved, without purpose. Falling into this cycle, next to my peers, we all fail to see that although we are partying in a penthouse, there's only 11 floors separating our lifestyle from the people below, struggling on the street.

On my off week, I become unglued. I fling myself into the world, searching for cheap thrills and distractions. When I come home, I walk crookedly down the hallway, using the walls for balance. I get into bed and stare at her empty crib until my eyes close.

I'm missing me, too. I don't recognize my face in the mirror. Five thousand spent on hair extensions, fake lashes to bat at whoever I want, whenever I feel like it, just for the rush. Skin aching for water and sleep, desperate for a day off instead of another night of blowing off steam. I've been left to my own devices, and the only ones that satisfy are the ones that burn me down. Drinks, parties, brash nights screaming in a bar, covering everyone's tab just because I can. Waking up the next morning and phoning the first friend who will jump in my truck and drink vodka Red Bulls and shop with me until the sun sets and it's time to start again. A pattern that keeps me present. Spinning out, but alive.

It's what everyone else was doing, wasn't it? I thought about the guys from the Hollywood parties, the ones with the unknowing wives and afterparty girlfriends. I thought about Bull, and our male friends, their late nights, their unkempt hair, the way no one challenged them for a second. The way people lit up when they got in the room because, finally, the life of the party had arrived. Living life like a big, stupid joke. I wanted in on it. To be that kind of untouchable. I grew out my armpit hair. I let my hair extensions tangle. In nothing but XXXL sweat pants and a bra top, I bought myself a diamond tennis bracelet, tried on fur coats with pro-athletes who winked at me in my DMs. Looking, but never touching. The perfect, infallible mother at the dance recital, drinking lean backstage at a rap show one week later.

I like being a contradiction—it's more realistic than trying to be one thing or the other. Perfect, or perfectly wild. Contradiction suits me. Like, when your life is falling apart and you get asked to host a national television show *and* write for a magazine.

Reassurance

"We live in separate houses, it's cool."

I'm so used to giving this response now that it just flows out of me, upbeat.

"Oh, damn. Like some real Hollywood type shit, huh?" Melissa asks, nodding.

"Yeah, something like that."

Melissa and Myke are my co-hosts on what MTV is calling their 'reboot' of TRL. But in six months, they'll call it one of their biggest budget blows in history. The show, live, was poorly planned and even more poorly executed, with audio drops and fistfights on set. I wasn't ever meant to be in this industry, but the panic I felt about money led me to it. Plus, who says no to something like this? People wait their whole lives for this kind of moment, and turning it down would be like spitting on their dreams—which initially, I wanted to. But then, I called Bull.

"Should I do it?" I asked him.

"Do you want to?"

In some ways, I did. More exposure was good for business, more money was good for stability. People spend their whole lives dreaming about this type of opportunity, and here it was, unprompted, in my inbox. Who the fuck am I to turn it down? But the one thing holding me back was the very reason why I didn't call this man mine anymore.

"I don't want to be famous," I told him.

Then, he laughed.

"Rachael, *hundreds* of people get T.V. shows. We don't know most of their names."

"You mean—?"

"This will not make you famous," he said. "Trust me."

I swung between my two new jobs, hosting for MTV and Vice. There was a huge paycheck difference between the two of them, but I definitely preferred one over the other—performing was hard for me, and that's exactly what hosting is. A performance. One where a team of suits leans over a couple of goofy male writers, scripting your slang and your attitude, before putting your name on it. I'm jealous of my friends who get to play characters instead of a caricature of themselves. Vice, in their attempt to remain a respected voice in the industry, wrote to make their hosts sound educated and smart, whereas MTV...well, they hosted golden television

252

moments like *Jersey Shore*. To them, everything was entertainment. And the days moved so fast, I couldn't even tell how I was coming off onscreen. It churned my stomach.

My cohosts were so good at navigating this—they were *made* for the camera. But not me. I'm an anxious mess, someone who used to think she wanted to do everything because it was the only way to find out what the world had to offer. Then, the cameras started rolling, and a man's voice was in my ear telling me to say the word "radical." When I got the call that the show had been axed and my contract was up, I walked away happily, never more sure about an ending in my life.

Bull once told me in a fight, "You can't do everything, Rach," and I took it so literally, like he was challenging me, but now, it feels like a lesson learned. I had spread myself too thin chasing opportunities, so much so that I didn't make the most of the ones that I had, the ones I was good at. I had spread myself so thin looking for happiness that I didn't cultivate it right here, from the career I fought so hard for. It sucks when the people who hurt you also teach you the lessons about yourself that you didn't want to learn, but I guess that's one of the themes of this book.

Titles Are Everything

"Is this what you had in mind?"

I walk around the office space, arms folded in front of my barely-covered chest. We're downtown in the sprawling arts district, on the cutting edge of a soon-to-be gentrified neighborhood with cheap rent and a lease that would certainly end as soon as the landlord realized he could double his earnings by pivoting towards startup bros. Wide windows, high ceilings. Good lighting. One of those big, dusty, industrial-but-cool buildings that could actually be photo worthy if you hung a few designs from the rafters. My head pulses with the remnants of last night's gin, and I can feel the realtor's eyes on me as I peek around the corners, knowing that the person who stepped out of her topless truck in cutoff shorts and combat boots was not the CEO *he* had in mind when he set up this showing.

"It's great," I tell him. "I'll take it."

Hot Lava was born in this fire, as an attempt to set myself apart from "us," and to nurture an urge to create something more me for *my* growing base, who proved to be a bit different from Bull's. I make it for my Tumblr readers, for versions of myself; some of me today, some of me at the skatepark. I make it for my friends in L.A. and as a tribute to the *CCS* catalogues that Butchie and I once pulled apart, looking at things we could never afford. The perspective of the brand comes from my experiences in the various countercultures and subcultures where streetwear was born. The places we, as women, have been excluded from yet still participated in, and in a way, the anger I feel about this carries Hot Lava's brand voice. My designs are an homage to the girls I saw in these spaces, the ones I interacted with. Clothes for me, clothes for Liz. This is my passion project. It's healthy and it's mine top to bottom, and my unwillingness to dip back into instability is my driving force. That, and dangerous levels of caffeine.

At lunch, I'd sneak off to a hotel with a valet service and rooftop pool that all felt very dated, in the way that all reality T.V. set in Los Angeles did at the beginning of the decade. In fact, sometimes I'd even bump into cast members from those shows behind the bar, mixing up cocktails for people who made slightly better choices in terms of agents, and were therefore able to spend their afternoon sipping mimosas and peddling detox skinny teas on Instagram for a living. The kind that was no longer popular in the way that they were no longer desirable; their stomachs have gained the soft weight that happens when a low-calorie diet meets high-calorie bar mixers and late-night snacks. Plus, you know, age. They haven't been offered more than a #brandambassador gig since followers became the primary measure of success.

Los Angeles has eaten them, and maybe it's starting to eat me in a slightly different way, too. Watching them makes me question my choices, like, is my celebratory 'I earned this right' lunch getting a little too close to their 'washed up and bored on a weekday' routine?

I sip a few more cocktails and feel the buzz put a healthy distance between me and my sadder-looking comrades. I remind myself that I'm on top of the world—on top of a roof at 1 o'clock!—and dip my foot into the pool before texting a friend to pick me up and take me back to the office just so I can feel like I aced a work day, but also so that I can throw on some samples and go out for the night. On our way back to the office, we'll take the back avenues that stretch through iconic city streets and tent cities alike, and in a frantic, made-for-the-big-screen moment I'm speaking and gesturing with my hands, liquid slick, reminding my friend that we need to make an upcoming turn when—*pop!* My wedding ring flies off my finger, directly out the window and onto the pavement. Just in time to catch the 3 p.m. industrial truck lines as they leave their bays. I see the gold shining back at me right as a five-ton gravel truck cements it into the street, the driver and I locking eyes, knowing there was no time on either end to react. We hold our stare until the last tire rolls over my forever band, and I jump awkwardly out of the car, feeling the snickers of those waiting to cross the intersection hit my back as I bend to pick up the ring. I dust it off, inspecting it for damage—scratched, covered in soot— knowing there's a metaphor somewhere in this moment, but the alcohol tells me not to care.

Steak's World

My rental house is twice the size of any house I've ever been in, and we got a deal because a girl who works with me told the landlord's son she would fuck him. 6,000 square feet, perched high up in the infamous Laurel Canyon. Down a dirt road I didn't know could exist in L.A.

Single, I'm seeing two men, both with the same name. I didn't plan it, but it keeps shit simple, keeps them both at a distance. With one eye squinted, I can call it a stable love life. Neither guy wants to slow down, and they let me know that right off the bat.

"Great, me either. I'm not looking for anything serious here."

With one of them, I bond over the fact that we both lost a parent the same year, and the way that we're both using our vices to run from that pain. He likes my playlists and my tight dresses and never once winces at my armpit hair, which passes the test. I actually grew it out to scare men off, and if they weren't scared, that was enough for me to at least entertain the idea of them. If you're wondering, it's a very good way to weed out weak men. I fly up to see him on my lonely weeks, which is great for eating up the time. By the time I come home, he's back to spending his nights out late, painting buildings with his friends, some high on PCP, unreachable. Not that any of that is good for him, but it's good for us. It makes sure that we never cross the line into seriousness.

When I'm looking for attention in L.A., the other one answers my calls, and that's the extent of our relationship. This one is calm and successful. The two of them together fits both of my types, my typical pendulum swing from wild to stable, but since neither of those have ever worked out for me individually, I keep them both on the line.

When I refocus on myself, throwing my energy into me, I feel this eerie sense of maturity. Long days of digital output and, yes, still day-drinking and going to events. Still, I find myself full and tired, satisfied with my work. What I am craving, though, is the comfort that you miss after a year of coming home to an empty house every other week. The thing I've been wired since birth to call love—a co-dependent, puddled mass. Someone to throw myself into, someone to memorize and anticipate. Someone to watch crime show marathons on the couch with.

Optimism, Age 30

Do-doot.

My phone has been dry for three days. Normally, I wouldn't stress about this, but sitting on my chest, straight-up and heavy, is the lack of connection I feel.

"Everyone sucks," I blurt out, eager to be held.

"No, dude. Not everyone. You're just shopping in the wrong departments."

Liz, like usual, is doing her best to reassure me, but not without an agenda. History has proved that life is better when both of us are up. Or, as up as we can be. We're standing outside a bar together, tipsy. She's smoking a cigarette, staring into my face.

"Who wants to *DATE*-date a mom?"

"You're not just a mom! You're a business owner, ex-T.V. host, a hustler. You have a lot going on, and you're hot. Anyone with a brain will want to date you, and if they're scared of your motherhood, then you shouldn't want them around."

"I guess."

"Anyways, it might be better if you just don't focus on this for a while. You know, take time for yourself?"

Liz has a point. I haven't been truly single since I was 13 years old. But the thrill of the new encounters, the 'what-ifs,' even the chaos of the aftermath that follows every time I answer those questions, that's an elixir to me. She's not hearing the undertones of what I'm saying, and I'm not ready to, either. But before I can admit to my fear of being alone, or even reflect on Liz's rant, the guy that's hanging onto her shoulder, begging for a drag of her cigarette, cut in.

"You can't date in L.A., man. You're not touchable," he says, sloppy and slurry, eyelids hanging low. "It's social suicide."

My mouth pops open, then shuts. Open, because he said exactly what I was thinking. Shut, because I'm fucking stuck—I know it, and so does Liz. I'm at the same bar on a Wednesday that my ex-husband will attend on Thursday. Our group is too mushed. We all still hang out, just like we used to. Our relationship was born this way, and to some outsiders, our relationship doesn't even appear to be over. Fuck. Even *this guy* knows it, and I don't even know who he is.

Liz swayed a few inches and let the guy slip, stumbling from her shoulder. She waved him away with the back of her hand.

"Shit. I just want someone to watch T.V. with," I sigh heavily, blowing bubbles with the tiny straw in my gin.

The empty cup is frozen and heavy in my hand. I glance over my shoulder once and heave it at the wall behind me; glass shatters, and the Wednesday night regulars laugh. Four people clap and the barback calls out to me.

"I'm adding that to your tab, Steak."

For a second, the bar seems illuminated. Everyone's face is tattered and flawed, floors stained and sticky, and I realize I'm not even entertaining myself anymore. This lifestyle is empty. I'm as big as it gets, as I'm *going* to get. I have everything I'm supposed to want, but what is it? Surrounding myself with the rappers and skaters I idolized as a kid. Finally using my social capital to impress myself. But still, I'm empty. And most of the text threads in my phone are about bar drama, about the people sitting around me. I don't even know their last names. I mean, except for my close circle, standing in front of me—but even they look just as sad as everyone else, just as wrinkled from lack of sleep, from the weight that looms over all of us.

Is this life? Is this the top?

Maybe I should leave L.A.

For a moment, the thought feels so freeing. Then, I remember the impossibility of it. Or, just the extreme effort it would take. Everything seems harder than just sitting here, in it, with this crew. I turn to the barback.

"That's fine. Could you please bring us another round? And a beer for you, too."

I stick him with a sweet southern grin, as if I were right back home, and he mirrors it back to me.

Do-doot.

I can feel a bottle-ache that's creeping around in the corner of my head, but it's not totally there yet, which gives me another hour or two of this mildly-nauseous, hyper-manic, half-drunk, flippant dream state before it's fully formed. I need to mobilize before I smack down on the hangover pavement. I scroll my texts for brunch invites so I can 'hair of the dog'-it into the next party.

6:17 a.m.

No one else is fucking up yet, lucky bastards. This whole city will probably sleep in until 10, something I haven't done in over a year.

Do-doot.

Do-doot.

Then, Snapchat noises. I never use that app. I open it up to assess whatever damage I might've incurred, posting drunkenly, forgetting.

I'm relieved when I find it's just a blurry selfie.

For a brief moment in Snapchat history, you could receive replies from anyone, anywhere. It's what I loved about the internet the first time I logged on, and why I stayed on, why I built my online presence. Tumblr,

Twitter, Instagram. I'm sure Snapchat took this feature away for a very good reason, but before it could, I saw a message from someone, replying to my selfie with one of his own.

Zak looks like he would have terrorized me in middle school and broken my heart on the mini ramp in tenth grade. I wonder how many people he might have sent this to, but at the same time, I don't care. The night before, I was convinced there was no man in the world for me, and yet here...this one seems to be made exactly for my eyes. Long hair. Tattoos. Full lips.

My heart pounds. I had desperately begged the universe for someone like this, but I knew better than to throw myself into him, no matter how fast he got my blood pumping before 7:00 a.m.

"Who's this?" I type back.

Something vague. Something that, if he screenshotted and sent it around, would be acceptable. I don't trust anyone.

Do-doot.

We go back and forth for weeks, keeping it light at first. Both of us sneaking in chances to get more information from each other, but trying to keep it surface-level with memes. Toeing the line of asking something that would be too much for the other to handle, avoiding things that might end the chat. Zak spends what seems like all of his long, on-the-clock hours at a western New York construction site talking to me, and the consistent access to him fills me up. I skip out on the thrills, the texts from friends inviting me here and there. All the conversation and excitement I need is right in my palm, so I stay wrapped in my down comforter, finding, for the first time, that it's the most magical thing to be wrapped in.

Can you imagine if you saw him working on the side of the road? In his hard hat? You would crash ur car.

My girls' group chat seemed to get it. But then, when weeks rounded out into a month, I couldn't take it anymore. I knew better than to keep things light forever, and I wasn't going to let myself get tangled up in someone who only wanted that. I wanted to see what more I could get from him.

"Call me or don't ever text me again," I challenged him.

"What? Like now? I can't, I'm at work," he responded, a little too quickly. Then, "I don't even have your phone number."

"562-***-****," I replied. Then, I closed the app.

Zak didn't call. I opened the app and closed it feverishly throughout the day, making excuses. Mourning the loss. I paced the house, trying to take my mind off him. I went to Whole Foods, staring into other people's carts, seeing what they were getting. I saw a very thin old woman pushing hers, filled with popcorn. So, I filled mine with popcorn, too. Popcorn and energy drinks. I came home and opened a bag, cracked a can. Scrolled in my bed for what felt like hours. My phone rang.

"Hi, I'm calling about the moped for sale on Craigslist."

I panicked, dropping popcorn all over my sheets. Was someone pranking me? I hung up the call, then typed the number into Google. Buffalo area code. I didn't connect the dots, not until two days later, when the same number called again.

"Hey, it's me," Zak said.

"What took you so long?"

"I was scared. And I did call—about the moped." Zak's voice was raspy from working outside in the cold. He was assertive and direct with his words, but he took long breaks in between them. And those breaks made me anxious, like his sentences were about to stop.

They didn't. We talked about his work day, he asked about mine. In the middle of the call, I heard muffled yelling. Then, Zak whispered, "Hold on, I think my brother is about to fight our neighbor."

In that instant, every ounce of me fell in love with him. We tell people we first fell in love after our trip to London, but for me, it was this. I fell in love with the fact that he didn't get mad at his brother, or annoyed, or loud. I fell in love with his narration of what was happening outside the window, the way he laughed at them both, but still told me he'd have to go down in a second to help him out. I fell in love with the dumb-assery of it all, and the way he was free of any judgment for that same dumb-assery. For a moment, I saw his entire world, and I wanted to be a part of it. To be shielded from judgment and coddled in that laughter, the kind of devotion that would have dragged him down the stairs and out in the street to fight alongside his brother if he had to.

You Already Knew

I fell in love with Zak again when he shyly asked if I wanted Cracker Barrel for dinner, as if apologizing on behalf of his hometown for having just three restaurants that stayed open after six o'clock on a snowy December night.

Then, for five days, Zak called out of work, and we spend that time twisting our bodies into shapes all over the hotel room. Ordering food, not answering our phones.

Zak says he fell in love with me when we were just sitting quietly, away from the anxious newness, the caffeine. Just breathing each other in.

On the fifth day, he decides he'd better go into work, so he wakes up at four in the morning to make it to his shift back in Buffalo; before he leaves, he taps his hand lightly on the small of my back. It's the first time anyone has ever touched me there.

"You have to get to work, too," he says, placing his hard hat on my head.

He was half-joking. We both knew what I had to do the next day, how insane I was for booking this trip in the way that I did. The way I was willingly putting myself through the whiplash of filling my heart and emptying it—staying with Zak, then visiting my mom's grave.

I stay in bed all day until he gets back. I tell myself I don't need to drink, that I'm not going to, but ultimately, I lose my hold at dinner. I push oysters and bread and butter and cheese into my mouth—four things I haven't eaten in years. Zak watches me excuse myself to get some vodka at the bar; he doesn't say anything, just gazes into my face as I gaze into his. Me, filling the quiet with babble and pretending it's because I'm carefree and cool but really, it's because I'm afraid that if I don't keep the words coming out, there won't be anything keeping me in motion. I grab a gin on our way out.

We go back to our hotel. Zak falls asleep right away, but I toss and turn until 11:30, unable to take the stillness of the room, of his breathing. I am itchy and I need to sprint, hard and fast. I grab a sweatshirt and go downstairs.

I walk wobble-legged into the snow. And throw myself at it, hard. Wanting to feel. Wanting to sink. But I land in the smallest bank, hitting the ground with a little *pooft*. I stay there for a moment, feeling the crystals seep into my clothes, the numbness creep in. Then, I pull myself up, icy and wet, and walk past the bar, thinking, debating.

I shake my head, feeling resolve, as if opting out of extra vodka nullified my previous intake, and I'd earned some kind of sobriety points. When I cross the threshold of the hotel and slam the 'up' button on the elevator, the front desk clerk coughs, letting me know there are eyes on me in case I decide to act any more belligerent.

That's when it occurs to me: I can't act anymore. I can't run.

As the elevator creeps up to the top floor of my hotel, every movement returns to me; all of the ways I tried distracting myself, everything I put out, is poured back in. My stomach flips. All of it fights inside of me. Oysters, cheese, gin, vodka, and water. I tear open the door of my room.

Zak doesn't move. His body is just a shadow, hair spread darkly over the pillows. I take a gulp of air and make a quiet lunge for the bathroom shower, jumping inside.

I slam on the hot water as it all comes up, warm water prickling my frozen skin as I retch. The shellfish see the light again, and I shove their creamy, masticated bodies down the drain with my numb, burning toes. They've been plucked, shucked, chewed, and now, they're circling the sewer. I mumble a promise to never eat another one of them again; once I'm sure that the yuck has been washed off of me, I peel my wet clothes off of my body, step out, and wrap myself in a towel, head ringing, booze reborn in the heat. Soaking wet, I climb into bed. No sooner have I decided that he's fast asleep, that I hear his voice, muffled against the bedclothes.

"You don't have to do that, you know."

I don't even ask what he means.

I wake up to snow. Feet of it. A shocking yet predictable part of being so close to the Great Lakes.

We quietly bundled ourselves in layers, mine lacking compared to his, as I'm still terrible at dressing for the cold. My throat burns. Zak's Jeep warms up fast for a '96, and I'm grateful to be seated again. I could fall back asleep.

"Take your coat off," he says, motioning to the air vents as if to say it's safe.

I wrestle out of it, whip it behind me, and hear a plasticky crunch. Under my jacket is a frozen Wegman's bouquet. The baby's breath is crushed, its blossoms, scattered like Skittles.

"What's all this for?" I ask, unprepared for the gesture.

"I dunno, I just thought we might need it."

By the time we get to the cemetery, there's four feet of snow on the ground. I feel like I've been here before. When Zak asks if I know where her stone is, I nod.

"Yeah, just around that statue, down by the big tree." Then, as we get closer, I continue, "It's okay, we can just drive by it. It's cold and covered in snow. I'll just say something from the window."

Zak pulls his Jeep up, parks it, and hops out of the door. I watch his long, thin legs run through the snow in the way that only people raised in these winters can, confused when he flings himself agilely over a fence, does it again, and bounds to the side of the car.

There's a shovel in his hands. He's digging a path for me, from the car door to the headstones, using a shovel he spotted propped up against a mausoleum two acres away. I unroll my window.

"Over here?" Zak asks, cheeks flushed.

"Yeah," I point, "just a little to the left."

The path is 15 feet long and leads right to her plaque. When he's finished, he motions for me to walk forward. I slink out of the passenger side door. Our arms graze each other as I walk towards the grave and he heads to the car.

Standing over her stone, an overwhelming amount of nothing washes over me. Nothing at all, no matter where I searched. I gulp at the cold air, fighting with the ache of my heart in my throat. Quietly, I stood there, waiting for the words. When nothing came, I went back to his Jeep, stepping over the rust on the runner board as I got in so that I didn't track any red slush inside.

"How ya feelin'?"

Honestly? Hungover. But I'm scared to say that. We've both let last night disappear.

"I'm good. Can we make one more stop?"

Grandma's house is around the corner from the cemetery. Which doesn't look ideal, typed out on a page, but I guess when you plan for death the way she does, with family plots and all, it might be a good thing. I know as we move towards it that we shouldn't stop, that I know better, but in my shallow breaths there's a desire to be forgiven for what I cannot see, or hold, or know. A need to be embraced by my family. "Real family," whatever that means. I want this time to be different.

Zak pulls into her driveway. The driveway of my grandmother's house, not a week after meeting me for the very first time, stepping into my most unresolved trauma with ease. You might think something else deserves that title, but honestly, this is one wound I simply can't reconcile with. It's too turbulent.

"You should just stay here, I'll be out in a second," I say, planless.

"Yeah fucking right," he laughs, ignition off, one foot out the door.

Grandma doesn't bring up mom, and for that, I'm grateful. She takes the plastic off of the tray of frostbitten cream puffs that she keeps just in case guests arrive, smiling at Zak. I don't hear what they're saying—I'm thinking about the day they put Mom in the ground, in a place so different from what she made me promise all those years ago. *At least there's a tree.*

263

Unconditional

Zak doesn't want anything from anyone else. He doesn't need anyone's admiration. All he wants is to positively affect the people closest to him.

It's been so long since I've met someone who isn't looking for what's next; instead, Zak goes out and gets the things he wants, and there's honesty to that. But he isn't perfect. Zak stays out late, is banned from a few Erie county establishments for shoplifting. He's scrappy. And he's got a fast mouth when he needs to speak up, can get quick and nasty and strong, but he only gets that way if it'll bring the peace. Mostly, he's quiet, someone with a good read on people's character.

We're different. I speak up to be heard, to make sure no one steps on my toes, to ensure that people don't misunderstand me or my worth or intentions.

But ultimately, we're both fighting for the children we once were, and while he has become that beacon that he needed, that provider of peace, I'm still waiting to learn to do the difficult things, for both myself and the little girl I still am inside.

Friends started to fall away, as Zak told me they should, just as I knew they would once I strove for a better version of myself. I complained about this to him, announcing that I was going to work to strengthen the friendships that I had that were based on actual substance.

"You can't give all of yourself to everyone, Rachael. Otherwise, there's nothing left for the people who matter," he said. Then, "A friend to everyone is loyal to none."

That cracked me in half. I think because of how he delivered it, like it was the truth, calm and forceful. No undertones detected, no judgment, no leaving me feeling like I should have known this all along.

The thing about Zak was, even when I didn't know things, even though I was still learning, he didn't make me feel bad. He told me that everything I was feeling was okay, and for someone like me, someone who has rounded the many corners of her life hiding her feelings, having them invalidated turn by turn—well, hearing that was what I needed. Sometimes, you just need someone who doesn't shy away from the fact that the world is hard and fucked up. You just want them to say, "You know what, babe? It's me and you, always. It's me and you."

Some of us don't need Zen. Some of us need to be angry, and to be validated in that anger. Peace can be dismissive. Zen can come later. Sometimes, anger is the first step, and maybe nobody has ever told us that that's okay. Maybe nobody has ever looked at us and cradled our souls with the one thing that matters most to people who have been abandoned: loyalty and validation, no matter what we're feeling.

"Do you think I'm dead?"

Zak perks up when I say this, looking worried. When he sees that my eyes are clear, he smiles. My head is on his chest. I'm looking outside at our green yard, feeling the clean sheets.

"Sometimes, I think I died," I continue, "doing the stupid shit I've done. And this is my new reality. Something I manifested. Or maybe this *is* a delusion, and I'm out on a corner of some hot intersection, sunbaked and out of my gourd. Imagining all this."

Zak waits until I'm done talking. Then, he pulls me in closer.

"No, Rachael. I think you're just safe."

Itch Relief

Heaven is our bed.

Heaven is in my head. It's right here. Pie at 2 a.m.—yes, we eat pie. I haven't lost control, just the need for control, in this moment, anyway. My body is brand new in his eyes. He doesn't say anything about my big, wide feet as I slip each one of my toes into his mouth.

Is this love or lust?

It's both. And it's a bit of luck, two people with similar traumas who are on the same path to healing them, who know how to love and to listen when someone needs to talk about them. It's setting yourself up with therapy. It's a combination of all of these things, ebb and flow.

It's constantly discussing your dreams and helping each other grow them. It's honesty about who you are and who they are and our insecurities and how to hold those, too.

I fall asleep as if I've been slipped a sedative. I have a physiological response to seeing his shape in the doorway, the sound of his car pulling up to the fence. My body knows it can finally rest. That with him, I am safe. The life I was scared of is opening up to me, the person I was so scared of, the space I was afraid of taking up, is needed, now. I have to do it in order to heal.

My disorders aren't healed, but they are being managed. They know how to find the doors and enter them, but thanks to active therapy, I know what to do when they come knocking, know why they're there, know what they're called. I have C-PTSD seizures. I take two pills a day for them, to keep them at bay. I know the eating disorder is the symptom of disfunction, the seizures, a symptom of trauma. The need for control. My company, Steak World, has 12 brands in its care, including Teenage, where I still work with Bully as a business partner. I can express my need for control through these brands, syphoning that energy into manipulating markets, trends, the thumping pulse of my customer base. Some people ask me how I do it and I tell them, I'm just myself. I've been selling me since the first day I walked alone in the mall.

Things are still, but they aren't itchy. My safety and value have all been contingent on the demands and moods of others but now, it's up to me to make things happen. The roof over my head is secured by me, not how satisfied someone is with me. And while this affects what I accept on my plate, what I take on for work, I need this. My sobriety, bank account, home—it's overwhelming, but when it gets that way, I have a thinned-out group of people waiting. My 'flat tire friends,' as I call them. The type of people that show up and help. These are the friends who get my energy now.

Whenever I feel like I'm broken in ways that can't be mended, I think of her.

She's always with me. When I wake up in the night, slamming my arm into Zak's chest, feeling for his body, kneading his legs with my toes. An overwhelming urge to assure myself. I'm the friend who panics when you're offline, the girlfriend who calls for help if she can't get ahold of you. I can't help this panic—it's part of me, now and forever. There are other ways she's still part of me, like when, on my busiest week of the year, I commit myself to cooking for six people. I buy a boxed lasagna from the store, melt some high-end cheese on top of it, and call it mine. That's Donna. The whole way.

Forgiveness

As I was writing this book, I became deeply upset that, as a woman, my narrative has been led greatly by the men I have spent time with. Upset that every chapter was hitched to a relationship. But if you don't have a strong family or support system, you have to anchor yourself to something so that you don't float away.

I forgive myself for anything I have done as a means of connecting, of learning, of loving.

The results of self-navigating out of necessity, out of a response to a lack of true, pure, impactful guidance, can be devastating. If we don't tell our children anything, we leave it up to the world to tell them, mostly in the hard way, sometimes the easy way. Through relationships, gut-wrenching and all, through bad friendships, by being a bad friend. Or, maybe that's how we all learn in the end? From being kicked and spat on. We'll go about things ass-backwards, with good intentions and bad execution, being harmed and causing harm, underprepared, naïve and alone. The world that we were left to learn from might eat us alive, and we'll have to carry on with those wounds, limping and bleeding.

The blacked-out pages are for me. In them hide stories I'm not ready to share, things about me maybe no one will ever know. The bones that have been broken by others, the things I've sold to survive, the dark things that could drive this storyline away from what I want to share, or what I think is important to know. There are happy things, too. Things just for me, that you aren't meant to read. Deeply magical intimacies. Secrets. For now, what's being held here, is right for me. Near me. Maybe one day, there will be a time when I share them aloud—I've started to recently with the ones that I love, the ones who are here today, the ones who can give me the validation I need. That is as free as I'll ever be. Or feel.

And if you are holding any inked pages, I hope you find the freedom I have in letting them out, even if it's just a few at a time. Don't tuck them away.

I sent the first transcript of my book from Tony Hawk's couch, where I was sitting with my friend Lizzie. She was just about to ask me to help her design her Olympic uniform. And I'm allowed to say all that, allowed to have this pride, double-spaced and, initially, written in Ariel Black, because my 15-year-old-self needed this book. In these pages, just like this.

Michael is still in Florida. We talk regularly, and have kept our promise to always check in with each other. My sister, Liz, is a self-taught marketing pro for a company that grosses four million a year; she was hired as an office manager and hustled to the top. She owns her house in California because we promised each other our first ones wouldn't be in our hometown. We celebrate every win we have together—not just birthdays and holidays—and when we do, it's perfect chaos.

Zak and I have three dogs and two kids. Our foster daughter falls asleep just like I did when Zak first made me feel safe, and I am happy to have this home that has a bed for her.

During my stay on Tumblr, I amassed 250k followers who followed me just to talk to me. Because they saw glimpses of experiences that I shared, or, even less, experiences that I was photographed having. I have spent years writing to them, answering their questions and listening to their pains. And when I need to be held, I tell them. I'm open and honest. It's my community. And even though it attracts the dark and vile bits of humankind, people who spill their hatreds on me, I've realized that I don't want to be without it. This has been my truest self, my subconscious. All that time I spent trying on and testing little pieces of me in the real world, was a waste. The real me, my full self, was here in these pages of writing all along.

The things that I have been through have shaped me into the woman I am right now. I am not a victim. Please do not call me strong—my strength came from never hearing that I didn't have to do it all. Nobody ever told me that I could crumble. That I could be both sides of the coin. I love being a walking, talking contradiction, challenging people to underestimate my abilities based on the shit they've seen or heard or read. I take up all the space I used to tiptoe in before. This year, I've let out my breasts in a post right next to one about me in *Forbes* magazine. Because of my past, I want to be dynamic in this way. I want people to scratch their heads, chew on their thoughts.

I wrote this, not because I am an expert—there are many things I haven't been told—but because I do not want to go without telling my daughters all that I have, just in case I'm not here to do it.

CPSIA information can be obtained
at www.ICGtesting.com
Printed in the USA
LVHW080057011022
729680LV00001B/21